Capt

Chief of Scouts

As Pilot to Emigrant and Government Trains, Across the Plains of the Wild West of Fifty Years Ago

William F. Drannan

Alpha Editions

This edition published in 2024

ISBN : 9789364733793

Design and Setting By
Alpha Editions
www.alphaedis.com
Email - info@alphaedis.com

As per information held with us this book is in Public Domain.
This book is a reproduction of an important historical work. Alpha Editions uses the best technology to reproduce historical work in the same manner it was first published to preserve its original nature. Any marks or number seen are left intentionally to preserve its true form.

Contents

PREFACE .... - 1 -
CHAPTER 1. .... - 2 -
CHAPTER II. .... - 18 -
CHAPTER III. .... - 43 -
CHAPTER IV .... - 58 -
CHAPTER V .... - 78 -
CHAPTER VI. .... - 94 -
CHAPTER VII. .... - 112 -
CHAPTER VIII .... - 138 -
CHAPTER IX. .... - 150 -
CHAPTER X. .... - 164 -
CHAPTER XI. .... - 176 -
CHAPTER XII. .... - 185 -

PREFACE

The kindly interest with which the public has received my first book, "Thirty-one Years on the Plains and in the Mountains," has tempted me into writing this second little volume, in which I have tried to portray that part of my earlier life which was spent in piloting emigrant and government trains across the Western Plains, when "Plains" meant wilderness, with nothing to encounter but wild animals, and wilder, hostile Indian tribes. When every step forward might have spelt disaster, and deadly danger was likely to lurk behind each bush or thicket that was passed.

The tales put down here are tales of true occurrences,—not fiction. They are tales that were lived through by throbbing hearts of men and women, who were all bent upon the one, same purpose:—to plow onward, onward, through danger and death, till their goal, the "land of gold," was reached, and if the kind reader will receive them and judge them as such, the purpose of this little book will be amply and generously fulfilled.

W.F.D.

CHAPTER 1.

At the age of fifteen I found myself in St. Louis, Mo., probably five hundred miles from my childhood home, with one dollar and a half in money in my pocket. I did not know one person in that whole city, and no one knew me. After I had wandered about the city a few days, trying to find something to do to get a living, I chanced to meet what proved to be the very best that could have happened to me. I met Kit Carson, the world's most famous frontiersman, the man to whom not half the credit has been given that was his due.

The time I met him, Kit Carson was preparing to go west on a trading expedition with the Indians. When I say "going west" I mean far beyond civilization. He proposed that I join him, and I, in my eagerness for adventures in the wild, consented readily.

When we left St. Louis, we traveled in a straight western direction, or as near west as possible. Fifty-eight years ago Missouri was a sparsely settled country, and we often traveled ten and sometimes fifteen miles without seeing a house or a single person.

We left Springfield at the south of us and passed out of the State of Missouri at Fort Scott, and by doing so we left civilization behind, for from Fort Scott to the Pacific coast was but very little known, and was inhabited entirely by hostile tribes of Indians.

A great portion of the country between Fort Scott and the Rocky Mountains that we traveled over on that journey was a wild, barren waste, and we never imagined it would be inhabited by anything but wild Indians, Buffalo, and Coyotes.

We traveled up the Neosha river to its source, and I remember one incident in particular. We were getting ready to camp for the night when Carson saw a band of Indians coming directly towards us. They were mounted on horses and were riding very slowly and had their horses packed with Buffalo meat.

With the exception of Carson we were all scared, thinking the Indians were coming to take our scalps. As they came nearer our camp Carson said, "Boys, we are going to have a feast".

On the way out Carson had taught me to call him "Uncle Kit." So I said, "Uncle Kit, are you going to kill an Indian and cook him for supper?"

He laughed and answered, "No, Willie, not quite as bad as that. Besides, I don't think we are hungry enough to eat an Indian, if we had one cooked by a French cook; but what will be better, to my taste at least, the Indians are bringing us some Buffalo meat for our supper," and sure enough they proved to be friendly.

They were a portion of the Caw tribe, which was friendly with the whites at that time. They had been on a hunt, and had been successful in getting all the game they wanted. When they rode up to our camp they surrounded Carson every one of them, trying to shake his hand first. Not being acquainted with the ways of the Indians, the rest of us did not understand what this meant, and we got our guns with the intention of protecting him from danger, but seeing what we were about to do, Carson sang out to us, "Hold on, boys. These are our friends," and as soon, as they were done shaking hands with him Carson said something to them in a language I did not understand, and they came and offered their hands to shake with us. The boys and myself with the rest stood and gazed at the performance in amazement, not knowing what to do or say. These were the first wild Indians we boys had ever seen. As soon as the hand shaking was over, Carson asked me to give him my knife which I carried in my belt. He had given the knife to me when we left St. Louis. I presume Carson had a hundred just such knives as this one was in his pack, but he could not take the time then to get one out. For my knife he traded a yearling Buffalo, and there was meat enough to feed his whole crew three or four days. That was the first Indian "Pow-wow" that I had ever seen or heard of either.

The Indians ate supper with us, and after that they danced "the Peace Dance" after smoking the Pipe of Peace with Uncle Kit. The smoking and dancing lasted perhaps an hour, and then the Indians mounted their horses and sped away to their own village.

I was with Carson off and on about twelve years, but I never saw him appear to enjoy himself better than he did that night. After the Indians had gone, Uncle Kit imitated each one of us as he said we looked when the Indians first appeared in sight. He had some in the act of running and others trying to hide behind the horse, and he said that if the ground had been loose we would have tried to dig a hole to crawl into. One of the party he described as sitting on his pack with his mouth wide open, and he said he could not decide whether the man wanted to swallow an Indian or a Buffalo.

The next morning we pulled out from there, crossing the divide between this stream and the Arkansas. Just before we struck the Arkansas river, we struck the Santa-Fe trail. This trail led from St-Joe on the Missouri river to Santa-Fe, New Mexico, by the way of Bent's Fort, as it was called then. Bent's Fort was only a Trading Station, owned by Bent and Robedoux. These two men at that time handled all the furs that were trapped from the head of the North Platte to the head of the Arkansas; the Santa-Fe trail, as it was then called, was the only route leading to that part of the country.

After traveling up the Arkansas river some distance, above what is known as Big Bend, we struck the Buffalo Country, and I presume it was a week that we were never out of the sight of Buffalos. I remember we camped on the bank of the river just above Pawne Rock that night; the next morning we were up early and had our breakfast, as we calculated to make a big drive that day. Carson had been telling us how many days it would take us to make Bent's Fort, and we wanted to get there before the Fourth of July. Just as we had got our animals packed and every thing in readiness to start, a herd of Buffalo commenced crossing the river about a half a mile above our camp. The reader will understand that the Buffalo always cross the river where it is shallow, their instinct teaching them that where the water is shallow, there is a rock bottom, and in crossing these places they avoid quicksand. This was the only crossing in fifteen miles up or down the river. We did not get to move for twenty-four hours. It seems unreasonable to tell the number of Buffalo that crossed the river in those twenty-four hours. After crossing the river a half a mile at the north of the ford, they struck the foot hill; and one could see nothing but a moving, black mass, as far as the eye could see.

I do not remember how long we were going from there to Bent's Fort, but we got there on the second of July, 1847, and every white man that was within three hundred miles was there, which were just sixteen. At this present time, I presume there are two or three hundred thousand within the same distance from Bent's Fort, and that is only fifty-eight years ago! In view of the great change that has taken place in the last half century, what will the next half century bring? The reader must remember that the increase must be three to one to what it was at that time.

After staying at Bent's Fort eight days we pulled out for "Taos," Carson's home. He remained at Taos, which is in New Mexico, until early in the fall, about the first of October, which is early autumn in New Mexico; then we started for our trapping ground, which was on the head of the Arkansas river, where Beaver was as numerous as rats are around a wharf.

We were very successful that winter in trapping. It was all new to me, I had never seen a Beaver, or a Beaver trap. Deer, Elk, and Bison, which is a species of Buffalo, was as plentiful in that country at that time as cattle is now on the ranch. I really believe that I have seen more deer in one day than there is in the whole State of Colorado at the present time.

In the autumn, just before the snow commences to fall, the deer leave the high mountains, and seek the valleys, and also the Elk and Bison; no game stays in the high mountains but the Mountain Sheep, and he is very peculiar in his habits. He invariably follows the bluffs of streams. In winter and summer, his food is mostly moss, which he picks from the rocks; he eats but very little grass. But there is no better meat than the mountain sheep. In the fall, the spring lambs will weigh from seventy-five to a hundred pounds, and are very fat and as tender as a chicken; but this species of game is almost extinct in the United States; I have not killed one in ten years.

We stayed in our camp at the head of the Arkansas river until sometime in April, then we pulled out for Bent's Fort to dispose of our pelts. We staid at the Fort three days. The day we left the Fort, we met a runner from Col. Freemont with a letter for Carson. Freemont wanted Carson to bring a certain amount of supplies to his camp and then to act as a guide across the mountains to Monterey, California. The particulars of the contract between Freemont and Carson I never knew, but I know this much, that when we got to Freemont's camp, we found the hardest looking set of men that I ever saw. They had been shut up in camp all winter, and the majority of them had the scurvy, which was brought on by want of exercise and no vegetable food. The most of the supplies we took him were potatoes and onions, and as soon as we arrived in camp the men did not wait to unpack the animals, but would walk up to an animal and tear a hole in a sack and eat the stuff raw the same as if it was apples.

In a few days the men commenced to improve in looks and health. Uncle Kit had them to exercise some every day, and in a short time we were on the road for the Pacific Coast. We had no trouble until we crossed the Main Divide of the Rocky Mountains. It was on a stream called the "Blue," one of the tributaries of the Colorado river.

We were now in the Ute Indian country, and at this time they were considered one of the most hostile tribes in the west. Of course there was no one in the company that knew what the Ute Indians were but Kit Carson. When we stopped at noon that day Carson told us as we sat eating our luncheon that we were now in the Ute country, and every one of us must keep a look out for himself. He said, "Now, boys, don't any one of you get a hundred yards away from the rest of the company, for the Utes are like flees liable to jump on you at any time or place."

That afternoon we ran on a great deal of Indian sign, from the fact that game was plentiful all over the country, and at this time of the year the Indians were on their spring hunt. When we camped for the night, we camped on a small stream where there was but very little timber and no underbrush at all. As soon as the company was settled for the night, Carson and I mounted our horses and took a circle of perhaps a mile or two around the camp. This was to ascertain whether there were any Indians in camp near us. We saw no Indians. We returned to camp thinking we would have no trouble that night, but about sundown, while we were eating supper, all at once their war whoop burst upon us, and fifteen or more Utes came dashing down the hill on their horses. Every man sprang for his gun, in order to give them as warm a reception as possible; nearly every man tried to reach his horse before the Indians got to us, for at that time a man without a horse would have been in a bad fix, for there were no extra horses in the company.

I think this must have been the first time these Utes had ever heard a gun fired, from the fact that as soon as we commenced firing at them, and that was before they could reach us with their arrows, they turned and left as fast as they had come. Consequently we lost no men or horses. We killed five Indians and captured three horses.

When the Indians were out of sight, Carson laughed and said, "Boys, that was the easiest won battle I have ever had with the Indians, and it was not our good marksmanship that done it either, for if every shot we fired had taken effect, there would not have been half Indians enough to go around. It was the report of our guns that scared them away."

It was figured up that night how many shots were fired, and they amounted to two hundred. Carson said, "Boys, if we get into another fight with the Indians, for God's sake don't throw away your powder and lead in that shape again, for before you reach Monterey, powder and lead will be worth something, as the Red skins are as thick as grass-hoppers in August."

Of course this was the first skirmish these men had ever had with the Indians, and they were too excited to know what they were doing.

About six years ago I met a man whose name was Labor. He was the last survivor of that company, with the exception of myself, and he told me how he felt when the yelling Red skins burst upon us. Said he, "I don't think I could have hit an Indian if he had been as big as the side of a horse, for I was shaking worse than I would if I had had the third-day Ague. Not only shaking, but I was cold all over, and I dreamed all night of seeing all kinds of Indians."

The next day we were traveling on the back bone of a little ridge. There was no timber except a few scattering Juniper trees. We were now in Arizona, and water was very scarce. The reader will understand that Carson invariably rode from fifty to one hundred yards ahead of the command, and I always rode at his side.

I presume it was between two and three o'clock in the afternoon when Col. Freemont called out to Carson, "How far are you going tonight?"

Carson studied a minute and answered, "I think, in seven or eight miles we will find good water and a plenty of grass."

A few minutes after this Freemont said, "Say, Carson, why not go to that lake there and camp? There is plenty of grass and water," at the same time pointing to the south. Carson raised his head and looked at the point indicated. Then he said, "Col. there is no water or grass there." Freemont replied, "Damn it, look. Can't you see it?" at the same time pointing in the direction of what he supposed to be the lake. Carson checked his horse until Freemont came up near him and then said, "Col., spot this place by these little Juniper trees, and we will come back here tomorrow morning, and if you can see a lake there then I will admit that I don't know anything about this country."

Freemont was out of humor all the evening. He had nothing to say to any person.

The next morning after breakfast was over and the herder had driven in the horses Carson said, "Now Colonel, let's go and see that lake."

Under the circumstances Freemont could not say "no." I think five of us besides Carson and Freemont went back. When we came to the place where the little Juniper trees were, Freemont's face showed that he was badly whipped, for sure enough there was no lake there; he had seen what is called a mirage.

I have seen almost everything in mirage form, but what causes this Atmospheric optical illusion has never been explained to my satisfaction. Some men say it is imagination, but I do not think it is so.

On our way back to camp a man by name of Cummings was riding by my side.
He made the remark in an undertone, "I am sorry this thing happened." I asked him, "Why?" In reply he said, "Colonel Freemont won't get over this in many a day, for Carson has shown him that he can be mistaken."

We laid over at this camp until the next day as this was good water and exceptionally good grass. Nothing interfered with us until we struck the Colorado river. Here we met quite a band of Umer Indians. Without any exception they were the worst-looking human beings that I have ever seen in my life. A large majority of them were as naked as they were when they were born. Their hair in many instances looked as if it never had been straightened out. They lived mostly on pine nuts. The nuts grow on a low, scrubby tree, a species of Pine, and in gathering the nuts they covered their hands with gum which is as sticky as tar and rubbed it on their bodies and in their hair. The reader may imagine the effect; I am satisfied that many of these Indians had never seen a white man before they saw us. Very few of them had bows and arrows; they caught fish. How they caught them I never knew, but I often saw the squaws carrying fish.

When we reached the Colorado river we stayed two days making rafts to cross the river on. The last day we were there, laying on the bank of the river, I presume there came five hundred of these Indians within fifty yards of our camp. Most of them laid down under the trees. One of our men shot a bird that was in a tree close by, and I never heard such shouting or saw such running as these Indians did when the gun cracked. This convinced me that we were the first white men they had ever seen, and this the first time they had heard the report of a gun. This incident occurred in forty-eight, which was fifty-eight years ago. I have seen more or less of these Indians from that time until now, and these Indians as a tribe have made less progress than any other Indians in the west. Even after the railroad was put through that part of the country, they had to be forced to cover themselves with clothes.

After crossing the Colorado river we came into the Ute country, but we traveled several days without seeing any of this tribe. About five days after we crossed the Colorado river, we came on to a big band of Sighewash Indians. The tribe was just coming together, after a winter's trapping and hunting. At this time the Sigh washes were a powerful tribe, but not hostile to the whites.

We camped near their village that night. After supper Carson and I went over to this village, at the same time taking a lot of butcher knives and cheap jewelry with us that he had brought along to trade with the Indians. When we got into their camp, Carson inquired where the chief's wigwam, was. The Indians could all speak Spanish; therefore we had no trouble in finding the chief. When we went into the chief's wigwam, after shaking hands with the old chief and his squaw, Carson pulled some of the jewelry out of his pocket and told the chief that he wanted to trade for furs. The old chief stepped to the entrance of the wigwam and made a peculiar noise between a whistle and a hollo, and in a few minutes there were hundreds of Indians there, both bucks and squaws.

The old chief made a little talk to them that I did not understand; he then turned to Carson and said, "Indian heap like white man."

Carson then spoke out loud so they could all hear him, at the same time holding up some jewelry in one hand and a butcher knife in the other, telling them that he wanted to trade these things for their furs.

The Indians answered, it seemed to me by the hundreds, saying, "Iyah oyah iyah," which means "All right." Carson then told them to bring their furs over to his camp the next morning, and he would then trade with them. He was speaking in Spanish all this time. On our way back to our camp Carson said to me, "Now Willie, if I trade for those furs in the morning I want you and the other two boys to take the furs and go back to Taos; I know that you will have a long and lonesome trip, but I will try and get three or four of these Indians to go with you back to the head of the Blue, and be very careful, and when you make a camp always put out all of your fire as soon as you get your meal cooked. Then the Indians can not see your camp."

The next morning we were up and had an early breakfast. By that time the squaws had commenced coming in with their furs. Uncle Kit took a pack of jewelry and knives and got off to one side where the Indians could get all around him. In a very short time I think there must have been a hundred squaws there with their furs.

They brought from one to a dozen Beaver skins each, and then the Bucks began coming in and then the trading began. Carson would hold up a finger ring or a knife and call out in Spanish, "I'll give this for so many Beaver skins!"

It really was amusing to see the Indians run over each other to see who should get the ring or knife first.

This trading did not last over half an hour because Carson's stock of goods was exhausted. Carson then said to the Indians, "No more trade no more knives, no more rings, all gone."

Of course a great many of the Indians were disappointed, but they soon left us. As soon as they were gone Freemont came to Carson and said, "What in the name of common sense are you going to do with all those furs?"

Uncle Kit said, "Col., I'm going to send them to Taos, and later on they will go to Bent's Fort." The Col. said, "Yes, but by whom will you send them to Taos?" Carson replied, "By Willie, John and the Mexican boy."

The Col. said, "Don't you think you are taking a great many chances?" "Oh, no, not at all. Willie here is getting to be quite a mountaineer. Besides, I am going to get some of these Indians to go with the boys as far as the head of the Blue, and when they get there they are, comparatively speaking, out of danger."

He then said, "Colonel, we will lay over here today, and that will give me a chance to pack my furs and get the boys ready to start in the morning."

We then went to work baling the hides; by noon we had them all baled. After dinner Carson and I went over to the Indian camp. We went directly to the Chief's wigwam. When the Indians saw us coming they all rushed up to us. I presume they thought we had come to trade with them again. Uncle Kit then told the Chief that he wanted eight Indian men to go with us boys to the head of the Blue River. At the same time he sat down and marked on the ground each stream and mountain that he wanted us to travel over. He told them that he would give each one of them one butcher knife and two rings, and said they must not camp with the Utes.

I think there were at least twenty Indians that wanted to go. Carson then turned to the Chief and told him in Spanish to pick out eight good Indians to go with us, and told him just what time we wanted to start in the morning.

We then went back to our camp and commenced making arrangements for our journey to Taos.

Carson and I were sitting down talking that afternoon when Col. Freemont came and sat beside us and said to Uncle Kit, "Say, Kit, ain't you taking desperate chances with these boys?"

This surprised me, for I had never heard him address Carson as Kit before in all the time I had known him.

Carson laughed and answered, "Not in the least; for they have got a good escort to go with them." Then he explained to Freemont that he had hired some Indians to go with us through the entire hostile country, telling him that the boys were just as safe with those Indians as they would be with the command, and more safe, for the Indians would protect them, thinking they would get his trade by so doing. Uncle Kit then explained to him that the Sighewashes were known to all the tribes on the coast and were on good terms with them all, and therefore there was no danger whatever in sending the boys through the Indian country. The Col. answered, "Of course, you know best; I admit that you know the nature of the Indian thoroughly, but I must say that I shall be uneasy until I hear from the boys again."

Uncle Kit said, "Wait until tomorrow morning, and I will convince you that I am right."

The next morning we were up early and had breakfast, and before we had our animals half packed the old chief and hundreds of the Indians were there. Those that the chief had selected to accompany us were on horse back, and the others had come to bid us farewell, and that was one of the times I was tired shaking hands.

When we were about ready to mount our horses and had shaken hands with Uncle Kit and the balance of the company, the Indians made a rush for us. Both bucks and squaws shouted, "Ideose, ideose," which means, "good bye, good bye," and every one trying to shake our hands at once, and of all the noise I ever heard, this was the worst. After this racket had been going on some fifteen or twenty minutes, I turned and saw Uncle Kit and Col. Freemont standing on a big log laughing like they would split their sides. Finally Uncle Kit motioned for me to mount my horse. I mounted and the other boys followed suit, and when we started of all the noise that ever was made this beat any I ever heard in all my life. At the same time the Indians were waving their hands at us.

As soon as we left the crowd of Indians Uncle Kit and Col. Freemont joined us. The Col. said to me, "Willie, this is one of the times you have had your hand well shaken, I really felt sorry for you, but I didn't see how I could assist you, and I am in hopes you will not get such a shaking up in a good while.

Now, my boy, be very careful, and try and get through safe and sound, and when we come along back next fall, we will all go to St. Louis together."

Uncle Kit told me to not let the Indians turn back until we crossed the divide at the head of Blue river. He said, "Then you will be out of the Ute country, and all danger to you will be over, but do not put too much confidence in these Indians although I think they are reliable and will do just as I have told them to do. But I want you to be on the lookout all the time yourself. I know there will be no danger in the daytime, and when night comes be sure and put your fire out before it gets dark, and when you get to Taos rest up a few days, and then hunt up Jim Bridger or Jim Beckwith, and they will advise you what to do. It may be that I will get home myself, in which case you will not need their advice."

We now bid them "good bye" and started on what would be called now a long, tedious and dangerous journey, but at that time we thought nothing of it.

How long a time it took us to make this trip I do not remember. The Indians traveled in the lead the most of the time. When near the middle of the afternoon, I would ask them in Spanish how far they were going tonight, and they would tell me the number of hours it would take to go but seemed not to understand the distance by miles. The Indians showed more judgment in selecting the camping ground than I expected they would.

In a few days we were in the Ute country, and we saw plenty of Indian sign every day. I think it was on one of the tributaries of the Green river we were traveling along one afternoon, we came in sight of a band of Ute Indians. They were in camp. We were in about a half a mile of them when we first saw them; they were directly to the north of us, and they discovered us at the same time we saw them. As soon as the Sighewashes saw the Utes they stopped, and two of the Sighewashes rode back to us and said in Spanish, "We go see Utes," and they rode over to the Ute camp. Probably they were gone a half hour or more, when they returned, and we surely watched every move the Utes made till the Sighewashes came back to us. When they came back they were laughing and said to us, "Utes heap good." Then I was satisfied that we were in no danger.

We traveled on some five or six miles when we came to a nice little stream of water where there was fine grass. I said to the boys, "We'll camp here. Now you boys unpack the animals and take them out to grass, and I will go and kill some meat for supper."

I picked up my gun and started; I didn't go over a quarter of a mile till I saw four Bison cows, and they all had calves with them. I crawled up in shooting distance and killed one of the calves. At the crack of my gun the cows ran away. I commenced dressing the calf and here came four of my Sighewash Indians running to me, and when they saw what I had killed, I believe they were the happiest mortals that I ever saw.

As soon as I got the insides out I told them to pick up the calf and we would go to camp. Some of them picked up the carcass and others picked up the entrails. I told them we did not want the entrails. One of the Indians spoke up and said, "Heap good, all same good meat". I finally persuaded them to leave the insides alone.

When we got back to camp, the boys had a good fire, and it was not long before we had plenty of meat around the fire, and I never saw Indians eat as they did that night. After they had been eating about an hour, Jonnie West said to me, "Will, you will have to go and kill more meat, or we won't have any for breakfast."

We soon turned in for the night and left the Indians still cooking. In the morning we were surprised to see the amount of meat they had got away with. What they ate that night would have been plenty for the same number of white men three or four days. The nature of the Indian is to eat when he has the chance and when he hasn't he goes without and never complains.

For the next three days we traveled through a country well supplied with game, especially Elk, Deer, and black bear. It was now late in the summer and all game was in a fine condition, it was no unusual thing to see from twenty five to a hundred Elk in a band. I have never seen since that time so many Elk with so large horns as I saw on that trip, which convinced me that there had been no white hunters through that part of the country before.

In traveling along there were times we were not out of sight of deer for hours; consequently we never killed our game for supper until we went into camp, and as a rule, the boys always picked me to get the meat while they took care of the horses. I remember one evening I was just getting ready to start out on my hunt. I asked the boys what kind of meat they wanted for supper. Jonnie West said, "Give us something new." Well, I answered, "How will a cub bear do?" They all answered, "That is just what we want." That moment I turned my eyes to the south, and on a ridge not more than three hundred yards from camp, I saw three bears eating sarvis berries. I was not long in getting into gun shot of them. There was the old mother bear and two cubs. I had to wait several minutes before I could get a good sight on the one I wanted, as they were in the brush and I wanted a sure shot. I fired and broke his neck; he had hardly done kicking before Jonnie West and some of the Indians were there. We made quick work getting the meat to camp and around the fire cooking, and it was as fine a piece of meat as I ever ate.

The next morning we bid the Indians good bye, but before they left us one of them stooped down and with a finger marked out the route we should take, thinking we did not know the country we must pass over, and strange to say, the route this wild Indian marked out in the sand was accurate in every particular. He made dots for the places where we should camp and a little mark for a stream of water, then little piles of sand for mountains, some large and some small, according to the size of the mountain we were to cross. After he had finished his work, I examined the diagram and I found he had marked out every place where we should camp.

From there to the head of the Arkansas river, I called Jonnie West and asked him to look at it. He examined it at every point and said, "This beats any thing I ever saw or heard tell of; with this to guide us, we could not get lost if we tried to."

We were now ready to start. Jonnie said to me, "Well, I feel we owe this Indian something. How many butcher knives have you?"

I said, "I have two." "Alright, I will give him this finger ring and you give him one of your knives."

We did so, and I think he was the proudest Indian I ever saw; he jumped up and shouted, "Hy-you-scu-scum, white man," which meant "Good white man."

The Indians all shook hands with us and then mounted their horses and were gone. We now pulled out on our long and dangerous trip to Taos, New Mexico, and strange to say, we never missed a camping ground that the Indians had marked out for us, until we reached the head of the Arkansas river, and the beauty of it was, we had good grass and good water at every camping place, which was very essential for ourselves and our horses.

When we struck the head of the Arkansas river we considered ourselves out of danger of all hostile Indians. Besides, we knew every foot of the ground we had to travel over from here to Taos, New Mexico. We camped one night on the river, down below where Leadville stands now, and I never saw so many huckleberries at one place as I saw there. After we had our horses unpacked and staked out to grass, I said to the boys, "Now you go and pick berries, and I will try and find some meat for supper." I did not go far when looking up on a high bluff I saw a band of mountain sheep. I noticed they had not seen me yet and were coming directly towards me. When they got in gun-shot, I fired and killed a half-grown sheep, and he did not stop kicking until he was nearly at my feet. This was the first mountain sheep I had ever killed, and it was as fine a piece of meat as I ever ate, and until this day, mountain sheep is my favorite wild meat. This was one of the nights to be remembered, fine fresh meat, and ripe huckleberries, what luxuries, for the wilds to produce.

In a few days we reached Taos, and here I met my old friend Jim Bridger. After laying around a few days and resting up, Jonnie West said to me, "Will, what are we going to do this winter? You are like me, you can't lay around without going wild."

I said, "That's so, Jonnie. Let's go and hunt up Jim Bridger, and ask him what he is going to do this winter."

We went to the house where Jim was boarding and we found him in one of his talkative moods. We asked him what he proposed doing this winter; he said, "I am going out a trapping, and I want you boys to go with me."

I asked him where he was going to trap, and he said he thought he would trap on the head of the Cache-la-Poudre, and the quicker we went the better it would be for us. "I have all the traps we will need this winter," he said; "now you boys go to work and mould a lot of bullets."

The reader will understand that in those days we used the muzzle-loading gun, and we had to mould all of our bullets. In a few days we were ready to pull out. I asked Jim if we could keep our horses with us through the winter. He said, "Yes, as the snow does not get very deep in that country, and there is plenty of Cotton Wood and Quaker Asp for them to browse on in case the snow gets deep. Besides, it will save one of us a long tramp in the spring, for we will have to have the horses in order to pack our furs on."

In a few days we were ready to pull for trapping ground. Each one of us took a saddle horse and two pack horses. We were on the road nine days from the day we left Taos until we reached our trapping ground.

We traveled down Cherry Creek from its source to its mouth, and across the Platte, where Denver City, Colorado, now stands. At that time there was not a sign of civilization in all that country.

After crossing the Platte a little below where Denver now stands, we met about five hundred Kiawah Indians, led by their old chief. The Kiawas were friendly to us, and the chief was a particular friend of Jim. He wanted to trade for some of our beaver traps. He kept bidding until he offered two horses for one trap. Jim refused to trade, but he made the chief a present of a trap. After Jim refused to take the horses, a young squaw came running out and offered to give me as fine a buffalo robe as I ever saw; I was in the act of taking it and was congratulating myself on what a fine bed I would have that winter when Jim said, "Will, don't take that. There is more stock on that robe than we can feed this winter. Open the hair and look for yourself."

I did so, and I saw the Grey Backs all through the hair as thick as they could crawl. I had never seen such a sight before, and the reader can imagine my horror. I dropped it so quick that Jonnie West laughed and asked me if it burnt me. The boys had the joke on me the balance of the winter. Most every day they would ask me if I didn't want a present of a Buffalo robe from a young squaw.

A few days after this, we were on our trapping ground, and our winter's work of toil, hardship, and pleasure had begun. We soon had our cabin built in a little valley, which was from a half mile to a mile wide and about eight miles long. On each side of the valley were high cliffs. In places there was a half a mile or more where neither man or beast could climb these cliffs, and we were surprised later on to see the quantity of game of various kinds that came into this valley to winter, such as Elk, Deer, and Antelope. I never, before or since, have seen so many Wild Cats, or Bob Cats, as they were called at that time, and also some cougars.

I remember one little circumstance that occurred later on; it was about the middle of the afternoon; we had all been to our traps and had returned to the cabin with our furs. Jim said, "Will, we will stretch your furs if you will go and shoot a deer for supper."

This suited me, so I took my gun and went outside the door to clean it. Just as I had got through, Jonnie West looked out and said, "Look, Will, there is your deer now; you won't have to hunt him."

I looked, and sure enough, there he was, in about a hundred yards of the cabin. Jim Bridger fired at him and knocked him down, but he got up and ran into a little bunch of brush. I ran to the spot, thinking he was only wounded and that I should have to shoot him again. When I reached the brush, to my surprise, I found five big wildcats, and they all came for me at once. I fired at the leader, and then I did some lively running myself. As soon as I got out of the brush, I called the boys, and we got the cats, the whole of the bunch, and the deer besides, which had not been touched by the cats.

We skinned the cats, and Jim afterwards made a cap out of one of them, and he wore it for several years.

Jonnie West and I were out hunting one day for deer when we discovered two cougars in the grass, and we could not make out what it meant. Finally one made a spring, and it seemed to us that he jumped at least twenty feet, and he landed on a deer, and for a minute or two there was a tussle. While this was going on Jonnie and I were getting closer to them, and when they had the deer killed we were within gunshot of them, and they didn't eat much before we killed them both. We skinned the deer, and also the cougars, and took them to camp, and when we went to Bent's Fort the next spring we got twenty dollars apiece for them, for they were extra large cougars, or mountain lions as they are sometimes called, and their hides are very valuable.

It seems wonderful to me when I think of the amount of game I saw through the country at that time, of all descriptions, some of which in their wild state are now extinct, especially the buffalo and the bison, and all other game that was so plentiful at that time is very scarce all over the west. I believe a man could have seen a thousand antelope any day in the year within five miles of where the city of Denver now stands.

We had splendid success this winter in trapping beaver. It was late in the spring when we left our trapping ground. Just before we pulled out Jim Bridger said, "Boys, I saw a pretty sight this evening out at the point of rocks," which was about a quarter of a mile from our cabin. Jonnie West said, "What did you see, Jim?"

"I saw an old Cinnamon bear and two cubs." Jonnie said, "Why didn't you kill her?"

"I didn't have anything to kill with," Jim replied. "I left my gun in the cabin, but we will all go out in the morning and see if we can find them."

We were all up early in the morning and ready for the bear hunt. Jim told us what route each should take. He said, "Now boys, be careful, for she is an old whale, and if you get in to a fight with her some one will get hurt, or there will be some running done."

I had not gone far when I looked up on a ridge ahead of me and saw what I took to be Mrs. Bruin; I crawled up within gun shot and fired and broke the bear's neck. I rushed up to her expecting to see the cubs. Imagine my surprise when I found only a small bear. In a few moments the boys were there; Jonnie laughed and asked Jim if that bear was the whale he set out to kill. Jim stood and looked at the bear quite a bit before answering. Then he said, "That is a Cinnamon Bear, but where are the cubs?" Jonnie said, "I will bet my hat you didn't see any cubs, Jim, you dreamed it." Jim grinned and answered, "Well, boys I guess you have the drop on me this time."

From then on, all the spring Jim's cubs was a standing joke. In a few days, we pulled out for Bent's Fort; we were late in getting to the Fort with our furs this spring. Mr. Bent asked us why we were so late in getting in. Jonnie replied that Jim kept us hunting for Cub bears all the spring, and as we couldn't find any, it took all our time. Of course they all wanted to know the joke, and when Jonnie told it in his droll way, it made a laugh on Jim. "If you will only quit talking about the cubs," Jim said, "I'll treat all around," which cost him about ten dollars.

After laying around the Fort a few days, Col. Bent and Mr. Roubidoux hired Jonnie and me to kill meat to supply the table at the boarding house for the summer, that being the only time of the year that the boarding house at the Fort did any business. At this time of the year all of the trappers and hunters were staying at the fort with nothing to do but eat, drink and spend their money that they had earned the winter before. It was no uncommon thing for some of these men to bring from three to four hundred dollars worth of furs to Bent's Fort in the spring, and when fall came and it was time to go back to the trapping ground, they wouldn't have a dollar left, and some of them had to go in debt for their winter outfit.

Jonnie and I had no trouble in keeping plenty of meat on hand, from the fact that buffalo and antelope were very plentiful eight or ten miles from the fort. I remember one little circumstance that occurred this summer. We were out hunting, not far from the Arkansas river, near the city now known as Rocky Ford, Colo. We had camped there the night before. We went out early in the morning to kill some antelope, leaving our horses staked where we had camped. We hadn't gone more than half a mile when we heard a Lofa wolf howl just ahead of us. The Lofa wolf was a very large and ferocious animal and was a terror to the buffalo. When we reached the top of a ridge just ahead of us, looking down into a little valley two or three hundred yards away, we saw five Buffalo cows with their calves, and one large bull, and they were entirely surrounded by Lofa wolves. Jonnie said, "Now, Will, we will see some fun." The cows were trying to defend their calves from the wolves, and the bull started off with his head lowered to the ground, trying to drive the wolves away with his horns. This he continued to do until he had driven the wolves thirty yards away. All at once a wolf made a bark and a howl which seemed to be a signal for a general attack, for in a moment, the wolves were attacking the Buffalo on every side, and I don't think it was five minutes before they had the bull dead and stretched out. Until then I had never thought that wolves would attack a well Buffalo, but this sight convinced me that they could and would kill any buffalo they chose to attack.

We went back to camp, packed up our meat, and pulled out for the fort. When we got there I told Jim Bridger about the fight the wolves had with the buffalos, and he said, "If you had seen as much of that as I have, you would know that wolves signal to each other and understand each other the same as men do."

CHAPTER II.

It was early in the spring of fifty when Kit Carson, Jim Bridger, and myself met at Bent's Fort, which was on the head waters, of the Arkansas river. Bridger and I had just got in from our winter's trapping ground and had disposed of our furs to a very good advantage; Carson had just returned from a trip back east. Carson said to Bridger, "Now Jim, I'll tell you what I want you to do. I want you and Will (meaning me) to go over to Fort Kerney and escort emigrants across to California this season, for the gold excitement back in the eastern states is something wonderful, and there will be thousands of emigrants going to the gold fields of California, and they do not know the danger they will have to contend with, and you two men can save thousands of lives this summer by going to Fort Kerney and meeting the emigrants there and escorting them through. Now boys, you must understand that this undertaking is no child's play. In doing this apparently many times you will seem to take your lives in your own hands, for the Indians will be worse on the plains this year than they ever have been. At the present time there is no protection for the emigrant from the time they get twenty-five miles west of Fort Kerney, until they cross the Sierra Nevada mountains, and there are to be so many renegades from justice from Illinois and Missouri that it is going to be fearful this season, for the renegade is really worse in some respects than the Indian. He invariably has two objects in view. He gets the Indian to commit the murder which is a satisfaction to him without any personal risk besides the plunder he gets. I know, boys, you can get good wages out of this thing, and I want you to take hold of it, and you, Jim, I know have no better friend than Gen. Kerney, and he will assist you boys in every way he can. I almost feel as though I ought to go myself, but I cannot leave my family at the present time; now, Jim, will you go?" Bridger jumped up, rubbed his hands together and said, "I'll be dog goned if I won't, if Will goes with me."

[Illustration: As soon as they were gone I took the scalp off the dead Chief's head.]

To which I replied, "I will go with you, and I think the quicker we start the better it will be for all parties concerned." Carson said, "You can't start too soon, for the emigrants will be arriving at Fort Kerney by the time you get there."

The next morning Jim and I were up and had an early breakfast and were ready to start. Uncle Kit said to us, "Now boys, when you come back this fall I want you to come and see me and tell me what kind of luck you have had, and all the news."

We now bid him good bye, and we were off.

I will here inform the reader that Carson had taught me to call him Uncle Kit when I was fourteen years old, and I always addressed him in that way. Jim and I were off for Fort Kerney, which was a journey of about three hundred miles and not a sign of civilization on the whole trip. It was a wild Indian country the entire distance, but we knew where the hostile Indians were and also the friendly Indians. Consequently we reached Fort Kerney without having any trouble.

We met Gen. Kerney, who was glad to see us. He said, "Boys, where in the name of common sense are you going to?"

We explained to him in a few words our business. After hearing our plans the Gen. said, "I am certainly glad to know that someone will take hold of this thing, for I am sure that there will be more emigrants massacred this year than has ever been in any other. I will tell you why I think so. All the Indians from here to the Sierra-Nevada mountains are in the war-path; in the second place the emigrants who are coming from the east have no idea what they have to contend with, and I dread the consequences."

While this conversation was taking place a soldier rode in that had been on picket duty and said to the Gen., "I saw some covered wagons going into camp down on Deer Creek about five miles from here. Where do you suppose they are going, Gen?"

To which Gen. Kerney replied, "They are going to California, and you will see hundreds of them inside the next two weeks."

Jim Bridger said, "Well, Willie, come on and let's see what we can do with them."

As we were leaving the Fort Gen. Kerney said to us, "Boys, come back and stay all night with me, I want you to make my quarters your home while you are waiting for the emigrants to arrive."

Bridger answered, "Thank you, Gen. We will be glad to do so, and we may want you to recommend us to the emigrants."

To which the Gen. answered, "I will take pleasure in doing so."

Bridger and I rode down to where the emigrants were in camp, and we found the most excited people I ever saw in my life. They had passed through one of the most terrible experiences that had ever occurred on the frontier. There were thirty wagons in the train, and they were all from the southeastern part of Missouri, and it seemed that there was one man in the train by the name of Rebel who at the time they had left home had sworn that he would kill the first Indian he came across. This opportunity occurred this morning about five miles back of where we met them. The train was moving along slowly when this man "Rebel" saw a squaw sitting on a log with a papoose in her arms, nursing. He shot her down; she was a Kiawah squaw, and it was right on the edge of their village where he killed her in cold blood. The Kiawahs were a very strong tribe, but up to this time they had never been hostile to the whites; but this deed so enraged the warriors that they came out in a body and surrounded the emigrants and demanded them to give up the man who had shot the squaw. Of course, his comrades tried not to give him to them, but the Indians told them if they did not give the man to them, they would kill them all. So knowing that the whole train was at the mercy of the Indians, they gave the man to them. The Indians dragged him about a hundred yards and tied him to a tree, and then they skinned him alive and then turned him loose. One of the men told us that the butchered creature lived about an hour, suffering the most intense agony. They had just buried him when we rode into the camp. The woman and some of the men talked about the dreadful thing; one of the men said it was a comfort to know that he had no family with him here or back home to grieve at his dreadful death.

On hearing this remark Jim said, "You are the most lucky outfit I ever saw. Any other tribe of Indians this side of the Rocky Mountains would not have left one of you to have told the tale, and it is just such darned fools as that man that stir up the Indians, to do so much deviltry."

Until this time there had been but a few of the emigrants near us. We were both dressed in buck-skin, and they did not know what to make of us. The young girls and some of the young men were very shy. They had never seen anyone dressed in buck-skin before. An elderly woman came to us and said, "Ain't you two men what they call mountaineers?" Jim answered, "Yes, marm, I reckon, we are."

She replied, "Well, if you are, my old man wants you to come and eat supper with we'ns."

Jim turned to me and laughed. "Shall we go and eat with them, Willie?" he asked. I answered, "Yes, let's get acquainted with everybody."

We went with the old lady to their tent, which was but a few steps from where we stood. When she had presented us to her old man as she called him, she said to him, "Jim, I know these men can tell you what to do." He shook hands with us, saying, "I don't know what in the world we are going to do. I believe the Indians will kill us all if we try to go any further, and I know they will if we go back."

By this time there was quite a crowd around us.

I said to Jim, "Why don't you tell the people, what we can do for them?" Jim then said, "why, dog gorn it, this boy and I can take you all through to California and not be troubled with the Indians if there is no more durned fools among you to be a-shooting squaws. But you will have to do just as we tell you to do." And looking over the ground he asked, "Who is your captain? I want to see him."

The old man said, "Want to see our Capt'n? We hain't got any capt'n, got no use for one." Jim then asked, "Who puts out your guards around the camp at night?"

"Guards? Didn't know we had to have any."

Jim looked the astonishment he felt as he said, "Why, dad-blame-it man, you won't get a hundred miles from here before all of you will be killed."

At that moment one of the men said, "Who is this coming?"

We all looked in the direction he was, and we saw it was Gen. Kerney. When he rode up to us Bridger said, "Gen., what do you think? These people have no captain and have no one to guard the camp at night."

The Gen. answered, "Is that possible? How in the name of god have they got here without being massacred?" And then, addressing the men that stood near he said, "Gentlemen, you had better make some arrangement with my friends here to pilot you across to California; for I assure you that if these men go with you and you follow their directions, you will reach your journey's end in safety."

Just then the Gen. looked down the road, and he said, "Look there!"

We all looked, and we saw another long train of emigrants coming towards us. They drove up near us and prepared to go into camp. This was a mixed train. Some came from Illinois, some from Indiana, and a few families from the state of Ohio.

Jim and I mounted our horses and rode with the Gen. down among the new emigrants. They had heard all about the skinning of the white man and were terribly excited about it. They asked the Gen. what was best for them to do. A great many of them wanted to turn and go back. Finally the Gen. said to them, "Here are two as good men as there are in the mountains. They are thoroughly reliable and understand the Indians' habits perfectly. Now, my friends, the best thing you can do is to organize yourselves into company, select your captain and then make some arrangement with these men to pilot you through, for I tell you now, there will be more trouble on the plains this year than has ever been known before with the Indians. Now gentlemen, we must leave you, but we will come back in the morning and see what decision you have come to."

At this time two men stepped up to Jim Bridger and me and said, "Why can't you two stay all night with us? We've got plenty to eat, and you both can sleep in our tent."

Jim answered, "We don't want to sleep in any tent. We've got our blankets, and we will sleep under that tree," pointing to a tree near us.

The Gen. said, "Mr. Bridger, you boys had better stay here tonight, for you have lots of business to talk over."

Jim and I dismounted, staked our horses out and went to supper. After supper Jim said, "Now, you want to get together and elect a captain."

One man said, "All right, I'll go and notify the entire camp, and we will call a meeting at once." Which was done. As soon as the crowd gathered, they called on Jim to tell them what to do. Jim mounted the tongue of a wagon and said, "Now, men, the first thing to do is to elect a Captain, and we must take the name of every able-bodied man in this outfit, for you will have to put out camp guards and picket guards every night. Now, pick out your men, and I'll put it to a vote."

Some called for Mr. Davis, and some for Mr. Thomas; both men came forward. Jim said, "now, Mr. Davis, get up on this wagon tongue and I'll make a mark, and we'll see if the crowd wants you for their Captain." Jim took a stick and made a mark on the ground from the wagon tongue clear out through the crowd. He then said, "All that want Mr. Davis for Captain will step to the right of this line, and they that favor Mr. Thomas will keep to the left of the line." About three fourths of the men stepped to the right of the line, which made Davis Captain. As soon as Davis was declared Captain, he said, "Now friends, we must hire these men to escort us to California; if there is anybody here that is not in favor of this let him say so now."

But everyone shouted, "Yes! yes!"

Davis turned to us and said, "What is your price for the trip?"

Jim said to me, "What do you say, Will?"

I replied, "It is worth four dollars a day each."

Jim told the Captain that we would go for four dollars a day to be paid each of us every Saturday night, and if at the end of the first week we had not given satisfaction, we would quit. Davis put it to a vote, and it was carried in our favor.

The balance of the evening was spent in making arrangements to commence drilling the men. In the morning Jim said to me, "Now, Will, I'll take charge of the wagons and you take charge of the scouts."

I told the Captain that I wanted him to select seven good men that owned their horses. I wanted to drill them to act as scouts. Jim said, "Yes, we want to get to drilling every body tomorrow morning."

We put in four hard days' work at this business, and then we were ready for the trail, and we pulled out on our long and tedious journey to the land of gold.

There were four hundred and eighty-six men and ninety women in the train, and they had one hundred and forty-eight wagons. Every thing moved smoothly until we were near the head of the North Platte river. We were now in the Sioux country, and I began to see a plenty of Indian sign. Jim and I had arranged that a certain signal meant for him to corral the wagons at once. As I was crossing the divide at the head of Sweet Water, I discovered quite a band of Indians coming directly towards the train, but I did not think they had seen it yet. I rode back as fast as my horse could carry me. When I saw the train, I signaled to Jim to corral, and I never saw such a number of wagons corralled so quickly before or since, as they were. Jim told the women and children to leave the wagon and go inside the corral, and he told the men to stand outside with their guns, ready for action, but to hold their fire until he gave the word, and he said, "When you shoot, shoot to kill; and do your duty as brave men should."

In a moment, the Indians were in sight, coming over the hill at full speed. When they saw the wagons, they gave the war whoop. This scared the women, and they began to cry and scream and cling to their children. Jim jumped up on a wagon tongue and shouted at the top of his voice "For God's sake, women, keep still, or you will all be killed."

This had the effect that he desired, and there was not a word or sound out of them. When the Indians were within a hundred yards from us, their yelling was terrible to hear.

Jim now said, "Now boys, give it to them, and let the red devils have something to yell about," and I never saw men stand up and fight better than these emigrants. They were fighting for their mothers' and wives' and children's lives, and they did it bravely. In a few minutes the fight was over, and what was left of the Indians got away in short order. We did not lose a man, and only one was slightly wounded. There were sixty-three dead warriors left on the field, and we captured twenty horses.

It was six miles from here to the nearest water, so we had to drive that distance to find a place to camp. We reached the camping ground a little before sunset. After attending to the teams and stationing the guards for the night Cap't. Davis came to Jim and me and said, "The ladies want to give you a reception tonight."

Jim said, "What for?" Davis replied, "Saving our lives from those horrible savages." Jim answered, "Why, durn it all, ain't that what you are paying us for? We just done our duty and no more, as we intend to do all the way to California."

By this time there was a dozen women around us. With the others was a middle-aged woman. She said, "Now, you men with the buck-skin clothes, come and take supper with us. It is now all ready."

Jim said, "Come, Willie, let's go and eat, for I am hungry and tired too."

While we were eating supper, three or four young ladies came up to us and asked me if I didn't want to dance.

"The boys are cleaning off the ground now, and I want you for my first pardner," she said with a smile and a blush. Jim said, "Will can't dance anything but the scalp dance." One of the girls said, "What kind of a dance is that?"

Jim replied, "If the Indians had got some of your scalps this afternoon you would have known something about it by this time."

Jim told them that when the Indians scalped a young girl, they took the scalp to their wigwam and then gave a dance to show the young squaws what a brave deed they had done, "and all you girls had better watch out that they don't have some of your scalps to dance around before you get to California; but if you wish us to, Will and I will dance the scalp dance tonight, so you can see how it is done."

When they had the ground all fixed for the dance, Jim and I took our handkerchiefs and put them on a couple of sticks, stuck the sticks into the ground and went through the Indian scalp dance, making all the hideous motions with jumps and screams, loud enough to start the hair from its roots, after which Jim explained to them this strange custom, telling them that if any of them was unfortunate enough to fall into the Indians' hands this was the performance that would be had around their scalps.

The girls said with a shudder they had seen enough of that kind of dancing without the Indians showing them. The lady who had invited us to supper said, "Now girls, you see what these men have done for us, they have saved our lives, and do you realize the obligation we are under to them? Now let us do everything we can for their comfort until we reach California."

And I must say I never saw more kind-hearted people than these men and women were to us all the way, on this long and dangerous journey.

We had no more trouble with the Indians until we had crossed Green river. We were now in the Ute country. At this time the Utes were considered to be one of the most hostile tribes in the West. That night Jim asked me what route I thought best to take, by the way of Salt Lake or Landers Cut Off. I said, "Jim, Landers Cut Off is the shortest and safest route from the fact that the Indians are in the southern part of the territory at this time of year, and I do not believe we shall have much more trouble with them on this trip." Which proved to be true. We saw no more Indians until we reached the Humbolt river. Just above the Sink of Humbolt about the middle of the afternoon I saw quite a band of Indians heading directly for the train. I signaled Jim to corral, which he did at once.

In a few moments they were upon us. As we were out on an open prairie, we had a good sight of the Indians before they reached us; I saw by the leader's dress that it was a chief that was leading them. His head dress was composed of eagles' feathers, and he rode some thirty or forty yards ahead of the other warriors. When in gun shot of me I fired at him and brought him down. When he fell from his horse the rest of the Indians wheeled their horses and fled, but the chief was the only one that fell. As soon as they were gone I took the scalp off the dead chief's head. When we went into camp that evening, Jim told the emigrants what a great thing I had done in shooting the chief. "There is no knowing how many lives he saved by that one shot in the right time."

Then all the emigrants gathered around me to see the scalp of the Indian; they had never seen such a sight before; each of the young ladies wanted a quill from the Indian's head dress; and they asked me what I would take for one of them; I told them the quills were not for sale.

At this time the lady who had invited Jim and me to eat with her so many times came up to us, and she said, "Girls, I can tell you how you can get these quills." They all asked at once, "How is that, aunty?"

"Each one of you give him a kiss for a quill," she laughed, and of all the blushing I ever saw the young girls that surrounded me beat the record. Jim grinned and said, "I'll be dog goned if I don't buy the scalp and the feathers and take all the kisses myself."

This made a general laugh. I told Jim that he was too selfish, and that I would not share the kisses with him, that I would give the scalp to him and the feathers to the elder lady, and she could divide the feathers among the girls. The girls clapped their hands and shouted, "Good! good!"

Jim said that was just his luck, he was always left out in the cold.

In a few days we were on the top of the Sierra Nevada mountains. We told the emigrants that they were entirely out of danger and did not need our services any longer, so we would not put them to any more expense by going further with them. As this was Saturday evening the emigrants proposed going into camp until Monday morning and that Jim and I should stay and visit with them. We accepted the invitation, and Sunday was passed in pleasant converse with these most agreeable people, and I will say here that of all the emigrants I ever piloted across the plains none ever exceeded these men and women in politeness and good nature, not only to Jim and me, but to each other, for through all that long and trying journey there was no unkindness shown by any of them, and if we would have accepted all the provisions they offered us it would have taken a pack train to have carried it through. Every lady in the train tried to get up some little extra bite for us to eat on the way back. The reader may imagine our surprise when Monday morning came and we saw the amount of stuff they brought to us. Jim said, "Why ladies we haven't any wagon to haul this stuff, and we have only one pack horse and he can just pack our blankets and a little more. Besides, we won't have time to eat these goodies on the road. Supposing the Indians get after us? We would have to drop them and the red skins would get it all."

We now packed up and were ready to put out. We mounted our horses, bid them "good bye" and were off.

Nothing of interest occurred until we got near Green river. Here we met Jim Beckwith and Bob Simson. Jim Bridger and I had just gone into camp when they rode up. After they had shaken hands with us Jim Beckwith said, "Boys, you are just the parties we are looking for."

Bridger asked Beckwith what he had been doing and where he had been since we parted at Bent's Fort last spring. Beckwith replied that he had been with a train of emigrants just now who were on the way to California, and they had camped over on Black's Fort. The cholera had broken out among them soon after they crossed the Platte River, and from then up to yesterday they had buried more or less every day. There had been no new cases since yesterday, and they were laying over to let the people rest and get their strength, and they expected to start out tomorrow morning, and turning to me Beckwith said, "Will, I want you to go with us for there is another train of emigrants over on the Salt Lake route."

At this time there were two routes between the Green river and the Humboldt; one by the way of Salt Lake and the other by Lander's Cut off. Beckwith said, "Those emigrants going by the Salt Lake route have no guide, and I am afraid when they strike the Humboldt they will all be massacred, for they will be right in the heart of the Pi-Ute country, and you know this tribe is on the war path, and I want you to go on and overtake them and see them safely through, or else stay with this train and I will go myself and take care of them. We want the two trains to meet at the mouth of Lone Canyon, and then we will go up Long Canyon to Honey lake and then cross the Sierra Nevada."

I turned to Jim Bridger and said, "Jim, what do you think of this proposition?"

Jim said he thought it a good thing for me to do; the responsibility would give me more confidence in myself. "You know, Will, you have always depended on Carson or me at all times, and this trip will teach you to depend on yourself."

I saddled my horse and went with Beckwith back to the emigrants' camp. It was arranged that I was to take charge of the scouts and Simson to take charge of the other train, and Beckwith would go on and overtake the other train, and the train that reached the mouth of Long Canyon where it empties into Truckey river first must wait for the other train.

At this point the two trails divided, one going up the Truckey by the Donna lake route and the other up Long Canyon by Honey lake, the latter being considered the best route.

The next morning we pulled out. I had good luck all the way through, having no trouble with the Indians, arriving at Long Canyon three days ahead of Jim Beckwith.

In my train there was an old man with his wife and a son and daughter; they seemed to be very peculiar dispositioned people, always wanting to camp by themselves and having nothing to say to any one. When we reached Long Canyon, Simson told the emigrants that we would wait until the other train arrived, which news greatly pleased the most of them, but the old man and his family seemed to be all upset at the idea of laying over, and the next morning they harnessed up their horses. While they were doing this, Simson called my attention to them and said, "Let's go and see what they mean."

I asked the man what he was going to do with his team. He replied that he was going to hook them to the wagon and was going to California. I said, "You certainly are not going to start on such a journey alone, are you? You are liable to be all killed by the Indians before you get twenty miles from here."

The old man shrugged his shoulders and said, "Why, gol darn it, we hain't seen an Injin in the last three hundred miles, and I don't believe there is one this side of them mountains," and he pointed towards the Sierra Nevada mountains. "And if we did meet any they wouldn't bother us for we hain't got much grub, and our horses is too poor for them to want."

I told him, he must not go alone, the road was too dangerous, and besides the other train might come at any moment, and then we could all pull out in safety. He said, "I own that wagon and them horses, and I own pretty much every thing in that wagon and I think I will do just as I please with them." I insisted on his waiting until the other train came up, he said, he would not wait any longer, that he was going to go right now. I left him and walked back to the camp; I asked the men if any of them had any influence with that old man out there.

"If you have for god's sake use it and persuade him to not leave us, for if he starts out alone he, nor any of his family will reach Honey lake alive."

Just then one of the men said, "I have known that man ten years and I know that all the advice all these people could give him would be wasted breath and the less said to him the better it will be."

I then went back to Simson who had charge of the wagons and said to him, "What shall we do with that old man? He is hitching up to leave us which will be sure death to him and his family. If he goes had we not better take his team away from him and save his life and his family's?"

Simson said, he would consult with the other men and see what they thought about it. After he had talked with the other men a short time, twenty or thirty of them went out where the old man was hitching up his team. What they said to him I do not know. When I got to him he was about ready to pull out; he said, "I'm going now and you men can come when you please and I don't give a D'. whether you come at all of not."

This was the last we ever saw of the old man or his son.

Three days later Jim Bridger arrived with his train, and then we all pulled out together by the way of Honey lake. The first night after leaving camp Jim Bridger, Simson and myself had a talk about the old man who had left us. Jim said. "I don't suppose we shall ever hear of him again," and turning to me he said, "Will, it will take us two days to go to Honey Lake; now tomorrow morning suppose you pick out of your scout force eight good men, take two days' rations and your blankets with you and rush on ahead to the Lake and see if you can find them. It may be possible that some of them are alive, but I don't think you will find one of them. Now, Will, be careful and don't take any desperate chances; if you find they have been taken prisoners keep track of them until we get there."

The next morning I and my men were off bright and early. We reached the lake about three o'clock in the afternoon, where we struck the lake there was scattering timber for quite a ways up and down and here we found the old man's wagon. The wagon cover, his tent, and his team, were gone; his cooking utensils were setting around the fire which was still burning. Almost every thing was gone from the wagon, but there was no sign of a fight. Neither could we see any white men's tracks; but moccasin tracks were plenty. We sat down and ate our luncheon: as soon as we finished eating we started to trail the Indians to find out what had become of the whites. We had gone but a short distance when I discovered the tracks of the two women; then we knew that they had been captured by the Indians. I said, "I want you men to take this side of the ridge and watch for Indians all the time, and you must watch me also; when you see me throw up my hat come at once and be sure to not shout, but signal to each other by whistling or holding up your hands and be sure to have your signals understood among yourselves. And another thing I want to say to you, if you see any Indian, signal to me, at once. Now I am going to take the trail of these white women, and if I need your assistance I will signal, and you must all get to me as quick as possible."

All being understood I started on the trail of the white women. I hadn't followed the trail over a half a mile, when I saw one of the men running towards me at full speed; when he reached me he said, "We have found a dead man, and he is stuck full of arrows."

I mounted my horse and accompanied him to where the body lay. I recognized it at once; it was the son of the old man who had left us three days before. His clothes were gone except his shirt and pants, and his body was almost filled with arrows. I said, "This is one of the party, and the other is a prisoner, or we shall find his body not far from here. Let us scatter out and search this grove of timber thoroughly; perhaps we may find the other body; and be careful to watch out for the Indians, for they are liable to run upon us any time."

We had not gone more than two hundred yards before we found the old man's body; it was laying behind a log with every indication of a hand-to-hand fight. One arrow was stuck in his body near the heart, and there were several tomahawk's wounds on the head and shoulders, which showed that he died game.

It was getting late in the afternoon so I proposed to the men that we take the bodies back to where we had found their camp, as we had no way of burying the bodies in a decent manner, we had to wait until the train came up to us. We laid the bodies side by side under a tree and then we went into camp for the night as there was good grass for the horses. We staked them out close to camp. We had seen no Indians all day, so we did not think it necessary to put out guards around the camp that night, and we all laid down and went to sleep.

The next morning we were up and had an early breakfast; that done, I said, "Now, men I want two of you to go back and meet Bridger and tell him what we have found and pilot him here to this camp, and he will attend to the burying of these bodies; I would rather you should choose among your selves who shall go back."

One man by the name of Boyd and another whose name was Taluck said they would go. These men were both from Missouri; I then told them to tell

Bridger that I was a going to start on the trail of the white women at once, and for him to camp here and that he would hear from me tonight, whether I found them or not.

The rest of the men and I started on the trail; three went on one side and three on the other, and I took the trail; I cautioned the men to keep a sharp look out for the Indians all the time, and if they saw any Indians to signal to me at once. I had followed the trail some five or six miles when it led me to a little stream of water in a small grove of timber. Here I found where the Indians had camped; the fire was still burning which convinced me that the Indians had camped there the night before. I also saw where the two women had been tied to a tree. I followed them a short distance and saw that the band we were following had met a larger band, and they had all gone off together in a northerly direction. We were now near the north end of Honey lake, and I had about given up hopes of ever seeing the women again, but I did not tell my thoughts to my companions. The trail was so plain that I now mounted my horse; we followed at a pretty rapid gate two or three miles, when we saw that a few tracks had turned directly towards the lake. I dismounted and examined them and found the two shoe tracks went with the small party. I was now convinced that this was a party of squaws going to the lake to fish; and I felt more encouraged to keep up the pursuit. We were within a mile of the lake at this time. We rode as fast as we could and keep the trail in sight. We soon came in sight of the lake; looking to the right I saw a small band of squaws building a fire. I called the men to me and told them that I believed the women we were looking for were with those squaws, and if they were, I thought we could rescue them.

"I think our best plan will be to ride slowly until they see us and then make a dash as fast as our horses can carry us; if the white women are with them, we will ride right up to them, if they are tied I will jump down and cut them loose," and pointing at two of the men I said, "You two men will take them up behind you and take the lead back, and the rest of us will protect you."

We did not ride much farther before the squaws discovered us at which they began to shout, "Hyha," which meant "They're coming they're coming."

In a moment we were in their midst, and sure enough the women were there and tied fast to a small tree, a short distance from where the squaws were building the fire.

What happened in the next few minutes I could never describe. The women knew me at once and with cries and laughter, touching, beyond description greeted me.

In an instant I was off my horse and cutting them loose from the tree, at the same time the men were circling around us with guns cocked ready to shoot the first squaw that interfered with us.

To my great surprise I did not see a bow or arrow among them or a tomahawk either; as quick as I had the women loose I helped them up behind the men I had selected to take them away from captivity back to meet the train. As soon as we had left them of all the noise I ever heard those squaws made the worst. I think they did this so the bucks might know that they had lost their captives and might come to their assistance. Where the bucks were I never knew. After riding four or five miles we slacked our speed, and the women began telling us how the whole thing had occurred. It seemed they had got to the camping ground early in the afternoon of the second day after leaving us and instead of staking out their horses they turned them loose, and about dusk the old man and his son went out to look for the horses, were gone a couple of hours and came back without them. This made them all very uneasy. The next morning just at break of day the old man and his son took their guns and started out again to hunt for their horses, and the mother and daughter made a fire and cooked breakfast. The sun was about an hour high, and they were sitting near the fire waiting for the men to come back when they heard the report of a gun; they thought the men were coming back and were shooting some game. They had no idea there was an Indian near them. In the course of a half an hour they heard the second shot, and in a few minutes the Indians were upon them, and they knew that the men were both dead, because the Indians had both of their guns and were holding them up and yelling and dancing with fiendish glee. The Indians grabbed them and tied their hands behind them and then they tore down their tent, took the wagon cover off and everything out of the wagon that they could carry off.

"The bucks did the things up in bundles, and the squaws packed them on their backs, and they were expecting every minute to be killed. After the squaws had gone the bucks ate everything they could find that was cooked, and the squaws that you found us with made us go with them to the north end of the lake and there they camped that night. They tied us with our backs to a little tree; we could not lay down and what little sleep we got we took sitting up; we had not had a bit of breakfast that morning when the Indians came upon us; it was all ready, and we were waiting for our men folks to come back, and we have had nothing since, but a little piece of broiled fish with no salt on it."

Until now I had not said anything about our finding the dead bodies of their men, I thought it better to tell them now rather than wait until we reached camp, as I thought the shock would be less when they came to see the condition they were in.

Before I had finished telling the condition of the bodies when we found them, I was afraid the young lady would faint, she seemed to take the horrid news much harder than her mother did.

When we got to camp we found that Bridger had been there some two hours ahead of us and had men digging the graves and others tearing up the wagon box to make coffins to bury the bodies in.

We took the women to a family they were acquainted with and left them in their care. After they had been given something to eat they went where the bodies lay and looked at them, and with sobs of bitter grief bent over them; which made my heart ache in sympathy for them in their loneliness.

The next morning we laid them away into their lonely graves in as decent a manner as we could, and in sadness left them.

Through the influence of Jim Bridger arrangements were made with two families to take these two ladies with them to California. Just before noon Jim came to me and said, "We will stay here until tomorrow morning; I would like you to take four or five men who have good horses and go around the north end of the lake and find out, if you can, if the Piutes are gathering together in a large band. It is about the time of year for the Piutes to leave this part of the country, but if they are gathering in a large band they are bent on giving us trouble, and we will have to make preparations to defend our selves. In three days more if we have good luck we shall be out of the hostile Indian country."

We had an early dinner and four others and myself set out for the head of the lake, we rode hard all that afternoon and to our great surprise we never saw an Indian. We passed a number of camps where they had been, but their trails all showed that they had pulled out for the north. Seeing this we turned back and struck the emigrant trail about ten miles from where Jim was camped. Just as we struck the emigrants trail I looked off to the south about a quarter of a mile and saw nine head of horses, and they were heading in the same direction we were going. I called the other men's attention to them and said, "Let's capture those Indian ponies." You may imagine our surprise when we got near them to find they were not Indian ponies but good American horses and several of them had collar marks on them showing that they had been worked lately. We drove them on to camp, and when we put them in the corral we found them to be perfectly gentle. Bridger and the balance of the men came to see them, and every man had his own view where they had come from. But we never knew for certain whom they belonged to. The next morning we pulled out very early. The third day we crossed the Sierra Nevada mountains without any thing of interest happening to us. In two days more we reached the Sacramento river. We were now about forty miles above Sacramento City, California. We camped here about the middle of the afternoon. It being Saturday Jim thought we would rest the balance of the day. After we had eaten our dinner Jim called all the men of the train together and told them that they were out of all danger now from the Indians and would have no further use for a guide and that our contract with them was ended, and that he and I would like to start back for New Mexico Monday morning. In a short time they settled up with us, paying us our due with grateful thanks for our care of them on their dangerous journey. I now went to the men who were with me when I found the horses. I said, "Some of those horses belong to you, how many do you want?"

They all looked surprised, and one said, "They are not our horses, they are yours. You found them."

I answered, "Now, boys, that is not fair; drive them up and let me select three and you may have the balance to divide as you choose among you."

This seemed to please them; and they drove the horses up at once. I chose the three I liked best, and I afterwards found them all to be good saddle horses. Bridger and I now went to work making our pack saddles and getting ready for our long and tedious journey back to New Mexico, a journey where wild beasts and still wilder savages might lurk behind any tree or bush, a journey where at that time all one could see for hundreds of miles was thick forests, and trackless prairies; a journey of danger and fatigue which the people of this later day of rapid travel could not be made to understand.

The next morning after breakfast was over a man came to me and said, Mrs. Lynch and her daughter Lizzie would like to see me. These were the two ladies I had rescued from the Indians. I had not spoken to them since I left them with Bridger at the camp near Honey Lake. As I came near to the elder lady she came to meet me and holding out her hand, clasping mine she said, "Are you going to leave us tomorrow?"

I answered, "That is what we intended to do."

She then burst into tears, and amid her sobs said, "We can never pay you for what you have done for us."

At this moment the young girl appeared, and as she gave me her hand her mother said, "He is going to leave us, and we can never pay him for what he has done for us"; at this the girl commenced to cry too and it was some minutes before I could talk to them. When they had quieted down I said, "Ladies, you owe me nothing, I only done my duty, and I would do the same thing over again for you or any one else under the circumstances that existed." Then the elder lady said, "If it hadn't been for you we might never have seen a white person again."

I asked her, what state they were from. She said they came from Wright country, Missouri, and that she had a brother there that was amply able to come and take them back, but she would not ask him to do so for she never wanted to cross the plains again. She said she had a few dollars left that the Indians didn't get, and she thought Lizzie and she could find something to do to get a living. I gave them all the encouragement I could, bid them good bye and went back to Jim.

By the time dinner was ready Jim and I had our pack saddles and every thing ready to put on our horses. While we were eating dinner as many as thirty ladies came to us to inquire what they could give us to take with us to eat on our journey. I was amused at Bridger. After each lady had told what she had to give us, some had cakes, some had pie, and some had boiled meat and some had bread; Jim straightened up and said, "Why dog-gorn it ladies, we ain't got no wagon and we couldn't take one if we had one the route we are going which will be through the mountains all the way with no road or trail. We are going horse back and we can only take about a hundred pounds on our pack horses. Now, ladies, we are a thousand times obliged to you all but all we want is some bread and a little meat, enough to do us a couple of days, and then we will be where we can shoot all the meat we want; it is a poor hunter that could not get enough grub for himself in the country we are going through."

The next morning when we were getting ready to start the women commenced bringing in bread and meat for us and we had to take enough to last us a week, we could not take less without hurting their feelings. When we were all ready to start, the whole company came to bid us "good bye." Men and women, old and young, all came, and amid hand clasps from the men and tears and smiles from the women we mounted our horses and were off.

We followed the trail we had come, back as far as Truckey river, and just below where Reno stands now, we met the remnant of an emigrant train and according to their story they had had nothing but trouble from the time they struck the head of Bitter Creek until the day before we met them. They said they had lost twenty seven men and fourteen women and a number of cattle and horses. They were very much surprised when we told them of the train we had just piloted through to California without losing one that staid with us. We told them of the dreadful fate of old Mr. Lynch and his son.

As night was coming on we camped in company with these people. Next morning we crossed Truckey river and struck out in a south east direction, leaving the site where Virginia city now stands a little to our right going by the sink of the Carson River. Here we camped and laid over one day to give our horses a rest. Before we left here we filled our canteens with water. Bridger told me that for the next fifty miles it was the poorest watered country in the United States. Said he: "There is plenty of water, but it is so full of alkali it is not fit to drink; it is dangerous for both men and beasts."

Jim took the lead all day, and when we came to a little stream of water he would get down and taste the water while I held the horses to keep them from drinking. It was about four o'clock that afternoon before we found water that was fit to drink; here we camped for the night.

Jim said, "From this on we may look for Indians; we are now in the Ute country and tomorrow night we will be in the Apache country. Now we must avoid the large streams for the Apaches are almost always to be found near the large streams at this time of year. Their hunting season is about over now, and they go to the large streams to catch fish and for the benefit of a milder climate. If we keep on the high ridges and mountains away from the large streams we will have no trouble with the Indians and what is better for us we can get all the game we want without any exertion."

The next day we were traveling along on a high ridge in the south east corner of what is now the State of Nevada. We looked off to the south at a little valley that was perhaps a half a mile from us, and there we saw a grand sight. There must have been at least a hundred elk and amongst them two very large old bucks fighting. Their horns were something immense, and strange to say all the rest of the band stood still, watching the fight. At last Jim said, "Will, I believe I will break up that fight."

He jumped to the ground, raised his gun and fired. At the sound of the gun all of the band ran away except the two who were fighting. I laughed and said, "Jim, I thought you were going to stop that fight."

He replied, "Give me your gun, and I will stop it."

This time I handed him my gun, and he squatted down and took a rest on his knee and fired. At the crack of the gun one of the elks fell to his knees, but got up and ran for all that was in him, and that was the last we saw of the elk. I told Jim he had spoilt the fun, and we had got no meat out of it. He grinned and said, "Oh durn it that old elk was too old to eat any way."

We went on and camped at the head of a little stream that emptied into Green river. The sun was perhaps an hour high, when we went into camp. As soon as we had staked out our horses Jim said, "Now Will, I will get the supper, if you will go out and see if you can get some meat."

I answered, "That suits me to a T. Jim."

I took my gun and started for a little ridge. I had not gone over a hundred yards when I saw five deer coming directly towards me. Among them were two spring fawns. I dropped down at the root of a tree and waited until they came to within fifty yards of me; I then fired and broke one of the fawns' necks, and the rest of the flock came near running over me, and over Jim also. I picked up my fawn and went back to camp. Jim said, "I don't want you to go hunting anymore Will."

I said, "Why not?" He said, "If you do I shall have to stand guard over the camp to keep the deer from tramping every thing we have into the ground"; and he pointed to the tracks of the deer not ten feet from the fire. This convinced us that these deer had never heard the report of a gun before. We were now in the extreme south east end of Nevada, and I don't imagine a white man had ever been through that part of the country before. On this trip we traveled some twelve or fifteen hundred miles, and we never saw a white person the whole way, and not even the sign of one.

At this time when a little more than a half of a century has passed there are portions of this same country that could not be rode over from the fact that it is all fenced in and cultivated. If we had been told then that we would live to see railroads crossing every part of this country we would have thought the person insane to ever think of such a thing at a time when there was not a foot of rail-road as far west as Missouri.

We had broiled venison for supper that night, the first we had eaten for some time, and the reader may be sure we enjoyed it.

Next morning we pulled out of here quite early and crossed Green river just above the mouth of Blue River. We were now in the greatest game country I had ever seen then or ever have seen since. We traveled up this stream three days, and I do not think there was a half an hour at any one time that we were out of sight of game of some kind. There was the Bison which is a species of Buffalo, Elk, Deer, Black Bear, and Antelope. We crossed the main divide of the Rocky Mountains at the head of the Arkansas River. That night we camped within a few miles of what since has become the far-famed camp and now city of Leadville.

We were now out of the hostile Indian country, and so we did not have to be so cautious in traveling days or camping at night.

While we were traveling down the Arkansas river I saw a sight I had never seen before and never have since. Two Buck Deer locked fast together by their horns. I had been told of such things and have since, but that is the only time I ever saw it myself. We were very near them before we saw them. They were in a little open prairie. I called Jim's attention to them as soon as I saw them. He said, "I'll be gol durned if that ain't the second time I ever saw such a sight, and now we will have some fun out of them bucks."

We dismounted and walked up near them, and by the looks of the ground which was torn and tramped for quite a distance we decided that they had been in that condition quite a while. Jim said, "How in the plague, Will, are we going to get these critters apart? They are too plaguey poor to eat, so we don't want to kill them, and they will die if we leave them in this fix; what shall we do, Will?"

I thought a minute and said, "Can't we take our little ax and chop one of their horns off?"

He said, "I hadn't thought of that, but bring me the ax and I will try it."

I ran to the pack horse and got the ax. He said, "Now you go back to the horses; for if I get them loose they may want to fight us."

So I went to the horses and looked back to see what Jim was doing. He went up to them with the ax drawn ready to strike but it was quite a bit before they were quiet enough for him to get a good hit at them. At last he made a strike and down went one of the deer. Instead of striking the deer's horn he struck him right back of the horn and killed him instantly; when Jim saw what he had done he made another hit at the dead buck's horn and freed the live one, which ran thirty or forty yards and stopped and turned around and shook his head at us a half a dozen times and then he trotted away as if nothing had happened.

Jim laughed and said, "He never stopped to thank us, did he? Well he ain't much different from some people." I said, "Why, Jim he meant "thank you" when he shook his head at us; that is all the way he could say it, you know," to which he replied, "Well, I saved one of them any way."

Nothing occurred of interest from this time on until we reached our journey's end at Taos, New Mexico. Here we found Uncle Kit and his wife both enjoying good health and a warm welcome for his boy Willie, and his old friend Jim Bridger.

After supper that night we told Uncle Kit that we had traveled from the Sacramento river, California to Taos, New Mexico in thirty-three days, and that we never saw a hostile Indian on the trip, and neither had had any trouble of any kind to detain us a half an hour on the whole trip. He said, "That is a wonderful story to hear, when there are so many wild Indians in that part of the country. Now boys tell me what route you came."

We marked out the route by different streams and mountains. He looked at the map we had drawn and said, "I will venture to say there is not two men in all the country that could make that trip over that route and get through alive. I will say again, boys, it is some thing wonderful to think of, and you must have been protected by a higher power than your selves to get through in safety."

We staid with Uncle Kit a couple of weeks and rested up, and then we struck out for Bent's Fort to make up our crew to go to our trapping ground for our winter's work.

Uncle Kit accompanied us to Bent's Fort; and all the trappers were anxious to get in his employ from the fact that the report had gone out that the Sioux and the Utes were on the war path, and all the trappers knew that these two tribes were the strongest hostile tribes in the west, and when fifty miles from Bent's Fort we never knew that we were safe and the trappers all had confidence in Uncle Kit's judgment that he seldom made a mistake in locating his trapping ground, and further more he had more influence with the Indians than any other man in the country, so they worked rather for him than take chances with any one else.

The next morning after we reached Bent's Fort I heard Mr. Bent and Mr. Roubidoux talking with Carson in regard to the trappers. Mr. Bent said, "Carson, I wish you would take as many as you can handle, for they all have an Indian scare on them and are afraid to go out, and every one of them is indebted to us for board now; and we can not afford to support them if they loaf around here all winter," to which Carson replied, "I can handle five or six of them, and that is all I want, I can not afford to take men out in the mountains and board them all winter for nothing." After thinking a minute Carson asked, "How many of the men have their own traps and blankets?"

Mr. Roubidoux said, he thought nearly all of the trappers at the Fort had their own trapping outfits with them. Carson said he would think it over and see what he could do for them. That afternoon Carson and Bridger had a talk with regard to how many men they should take with them. Uncle Kit said, "We haven't horses enough to carry more than three or four besides us three." Bridger said, "That will not make any difference, if they want to go they can foot it from here to the head of South Platte as that's where we are going to trap this winter; and when they are through in the spring they can foot it back again. We have nine pack horses besides our saddle horses, and we can pack out to the trapping grounds, an outfit for five or six men besides our own all in good shape."

That afternoon Uncle Kit and Bridger made arrangements with six men to go with us to the head of South Platte to trap Beaver that winter. Carson and Bridger agreed to furnish them with flour, coffee, salt, and tobacco for which Carson and Bridger were to have half of the furs that each man caught, Carson and Bridger to pack the grub and every thing else out to the trapping ground and also to pack the furs and all their other things back to Bent's Fort in the Spring. After Carson and Bridger had selected the six men they wanted, it seemed as though all the trappers at the Fort wanted to go with them. Carson told them he had engaged all he could handle. The next two days we spent in getting ready to go to our trapping grounds. On the morning of the third day every thing in readiness we bid farewell to all the people at the Fort and struck out for the trapping grounds and our winter's work. The men that had to walk did not wait for us but started as soon as they had breakfast.

Uncle Kit told them where we would camp the first night. They got there before we did, and they had killed the fattest deer I ever saw and had killed a Cub Bear. They were skinning them when we got to camp. The deer was a spike buck and when he was skinned he was as white as a sheep from pure fat. The reader may be sure we were not long in unpacking and getting ready for supper; every one was tired and hungry for we had not had any thing to eat since morning. For my supper I roasted two of the cub's feet, and I have never enjoyed a meal since that tasted better. While we were eating Jim Bridger looked at me and said, "Will, you have the best of me tonight, but when we get to the Beaver grounds I'll have a Beaver's tail roasted for my supper and then I'll be even with you."

I never saw a band of men enjoy a meal more than those men did that night. In this climate people have better appetites than any climate I have ever been. I think the reason for this was the air was so pure and invigorating and it naturally required more food to sustain the body and keep it in good health, and at that time sickness was very rare in that part of the country. It would seem unreasonable to tell how much meat a man ate at one meal, especially when out on a trip like this when he was out in the open air all the time, night as well as day.

The third day after leaving this camp we struck the South Platte river, and now we had another change of meat, which was mountain sheep. This is in my opinion the best wild game that roams the forest.

We made an early camp that night and Uncle Kit said to Jim Bridger and me, "You two boys get the meat for supper and the rest of us will look after the horses." We picked up our guns and started up the river; we had not gone far when in looking up on a high bluff we saw a band of mountain sheep. Jim said, "Now if we can reach that little canyon," and he pointed to one just ahead of us, "without them fellows seeing us we will sure have something good for supper." This we succeeded in doing and then we crawled around until we were within fifty yards of our game. We selected a couple of spring lambs and fired and brought them both down. When the men at the camp heard the firing a couple of the men came running to help us bring our game to camp. We soon had it dressed and ready for cooking, and it was good and every one of the men ate as if they enjoyed it as much as I did. While we were eating supper Jim told us a story of his coming in contact with a panther that had just killed a sheep, and he said it was a miracle that it did not kill him. He was coming down a bluff on a little trail and as good luck had it he had his gun in his hand. The panther had the sheep behind a rock and as the panther sprang at him he fired and broke its neck.

"It was the luckiest shot I ever fired," said he, "for if I had not had my gun all ready to fire he would have torn me to pieces before I could have helped myself."

Uncle Kit said, "Well, Jim, you were in about as close a place as I got into once. I went out from my camp fire one night perhaps forty yards to a small tree. I didn't have any pistol or gun with me, I had nothing but my hunting knife to protect myself with when a half-grown panther sprang out of the tree on me and, maybe you think I didn't have a lively time there with him for a few minutes, but I finally got the best of him by cutting him almost to pieces. He tore my buck skin breeches and coat pretty near off me and left this scar on my arm before I finished him," and Carson pulled his sleeve up and showed us a scar that must have been torn almost to the bone.

Two days from this we reached the place where we made our headquarters for the winter. That night the men talked it over and made their plans how many should camp together. They agreed that there should be three in each camp as there were nine of us in all. That made the number even in each camp. Next morning they all put out leaving me to look out for the horses and things in general.

For the benefit of the reader I will explain how we arranged a camp where a number of men were associated together in trapping beaver. We built our camps about four miles apart which gave each camp two miles square to work on, and this was ample room, for this was a new field and Beaver was as thick as rats around a wharf.

While they were gone I took my gun and started out to take a little stroll around where the horses were feeding. I had gone but a short distance when I looked up. On a mountain, north of me I saw a band of elk with perhaps seventy five or a hundred in it, and they were coming directly towards me; I was satisfied in my mind that they were going to the river to get water. I dropped down behind a log and waited for them to come close to me. The nearest one was twenty yards from me when I fired. I shot at a two-year-old heifer and broke her neck. I then went back to camp to see if any of the men had come in as it was near noon. I thought some of them would be back and sure enough in a few minutes they all came together; I told them what I had done, and Uncle Kit said, "Jim and I will get dinner and the balance of you go and help Willie bring in his cow."

We found her in fine condition. We soon had her skinned and in camp, and we found dinner ready when we got back. After dinner Uncle Kit said, "Come boys let's pack up and move to our camp which is only about a half a mile from here, and tomorrow, while Jim and me are at work on our shanty, Willie can help you to move to your quarters, and you can be building your shanties, so we can get to work as soon as possible."

We gathered every thing together and moved it to the ground where we were going to make our winter quarters, and Uncle Kit and Jim selected the place to build our cabin, and the men all turned to and went to chopping the logs and putting up the cabin. By night the body of the cabin was almost up, but the reader must bear in mind that this was not a very large house. It was ten feet one way, and twelve the other, with a fire place built in one corner. They built the walls of the shack seven foot high and then covered it with small poles, covered the poles with fine bows and then there was from six to eight inches of dirt packed on them and the cracks were stuffed with mud. The door was split out of logs called puncheons and was fastened together with wooden pins, driven into holes, bored with an auger. This way of building a house to live in through the winter may seem strange to the readers who are accustomed to all the luxuries of the modern home of civilization; but we considered our cabin very good quarters, and we were very comfortable that winter.

The first morning after we were settled in our new home we commenced setting traps for Beaver. Jim Bridger was the lucky man of the whole outfit in catching Beaver all that winter. Each man had twelve traps which was called a string, and a number of times that winter Bridger had a beaver in every one of his traps in the morning. I had watched him set his traps many times and I tried to imitate him in every particular, but I never had the luck he had.

Uncle Kit told me a number of times that winter that it was a good trapper that made an average of catching five Beaver a day, during the trapping season. We were all very successful this winter. Beaver was very plentiful, as there had never been any trappers in this part of the country before, and besides that was an exceptional good winter for trapping. The winter was quite cold, but there was not much snow all winter for that country. We stayed here and trapped until the very last of March, and when we had the furs all baled and ready for packing we found we did not have horses enough to take them all out at one time, so Uncle Kit and Jim Bridger packed the seven horses and rode the other two and struck out for Bent's Fort, telling us they would come back as soon as they could make the trip; and to our surprise they were back on the tenth day.

We had everything ready for them to break up camp when they came back, and we had all we could carry the second time. All of the nine horses were packed, and we all had to walk to Bent's Fort.

After we left the Platte we took up a stream called Sand Creek which leads to the divide between the Platte and the Arkansas rivers. After we camped that night Carson said to the boys, "Now we have had a pretty good variety of meat this winter, but we haven't had any antelope, but we are in the greatest country for antelope in the west now. Can't one of you boys kill one tomorrow for supper? But I am sorry for Jim and Will for Jim can't get a Beaver's tail off of it, and there won't be any bear's foot for Will to eat."

Jim answered, "You needn't worry about Will and me, for we may make you sorry twice, for when we get at the Antelope there may not be enough for the balance of you."

After breakfast next morning two of the men struck ahead in order to get the antelope. Near the trail about ten o'clock we overtook them, and they had killed two nice young antelope. One said that if they had had ammunition enough with them they could have loaded the train with antelope. That day we saw a number of bands of antelope, and I venture to say there were as many as eight hundred or a thousand in each band.

At supper that night Jim Bridger and I convinced Uncle Kit that we had not lost our appetite, if we didn't have Beaver's tail and Bear's foot for supper.

The second day after leaving this camp we landed at Bent's Fort about the middle of the afternoon. That evening and all the next day Carson and Bridger were counting the pelts and paying off the men for the furs they had trapped during the winter. Each man had a mark of his own which he put on all his hides as he took them off the animal. I noticed one man always clipped the left ear; that was his mark. Having a private mark for each man saved a great deal of trouble and dispute when the time came to separate the furs and give each man his due.

I heard Carson and Bridger talking after they had settled with the men, and Bridger said, "We have done twice as well as I expected we would do the past winter."

Carson answered, "Jim, we had an extra good crew of men. Every man worked for all that was in him and when they earned a dollar for themselves they earned one for us. I am more than satisfied with our winter's work and what it brought us."

He then asked Jim and me what we intended to do that summer; Jim answered, "We are going back to Fort Kerney to pilot emigrants across to California, and it is time we were off now, for I believe by the first of May there will be lots of emigrants there, and we want to get there, and get the first train out, and if it is possible we are going to make two trips across the plains this season."

CHAPTER III.

The next morning Carson left Bent's Fort taking his four horses with him going to his home at Taos, New Mexico, and Jim and I, taking five horses, pulled out for Fort Kerney. Nothing of interest happened to us on the way; and we made the trip in eleven days. As soon as we got to the Fort, we called on the General; he was very glad to see us, and invited us to stay all night with him. We accepted his invitation. That evening at supper General Kerney mentioned my rescuing the two women at the head of Honey Lake the year before; he recounted the incident very much as it took place.

I said to him, "General, how in the name of common sense did you hear of all that?"

He said, "Why the eastern papers have been full of it; and it will be the best thing for you two men that could have happened; for no doubt there will be hundreds of people here on their way to California, and when they see you two men who are the heroes of that expedition they will all want your services to pilot them across the plains, and I assure you if there is any thing I can do to assist either of you in any way I am more than willing to do it. I heard yesterday that there were several small trains on the way coming from St. Joe, and they will be here in a few days, so you are in good time to catch the first of them, and I want you both to stay right here with me until you make arrangements to leave for California. We will take a trip down the road every day, and if there are any emigrants coming we will meet them."

[Illustration: The first thing we knew the whole number that we had first seen was upon us.]

After breakfast next morning an orderly brought in our horses, all saddled, the General's as well as ours. We all mounted and started down the road. We had made five or six miles when we saw an emigrant train coming towards us. The General said, "Look, boys, there they come now. Let me do the talking."

The General had his uniform on, and Jim and I were dressed in buck-skin from head to foot, and we were a rather conspicuous trio, as we rode up to them. There were six or eight men on horse back, riding ahead of the train. As we met them the General saluted them. One of the men said, "Is this the commander at the Fort?"

The General answered, "I am. My name is Kerney."

One of the men said, "General, can you tell us whether the Indians are on the war path or not between here and Salt Lake?"

The General answered, "I surely can. Every tribe of Indians between here and the Sierra Nevada mountains is on the war path, and the emigrants who get through this year without losing their lives or their stock may consider themselves lucky," and pointing to Jim and me, he continued. "These two men took a train through last year and only lost two men and would not have lost them if they had obeyed orders."

One of the men asked, "Are these the men that piloted a train across and had the trouble at Honey Lake last year?"

The General answered, "Yes, sir, they are, and that boy sitting on that iron gray horse is the boy that planned and led the rescue of the two women from the Indians."

One asked, "Are these the two men the papers said so much about last fall? I think one was named Jim Bridger and the other's name was William Drannan."

General Kerney smiled and answered, "Yes, these are the very men."

By this time the train had come up, and the other men of the company gathered around us and being told who we were they all shook hands with us, besides a great many of the ladies got out of the wagons and came to us offering their hands. The people were all from Missouri and Illinois. A man by the name of Tullock from Missouri asked us what we would charge to pilot their train to California. Jim Bridger turned to me and said, "Will, what do you think it would be worth?"

I said to the man who had asked the question, "Drive on about five miles, and you will find a little creek and plenty of grass. Go into camp there and select five or ten men to act as a committee, and we will be there at four o'clock to meet you. You must give your committee full power to deal with us. The committee must know the number of wagons, the number of men, and the number of grown women; it will be more satisfactory to you as well as to us to deal with a few men than for the whole train to take a part in the business."

This plan seemed to meet with the approval of the men, so General Kerney, Jim Bridger and I left them and rode back to the Fort. On the way back the General asked Bridger how much he meant to charge the emigrants to take the train across.

Bridger said, "What do you say, Will?"

I answered, "Jim, I look at it this way, we are held responsible for the people's lives as well as their stock to get them to California in safety; just think of the responsibility we are assuming; and as far as I am concerned I will not undertake the job for less then four dollars a day."

Bridger answered, "That settles it, Will, that's just my price."

The General said, "I think you are very moderate in your charges; I should think they would jump at such a chance; for I assure you, you will have your hands full day and night."

After we had eaten our dinner at the Fort Gen. Kerney accompanied us back to the emigrant's camp. On our arriving there we found the committee waiting to receive us. Mr. Tullock introduced us to the others, and then said, "We want you to tell us what amount of money you will charge us to pilot us across the plains to California."

I said, "Gentlemen, I want to ask you a few questions before I answer yours; how many wagons have you in this train?" Mr. Tullock answered, "Sixty four." "How many men?" "One hundred and forty-eight." "How many women?" "Sixty four."

I then said, "I will now answer your question as to our price. If we take charge of this train from here to California our price will be four dollars a day to each of us, with this understanding that Mr. Bridger has entire charge of the wagons both day and night, and I to have the charge of the scout force. Now, gentlemen, I don't suppose any of you know what the duty of a scout is, and I will explain it to you. Twenty miles from here we will strike a country where all the Indians are hostile, and for the next twelve hundred miles they are all on the war path; now, if we undertake this job we shall want twelve good men to help me in scouting; each of the twelve to be mounted, and our duty will be to protect the train; three men to ride in the rear of the train and three on each side, each three to keep about a half a mile from the train, and the other three in the lead, and the duty of these scouts will be when they see Indians coming towards the train to notify Mr. Bridger at once, so he can corral the wagons to protect the women and children and the stock, and my duty will be to ride to the highest hills on either side of the road to keep a lookout for Indians all through the day, and at night to watch for their camp fires. Now, gentlemen, I have told you our terms and if you decide to employ us, it will take four or five days to drill the outfit so it will be safe for us to start on this long and dangerous journey. Now, it is for you to say what you will do."

Gen. Kerney then spoke for the first time. "Let me say a word, gentlemen. These men know every camping ground and every watering place and also every Indian run way from here to the Sierra Nevada mountains, and you could not find better men for guides on the frontier, and the price they ask for the dangerous service they will give you is the least you can expect to give."

The committee walked away from us a short distance, and talked among themselves about a half an hour, and then came to us, and said they would accept our offer. Bridger then said, "Now gentlemen I want you to pick out twelve men that are not afraid to ride alone and have number-one eyesight and good hearing, for no doubt there will be many times when the fate of the whole train will depend on these twelve men. Will will start in to train them tomorrow morning if they are ready, and he will tell them and show them just what they have got to do; and I want every teamster to have his team hooked to his wagon by nine o'clock in the morning. It is not necessary for you to take down your tents or move any of your camp equipage at all; for I will drill the teamsters out on that little prairie yonder," and he pointed to a clear space a little ways up the road.

After these arrangements were made General Kerney went back to the Fort, and Jim and I staid at the emigrants' camp that night, so we could be up early the next morning to commence our work of drilling the men for the coming trip. My men reported to me soon after breakfast, and they were all fairly well mounted and well armed, each man having a pistol and a rifle. We mounted our horses and rode about a half a mile away from camp. We stopped and I explained to them what we had to do. After showing them and drilling them about two hours I asked them if any of them had ever shot from his horse's back. They said they never had; neither had they ever seen any one shoot that way. I went a short distance to a tree and made a cross mark with my knife. I then said to them, "Now, my men I will show you what you must learn to do."

I then rode a hundred yards from the tree I had marked, turned my horse, put spurs to him and had him running at his best. When I came near the tree, I fired my pistol and also my rifle as I passed the tree and didn't miss the mark over a foot with either shot. When I returned the men were examining the bullet holes I had put in the tree. One of them said, "That is wonderful shooting. But what seems to be a mystery is how you can use both your gun and your pistol so near together."

I showed them how it was done, and then I said to them, "You will have to practice this way of shooting when fighting with the Indians. They never stand up and fight like a white man does, and if they should attack us they will be on horse back, as that is their general mode of fighting, and you are liable to meet them any moment, and you will be in a country some of the time where you can not see a hundred yards ahead of you, and you must always be prepared to give them a warm reception. When we come out here this afternoon I want you to all try your hand at shooting the way I have just done, from off your horse's back with him on the run."

I met Jim at dinner, and asked him what success he had training his teamsters. He answered, "Why, we will get there bye and bye, for every man tries to do his best."

At that moment two of the committee came to where Jim and I stood talking and said, "There is another large train of emigrants in sight. What are you going to do with them?"

"I don't intend to do any thing with them," Jim answered. "It is the business of you men of the committee to look after them, but if they join this train they will have to bear their share of the expense, the same as you do."

One of the men asked how much extra we would charge to take the other train under our protection. Jim answered, "If there are forty wagons or over that number, we will require one dollar a day extra and that will lighten the expense on this train, and they must comply with all the rules this train does; and if they are going to join us, I want them to do so at once, for I want to get away from here day after tomorrow."

The man said he would attend to the matter at once, which he did, and all of the new train joined us with the exception of four wagons and eleven men. These eleven men claimed they could take care of themselves at all times and in every place, and they pulled out alone.

The train over which Jim and I had control now numbered one hundred and four wagons, and we had to work day and night to get them in shape to start out on the road. We left there the third day after taking charge of the train. That afternoon when I took my scouts out to practice shooting, I had considerable sport at their expense. They were all perfectly willing to try their guns and pistols, but they wanted some one to take the lead. No one was willing to be the first one to shoot. So I said, "I will settle the matter this way. I will call the name of a man, and he must take his place and shoot." The first man I called rode out saying, "I have never shot from the back of a horse." I answered, "Well, there is always a first time for everything, and the quicker you start in the sooner you will learn."

He rode off a short distance, whirled his horse and started for the tree. When he got to within a few steps of the mark he fired his pistol, and made a very good shot, but the report of the pistol frightened his horse, and he wheeled and ran in the opposite direction of the one he was going, and he had run about two hundred yards before he could stop him. When the man rode back and saw the shot he had made, he felt encouraged, and said, "I want to try that over again."

I answered, "All right, load your pistol and try again, and I will ride by your side and perhaps that will quiet your horse."

This time he did fine for a green hand at that way of shooting. The next man I called on fired his pistol before he got near the tree, and his horse commenced to jump, and he dropped his gun. At that moment Gen. Kerney rode up to us and said to the man, "That is one time, young man, when if you had been in an Indian fight you might have lost your scalp and you surely would have lost your gun. You must do better than that. You must all take an interest in what Mr. Drannan is trying to teach you to do, for you will need all the knowledge you can get to protect not only your selves but the whole train before you get to California. The Indians are all on the war path and you are liable to have a brush with them any day after you leave Fort Kerney, and Mr. Drannan is fully competent to teach you how to meet them, if you will follow his instructions."

After talking a little longer to the men the Gen. rode away; and I was glad to see that his advice had a good effect on the men; they all seemed anxious to try their hand at shooting instead of being backward as they had been before, and I heard one of them remark to another, "Say, man, we have got to learn to shoot from our horses for that General knows what he is talking about, and now let's get in and learn as quick as we can."

After they had all had a try single handed at the mark on the tree I said, "Now men, we will take a shot all together."

I then made a mark on the ground, about twenty steps from the tree we had been shooting at. I then said to them, "We will go back to our starting place," which was about two hundred yards, "then we will form in, line, and we will make a dash as fast as our horses can carry us. When we reach this mark I have made on the ground I will shout, "Fire!" and every man must be ready to fire together, and be careful that you keep in line together; for if you break your ranks in an Indian fight you are almost sure to lose the battle; this drill will train your horses at the same time it is training you."

We rode back, formed in line, and made the charge, and I was very much surprised at the way the men all acquitted them selves. When I gave the word "fire," the report was almost as one sound, so close were their shots together. I went up to the tree and I found that every man had the mark. I told them that they had done exceptionally well.

"It is getting near night, so we will go back to camp and after supper we will practice signaling for one to use in case of danger to the others."

When we got back to camp Bridger had just finished corralling the whole train, and I was surprised to see how neatly it was done considering the short time they had been drilling; I asked Jim when he would be ready to pull out. He answered, "I am going to order an early breakfast for tomorrow morning; and we will pull out as soon as we can after we have eaten it. I want to make it to the crossing of the Platte tomorrow, and it will take us all of the next day to cross the river, and as the river has commenced to rise, the quicker we get across it, the better it will be for us; after we cross the Platte we will have no more trouble with high water until we get to Green river."

After supper I got my scouts together, and we went outside of the corral; we all sat down on a log. I then asked them if any of them could mimic a Coyote; they all looked at me a moment, and then one said, "I don't think any of us ever saw a Coyote. What are they? What do they look like?"

I could not help laughing, for I thought everyone knew what a Coyote was. I told them that a Coyote was a species of Wolf, not as dangerous as the Grey Wolf but three of them could make more noise than all the dogs around the camp could, and I said, "You will see them in droves between here and California, being so numerous the Indians pay no attention to them; and we scouts often use the howl of a Coyote as a signal to each other because this noise will not attract the attention of the Indians; I will now show you how the Coyote howls."

I then gave two or three yelps mimicking the Coyote, and before I had given the yelp the Coyotes answered me. They were about two hundred yards from us in the brush. Some of the men jumped to their feet exclaiming, "What was that?"

When I could stop laughing I told them those were my Coyote friends, answering me.

The Coyotes and I kept up the howling several minutes, and quite a crowd of men and women gathered around me, listening to the noise, and they all wanted to know what it was that I was mimicking. Before I could answer them Jim Bridger, who had come near unobserved by me, said, "Will, suppose we give them the double howl?"

I said, "All right," and we howled together just a few times when the Coyotes in the brush turned loose and such howling I never had heard before in all my experience among them. A number of the women rushed up to Jim and me, frightened nearly into spasms, crying, "oh, is there any danger, of those dreadful beasts attacking the camp?"

Jim laughed heartily and assured them there was no danger as the Coyote was the greatest coward in the forest and would run at the sight of a man. I told the men that they would not have any scout duty to do until after we crossed the Platte river, so we could all ride along the trail together and practice the coyote signal, for they would need to know it as soon as they crossed the Platte river.

The next morning we were astir very early, had our breakfast and were on the road. A little after sunrise that morning, just as we were pulling out, Jim said to me, "When we are within five or six miles of the Platte I want you to go on ahead of the train and select a camping ground as near the crossing of the river as you can; for if we camp near the crossing we can get the train over the river very much quicker than we can if we camp a distance back."

I left them in time to reach the river an hour before the train and had good luck selecting a place to camp not a quarter of a mile from the crossing. I found a little grove of timber with a beautiful little stream of water running through it which I thought was just the place for us to camp that night. I went back and reported to Jim. He said, "Why, I ought to have remembered that little grove, but I clean forgot it."

As soon as Jim had corralled the train, we turned our horses over to the herders and struck out down to the river to see what condition the water was in, and to our satisfaction we found that it had just commenced to rise. Jim said, "As soon as you have eaten breakfast in the morning, Will, I wish you would ride down here and cross the river and see if the ford is clear of quick sand. If there is nothing of that kind to bother us we ought to get the whole outfit over by noon."

When we returned to camp supper was ready. While Jim and I were eating, about a dozen ladies came to us; among them was an old lady who said, "Can't you men coax the wolves to howl again to night?"

Jim answered, "Yes, but I will bet my old boots that before another week has passed you will want us to stop their howling so you can sleep," to which she answered, "Well, where do they live? We don't see or hear them in the day time."

Jim told her that the Coyotes stayed in hollow logs or caves or in thick brush in the day time anywhere out of sight. Just at that moment a Coyote yelped; he was up the river a short distance and for the next two hours there was a continual howl. I asked the old lady if she thought the wolves needed any coaxing to make them yelp. She said, no, she guessed, Mr. Bridger was right when he said they were noisy. Early in the morning I did not wait for breakfast but mounted my horse and went down to the river. I crossed it at the ford to ascertain whether there was quick sand in the ford enough to interfere with the crossing of the emigrant train.

I will here explain to the reader that it was very necessary to examine the fords of the Platte river, as it was a treacherous stream in the way of quick sand, but this time I found nothing in the way to interfere with our crossing. When I got back to camp they were just sitting down to breakfast. I told Jim that there would be no trouble in crossing the river, to which he replied, "All right, when we get ready to cross I want you to lead the train. We will cross twenty-five wagons at a time, and I will have all the mounted men ride on each side of the wagons to keep the teams in their places."

We were successful in landing all the wagons in safety and were all on the other side by eleven o'clock. I asked Jim where we should camp that night; he asked me how far it was to Quaking Asp Grove. I told him I thought it was about nine miles to that place.

He said, "Well, I think we can make it there in good season and that will be a good place to camp."

I now instructed my scouts what their duty was, and we pulled out, I taking the lead from one to two and a half miles ahead of the train.

Late that afternoon I discovered considerable Indian signs where they had crossed the main trail. I followed their trail quite a way and decided that they had passed that way about two days before.

After we went into camp I rode to the top of a high hill about a mile away to look for Indian camp fires. I was soon convinced that there were no Indians near us and started back to camp. I had got within a quarter of a mile of the camp when I saw two men sitting on a log just ahead of me; I rode up to them, and when I spoke to them I recognized them as two of the eleven that left us with the four wagons at Fort Kerney. I said to them, "Men, what are you doing here, and where are your teams and the rest of the men who went with you?"

They answered, "The rest of the men are all dead, killed by the Indians night before last; we made our escape by running off in the dark, and we haven't had a bite to eat since supper that night, and in fact we did not have much supper then, for the savages came on us when we were eating."

I said, "What became of your wagons and teams?"

They said they did not know what became of them, for they made their escape as soon as the Indians came upon them; that they ran a little ways and stopped and listened to the cries of the others as long as there were any left, and then wandering around through the woods ever since, not knowing where they were or what would become of them, and they continued, "We sat down here because we were so weak we could go no further."

One then asked where the rest of the train was. I replied, pointing, "It is about a quarter of a mile over there."

At that, one said to the other, "Let's go and get something to eat." I showed them the way to the train, and as they were intimately acquainted with some of the emigrants they soon had their hunger appeased.

While they were eating, they told us their experience. Three or four miles before they camped for the night they saw the Indians. There were at least seventy-five of them. They were on the north side of the road. They would come close to the road and then disappear again.

"We tried to get near to talk to them, but they ran away as if they were afraid of us. When we camped that evening there were about twenty-five of them on a hill not more than a hundred and fifty yards from us. Two of the men started to go up to them, but they ran away, and that was the last we saw of them, and so we made up our minds that they had gone, and we thought no more about them. It was good and dark when we sat down to supper, and how so many of them came upon us without making any noise is a mystery to us. The first thing we knew, the whole number we had first seen was upon us, and of all the noise, the yells and whoops we ever heard, they made the worst. If they had come up out of the ground, we would not have been more surprised, and the arrows were flying in every direction. As it happened we two were sitting a little away from the rest of the men eating our supper, and at their first yell we jumped up and made for the nearest brush; our guns were all in the wagons, and the Indians were between us and the wagons, so we had no way to defend ourselves. We went a little ways into the brush, and then we looked back and saw the Indians using their tomahawks on the men we had left, and in a few minutes all the noise was over and we supposed all the nine were killed."

Jim Bridger then said, "You two men are the luckiest chaps I ever heard of. You may be sure that the Indians did not see you that night, or they would have trailed you up and had your scalps before the next morning."

One of the committee men came to where Jim and I were sitting and said, "What shall we do about finding and burying those bodies?"

Jim answered, "That, sir, is your business, not ours. It is our business to see that the people under our care do not meet with the same fate these men have met, and I do not intend to put the lives of all this train in danger by stopping to hunt for the remains of men who refused with scorn to stay with us and share the protection we offered them; they brought the trouble and their own deaths on them selves, but I will say this, if any of you men want to hunt for these bodies and take the time to bury them, I have no objection, but you must understand that when you get outside of the scout force we shall not be responsible for any thing that may happen to you."

At that moment more than twenty men spoke together, saying, "Mr. Bridger is right, Mr. Bridger is right; he proposes to do just what he agreed to do, and no one can blame him." One of the men then asked if we would be willing to stop long enough to bury the bodies if we found them; Jim said, "We have no objections to stopping if it is a suitable place to make our camp, but if it isn't we can't afford to lose the time, as we must make certain places to camp every day, for we are now in a hostile Indian country, and in order to protect our selves we must camp in certain places, for without we take this care this train will not be in existence a week, and Will and I feel the responsibility that rests upon us, for the lives of your women and children as well as your own are in our hands."

At this moment a middle-aged lady who stood near us with the tears running down her cheeks said, "Why don't you let Mr. Bridger and Mr. Drannan have their way? You see what these other men came to by not obeying their orders, and do you want to bring us all to the predicament they are in?" At this Jim said, "I'll be dog goned if they will."

This settled the controversy for the time being.

That evening before we turned in for the night Jim and I talked the matter over together; and we decided that after I put out the scouts in the morning I would take ten men all mounted on horses and keeping about five miles ahead of the train, and if we found the bodies I should set the men I had with me to work digging graves, and I should turn back and report to Jim what we had found, and the condition we found them in.

As soon as possible the next morning the men I had selected and myself pulled out. We had made eight or nine miles when we found the bodies we were looking for. They were all laying near together, around what had been their camp fire, and all of them were scalped.

There was nothing about them to indicate that they had made any effort to protect themselves. Every one of the heads was split, showing they had been tomahawked, proving what the two survivors had told us about the suddenness of the attack to be correct. We found their wagons nearly empty. The covers had been torn off, the most of the bedding was gone and some of their clothing. The eatables such as bacon and flour and dried fruit was laying on the ground. I told the men I thought the best way to bury them would be to dig one large grave and put them all into it, and they seemed to be of the same mind. After helping to select a spot for the grave, I left them and rode back to meet the train and report our find. I told Jim all about the condition of things at the dead men's camp, at which he said, "I guess we had better stop there a couple of hours, which will give us time to bury the dead, and we can reach our camping ground before night."

On reaching the place Jim corralled the train, and he then went to all the families and told them that two hours was as long as we should stop there. I said, "I will take a stroll around through the brush and see if I can find some of their cattle."

I hadn't gone more than a quarter of a mile when I found twelve head of their oxen. When I drove them back to the wagons, the two men said they were just half of the original number. They yoked them up and hooked them to two of the wagons and took what they wanted of the provisions and clothes and left the rest laying on the ground. As we were about to leave Jim said, "It is too dog goned bad to leave all that grub for the Coyotes to eat. That meat and flour will be worth fifty cents a pound when you get to California."

Then several of the men and women commenced to gather up the stuff, the men carrying the flour and the women the bacon, and they soon had it all stowed away in their wagons.

Having laid the dead away in the best manner we could under the circumstances, and every thing else being in readiness, we pulled out for Barrel Springs. I told Jim not to look for me until about dark, as I intended to climb the tall hills that we could see in the distance to look for Indian camp fires. This being understood, my twelve scouts and myself left the train in Jim's care. After giving the eleven scouts their orders, I took the other one with me and took the lead. Nothing of interest occurred until we had nearly reached the place where we were to camp that night. Happening to look up on a high ridge to the north of us, I saw a large band of Buffalo coming towards us, and I thought by the lay of the ground that they must pass through the spot where we were going to camp. I said to my companion, "Let's hitch our horses and get those trees," pointing to a little grove of timber, which stood near the springs. "Those Buffalo are going to come down there, and we want to get as many of them as possible. Now don't shoot until they are opposite us, and then aim to break their neck every time, and load and shoot as fast as you can after you commence."

We only had a few minutes to wait. When we reached the timber, the Buffalos were opposite us. They were within thirty feet of us. We both fired and two Buffaloes fell. Now it was a race to see who could load first. I was the quickest and got the next one. They were now on the stampede, and it was a sight to see the number that was passing us. I got three of them with my rifle and one with my pistol. My companion shot three with his rifle. The one I shot with my pistol I don't think was over ten feet from me when she fell. She was the nicest little two-year-old heifer I had ever killed, and her meat was almost as tender as chicken. We went to work dressing them and had them pretty well underway when the train arrived.

Barrel Springs was one of the prettiest places for a camping ground I ever saw. It was in a small, open prairie, surrounded by scattering timber, a stream of cool and pure sparkling water running through the center, and the grass was almost to the horses' knees.

As soon as Jim had corralled the train, he rode to where we were at work and said, "Boys, I'll be gol durned if this ain't one of the times, you done two good jobs at once."

I said, "How is that, Jim?"

He answered, "In the first place you provided meat for our supper, and in the next, you drove the Buffalos off so we have plenty of grass for the stock for their supper."

By this time nearly all the women were standing around us. This was the first Buffalo they had ever seen and they were a great curiosity to them. With the rest was a middle-aged lady, and with her she had two daughters nearly grown. The mother stood near me watching me work.

She said, "Mr. Drannan, may I have a piece of that yearling's hind quarter? I will tell you what I want to do with it; my girls and I have picked a lot of wild onions today, and I want to make a stew, and we want you and Mr. Bridger to come to our tent and eat supper."

I assured her she could have all the meat she wanted from my little heifer. One of the girls ran to their wagon to get an ax and her father to come and chop it off for them. By this time the men had about finished dressing the Buffalo, and every body helped themselves to what part they wanted. There was plenty for all, and some of the rough part left over. It did not seem long to me when one of the girls came to Jim and me and told us that her mother had sent for us to come and take supper with them, and I think that was one of the times we did justice to a meal, for a stew with onions was a rare dish for us woodsmen, and a woman to cook it was a still more rare occasion. As soon as we had finished eating, Jim stood up and in a loud voice said, "Ladies, how many of you can dance?"

I think there were as many as twenty-five answered, "I can dance."

Jim said, "All right, get ready, and after dark we will have lots of music."

One of the men asked, "Where are you going to get your music?"

Jim answered, "Why dog gone it, Will and Mr. Henderson have engaged a band to play for us to night."

And in a few moments the band struck up in a Coyote howl, and Jim laughed and said, "There, didn't I promise you a band? Isn't that music?" And from then until midnight the howling never ceased. It was something fearful to listen to. The smell of the Buffalo blood made them wild, and they howled worse then usual that night. A great number of the emigrants did not lay down until after midnight, and time after time asked me if I thought there was any danger of them attacking the camp. I told them there was no danger from them, and that if I knew there weren't any Indians within twenty miles of us I could stop their yelling in five minutes. They asked how that was possible. I told them that if I was sure there were no Indians in hearing, I would fire my gun off a time or two, and we would hear no more of the Coyotes at night. After midnight they quieted down and every one went to sleep, except the guards who watched the camp.

Jim and I were up very early the next morning and called all the others to have an early breakfast, telling them we had to make twenty miles that day to get to water and grass so we could camp that night. As soon as breakfast was over Jim said to the women, "Now ladies, you won't have any more music to dance to for the next three nights, for you will see no more Buffalo, hear no more Coyotes, or see any Indians until we cross Green River."

Several of the ladies said they would be glad if they never heard any more Coyotes howl. They did not like that kind of music to dance to, or to be kept awake all night listening to them either.

For the next three days everything passed along smoothly; when we reached Green River, it was rising rapidly, and we had a great deal of trouble crossing it. We had to hitch three teams to one wagon and six and eight men had to ride each side to keep the teams straight.

Green River is a mountain stream and flows very rapidly, and at this place was very narrow, and if the team should get ten feet below the Ford they would be lost so swift is the current. We worked hard two days getting everything across the river, but we got everything over in good shape at last.

That night, after supper was over, we told all the people of the train to be ready for starting on the road by sunrise in the morning, as we had a long drive before us and it was all gradually uphill at that. Several of the women asked when we were going to give them some more Buffalo meat. Jim burst out laughing and asked them if they wanted some more music to dance to. One girl said, "Have we got to have music every time we have Buffalo meat?"

Jim told her that for the next two weeks we would have music every night whether we had Buffalo meat or not, and very likely there would be times we would hear Indian yells during the day.

"By that time," he said, "we shall be in the Ute country, and they are the meanest tribe of Indians in the west, and we may look for trouble with them any moment, day or night." And addressing the men he said, "I want you to keep your guns loaded and ready for use at a moment's warning, and you must stay with the wagons, all but the scouts, who will be under Will's control, for if they attack us I want to give them as warm a reception as we possibly can, for if we whip them in the first battle, that will settle it with that bunch. They will not trouble us again."

The next night we camped at Soda Springs. There were three springs close together. Two of them were mineral, one strong with soda, and the other was very salt, and the third one was pure cold water. As soon as the wagons were corralled, several of the young girls took buckets and started for the springs to get water, and as luck had it they all went to the Soda spring. Not one of them had ever even heard of a soda spring until they tried this one. They had not had any water to drink since noon and were very thirsty, so drank very heartily without stopping to taste, but as soon as the water was down, there was a cry from as many as had drunk, and they all ran back to the wagons, screaming, "oh! oh! I am poisoned, oh! What shall I do?" And with their hands pressed to their breasts and the gas bursting from nose and mouth they did make a sad sight to those who did not understand the effects of soda springs, but to Jim and me it was very amusing, for we knew they were in no danger of poison.

Some of the sufferers cried as well as screamed. I could not speak for laughing, for I remembered my own first experience in drinking from a soda spring, but Jim told them they were not poisoned and told them what kind of water they had drunk. In a few moments all the crowd was at the soda spring, drinking its poison water as the girls still called it. The older women asked what they should do for water to cook with. I pointed to the salt spring and told them to go and get water from that if they had fresh meat to cook, and the water would salt it and for coffee I pointed to the spring of water farthest from us, and I told the girls they could drink all the water they wanted from that spring and not have to make such faces as they did after they drank the soda. One of the girls said she reckoned I would have made a face if I had felt as she did. Jim stood near us with a smile on his lips, which I knew meant mischief of some sort. He said. "Will, why don't you tell the girls how you enjoyed your first drink of soda water?" And seeing how I blushed, for my face was burning, he said, "I guess I had better tell them myself. I don't think you know how comical you looked." And in the most ridiculous way he could think of he described how I looked and acted on that to me never-to-be-forgotten occasion, "My first drink from a soda spring."

I have been told there is a large town at this place now, and that it is a great resort for the sick. They use this salt water, which I forgot to say was also hot as well as salt, for bathing, and is considered a great cure for many diseases.

[Illustration: Waving my hat, I dashed into the midst of the band.]

CHAPTER IV

The next morning we pulled out of this place by the way of Landers. That afternoon about two o'clock I saw a small band of Indians coming directly towards us. They were about a mile away when I first saw them. I rode to the foot of a little hill which was close to me at the time I saw them. I dismounted from my horse and tied him to a sage brush, and then I crept to the top of the hill to see how many there were of them. I watched them until they were within a half a mile of my hiding place; I then counted thirty. I took them to be a hunting party by the way they were traveling. I signaled to my scouts to come to me at once. When they reached me, the Indians were less than a quarter of a mile from me. I told them what was coming down the ravine and told them to see that their guns and pistols were in order, "for, as soon as they round that little point yonder, we will charge on them, and we will kill every one we can. Now, don't shoot until we get within thirty yards of them. I will say, "fire," then I want every man to get an Indian. Now don't get rattled, but shoot to kill and shout as loud as you can. It don't make any difference what you say, only make as big a noise as you can, and as soon as you empty your guns, pull your pistols and go after them."

In a moment more the time had come to act, and when I said, "Charge," every man responded and did his duty. I had been in several Indian fights before, but I never saw Indians so taken by surprise as this band was. They did not draw their arrows or run, until we had fired into them, and after they turned to run, they had gone at least two hundred yards, before I saw them try to shoot an arrow.

We got fourteen of them in the first charge, and inside of three hundred yards we got six more. The remainder had reached the thick brush, so we let them go.

We now commenced catching the horses. We caught sixteen horses, and they all had good hair ropes around their necks. We tied them all together, and I left them in charge of two men, and the rest of us went to take the scalps of the Indians, and I was surprised to find when I said, "We will take the scalps of these Indians," that the men did not know what I meant. I showed them how to take the scalps off, and then they asked what I was going to do with them. I told them I was going to give them to Jim Bridger, and he would make guards out of them. "Jim wouldn't take the biggest hundred dollar bill you could offer him for these scalps, when he gets his hands on them."

One of the men said, "What will Bridger do with them horrid bloody things?"

I told him to just wait until night and then Jim would explain the use they would be to him. I tied the scalps to my saddle, left two men to care for the horses we had captured and biding the others to follow me I struck out for the place where we were to camp that night.

Jim told me that night how surprised the emigrants were when the train came to the men who had charge of the horses, and seeing the bodies of the dead Indians.

He said, "I had to let them stop the train a few minutes so they could all look at them." He said, "Some of the women wanted to know what had become of the hair off the top of their heads. I told them that I reckoned Will had taken them to give to me."

"And what are you going to do with those horrid Indians' hair?" one woman inquired.

"I am going to protect you and the rest of the train with them," he answered her.

The place we had picked out for camping ground that night was Sage Creek. There was no timber in sight as far as one could see; there was nothing to see but sage brush, but there was plenty of good water and fine grass.

We had been riding around looking for signs of Indians, so we did not reach the camping ground until Jim had the wagons corralled. I gave him the scalps I had taken and I told him I was going to get some meat for supper. He said, "What have you found? Bison or Antelope?"

I answered, "There are four or five hundred head of Antelope over beyond that hill yonder," and I pointed to the ridge a short distance from camp, "and I think I can take my scouts with me, and we can get an Antelope apiece and get back here before sundown." Jim answered, "All right, Will. I busy myself by hanging up my scalps while you are gone."

My men and I struck out up a ravine that led up close to where the Antelope were feeding; we were screened from their sight by the high banks. When we were close enough to them we dismounted and tied our horses to some bush. I then crawled up the bank alone to see just where the Antelope were, and to my surprise I found that there were two or three hundred of them feeding almost on the edge of the ravine in close gunshot to us. I slipped back down the bank and got to the boys as quick as possible and told them that the Antelope were on the top of the bank in close gun shot of us. We scattered along down the ravine for perhaps a hundred yards. I took my handkerchief out of my pocket and told them I would tie it around my ramrod. "And now don't any of you shoot until you see this red handkerchief waving, for the color being red it will attract their attention, and you will see more heads looking towards it then you ever saw in your life before. Now take good aim and be sure and hit your game, and as soon as you have emptied your guns pull your pistols and get some more while they are running away; we ought to get at least twenty Antelope out of this band."

When I waved the handkerchief, it seemed as if every rifle cracked at once, and it was a lively time for a few minutes for all of us. When we counted the Antelope we found we had shot twenty-two. We each took an Antelope in front of us on our horses and put out for camp. When we got there we unloaded, and some of the men that were at the camp commenced dressing them and cutting them up in pieces to cook, while the other boys went back to get those we had left where we killed them.

The women had the fires burning when the meat was ready for cooking, and when supper was ready all the Antelope were dressed and distributed around among the emigrants, and there was enough to last until the second day.

Jim had cut long sticks and had hung the scalps on the wagons so they could be seen quite a distance away. After he had them all fixed, he and I were standing together talking, he telling me the effect the sight of the dead Indians had on the emigrants and especially when they saw that their scalps had been taken off.

Two of the women came to us and invited us to eat supper with them at their tent. I will here explain to the reader that every family in the train had their own separate tent and cooked at their own fire. Jim and I accepted the invitation as we always did of the first that invited us to each meal.

As we finished eating it seemed as though all the women of the train gathered around us. There was one old lady in the crowd who seemed to be the one selected to do the talking. She said, "Mr. Bridger, I want you to tell me truly, don't you think it was awfully wicked to cut those scalps off those Indians' heads and then hang the dreadful, bloody things up on the wagons for us to look at?" and the tears were in her eyes as she finished her question.

Jim replied, "The best thing that has been done since we started on this trip is killing those Indians, and better still taking their scalps. I did not hang those scalps up on your wagons for you to look at. I hung them up for the Indians that are alive to look at, and I will tell you this, the Indians will never attack the train as long as they see those same bloody things hanging there, for they will think they will lose their own scalps, if they do. I would rather have these Indian scalps to protect you with than a hundred of the best soldiers in the United States Army. The Indian does not fear death, but he dreads the thought of having his scalps taken off his head, for it is the Indian's belief that he cannot enter the happy hunting grounds after death if his scalp has been taken off his head, and I want to impress on your minds that if this train should be attacked, every one of you that fell into the hands of the Indians, it would not matter whether they be men or women, would have their scalps torn off, and the same scalps would be hanging up on the Indians' wigwams for the squaws to dance around, and I want all you ladies to distinctly understand that Will Drannan or myself will do nothing while we have charge of this train but what will be of benefit to you all, and will bear the strictest investigation."

By this time everyone in the train had surrounded us, and turning to the men of the train, Jim continued, "If any of you are dissatisfied with our actions, now is the time to say so, and we will quit right here, and I will guarantee that the Indians will have all of your scalps before you are a hundred miles from here."

At this moment the committee came to us and said, "We want you two men to understand that there is no fault to be found with what you have done since you took charge of this train. We realize that every move you have made has been for our benefit. Mr. Bridger, you have no doubt found out long before this time that in a large company like this, everyone can not be satisfied. No matter how hard you may try to please them, there will still be some growlers and, pardon me for saying, there are cranks among the women as well as among men."

At this the old lady who had called Bridger wicked stepped up to Jim and said, "Mr. Bridger, I hope you will excuse me, for what I said. I will admit that I did not know what I was talking about, and if you will forgive me this time I will find no more fault with you."

Jim made no reply to the lady's remarks, but turning to the rest of the company he said, "Now get ready to have a good dance tonight, for we are going to have lots of music, for the Coyotes will smell the blood of the Indians on one side of us and that of the Antelope on the other side, so there will be music from a double band."

This was the last word of complaint that was expressed, while we were with this train. Everyone seemed satisfied, and all things went pleasantly from this time on. But talk about Coyotes' howling. This was one of the nights when they did howl. They came so close to us that we could hear them snap their teeth. Apparently there were hundreds of them around us.

After leaving this camp we had no more trouble for two days. The second night we camped on a little stream which was a tributary to Snake river. In the morning before we camped at this place, I told Jim when I left him with my scouts that he need not expect to see me until supper time. "You know, Jim, that we are in the heart of the Ute country, and I shall prospect every hill or ravine where there is liable to be found signs of Indians."

That evening it was perhaps a couple of miles before we got to the camp and a mile or so away from the other scouts, I ran on three wagons standing right in the middle of the road. After examining them a few minutes, I came to the conclusion that they had been standing where they were all winter. I saw that there had been ox-teams attached to them some time, but there was no sign of yokes there. The covers were still on the wagons, so I got off my horse and climbed into one of them. I found some flour and probably three hundred pounds of bacon in the three wagons. There was no bedding, but some clothing for both men and women, which was quite old and worn. On the front gate of one of the wagons I found considerable blood, and there was blood on the tongue of the same wagon. I now made an examination of the ground to see if there were any signs of a fight. After I had looked around some time, I was convinced that the owners of the wagons, whoever they had been, had been massacred by the Indians.

About forty steps from the wagons I found the remains of three people. One was a large body, that of a man, and one a medium size, which I took for the body of a woman, and the other was a small child. All there was left of them was their bones and some hair, the Wolves having stripped the flesh entirely from them.

I signaled to my scouts to come to me. As soon as they came, I told them to take all the grub out of the wagons and put it in a pile, and I would go back and meet the train and have three men appointed to distribute the stuff among the families. I told the boys that there were two trunks in the wagons and to break them open and see what was in them.

They did so and found them full of women's clothes, some of the garments of very nice material. I rode back and met the train and told Jim what I had found, and what I thought we had best do.

He selected three men to divide the provisions among the families of the train. I never inquired what they did with the clothes that was in the trunks.

We hunted all around in every direction, but we could find no more bodies, so if there had been others, the Indians must have taken them into captivity or, what was more likely, the Coyotes had dragged them away into the brush beyond our reach.

After the emigrants had stored the provisions in their wagons, we went on to the place we had selected for a camping ground for that night. I preceded the train a half a mile, and I found plenty of Indian signs, but they were all old. All their trails were pointing south that night. I asked Jim why all the Indians were going south this time of the year. He told me that they were going to hunt big game such as Buffalo, Bison and Elk, and they had to go further south to find such game, and he said, he should not be surprised if we did not see another Indian until we struck the Sink of Humboldt.

"But you may look out then, for we will find them then in plenty." As Jim finished this remark, one of my scouts came riding into camp at full speed. Jim and I went to meet him, for we suspected that something was up. As soon as he got in speaking distance he said to me, "There are a thousand Indians up on that ridge yonder, and they are coming this way; they are all on horse back, and there are women and children with them." Jim asked how far off they were. He said he didn't believe they were over a mile from camp at this minute; Jim mounted his horse and went to the herders and ordered them to corral the stock at once, at the same time telling every man to get his gun and form in line for the Indians were coming upon us, and the reader may be sure that everybody and every animal in that train was moving lively for a few minutes.

As soon as the stock was corralled, Jim rode up to me with one of the sticks that had a scalp on it in his hand. Handing it to me, he said, "Here, Will, take this and ride out a little ways from the corral, and when the Indians come where they can see you, wave it over your head so they will be sure to see the scalps, and I will get another bunch and I will stand close to you at the same time."

In a few minutes more the Indians hove in sight. They were in less than a quarter of a mile of us before they could see the whole train. As soon as they got a good sight of us the whole band stopped. The leader of the band was a war chief. We knew this by his dress. As soon as they stopped, Jim and I rode out towards them, waving the scalps like a flag.

The old chief looked at us a moment, then turned and seemed to be talking with some of the other braves a few minutes. Then the whole tribe pulled out in a westerly direction from us, and in a short time they were out of our sight, and their pace was lively the reader may be sure for the sight of the scalps had frightened them, as they feared they would meet the same fate if they did not get away from us quick.

I followed them quite a distance to make sure that they had gone. When I got back, everything had quieted down and the company was just sitting down to supper.

After Jim and I had got through eating, two of the committee came to us and as many as forty or fifty women, old and young, were with them. The men said to us, "These women have asked us to come to you and tender their most heartfelt thanks to you for what you have done for them today, for we are all sure we would have fallen victims to the savages if you had not been with us to protect us from them. It was the easiest-won battle that I ever heard of, and all because you knew how to fight the savages with their own weapon."

Jim answered, "Didn't I tell you that them scalps was worth an army of soldiers to us, and hasn't this proved my words to be true? What would a hundred soldiers have done with that whole tribe of Indians? There wouldn't have been a man of them left in an hour to tell the story, and every one of their scalps would be hanging to the Indians' belts, and I want you to all bear in mind that for the next three hundred miles we are liable to have just such another experience any hour of the day or night, and I want to ask you all to do as you done this time. Only keep cool and obey our orders, and I think we will get you through in safety, and I want to say this for the ladies, they showed great bravery today in keeping so quiet and having good sense staying under cover, and I did not hear a sound from any of them, and I will tell the girls that I will recommend them to the best-looking young frontiersmen I am acquainted with, as wifes, especially if they learn to dance to the Coyote's music."

This made a laugh all around and took the edge off of the danger that had clouded the people's faces, which was the motive Jim had in view in making the joking remarks, for no one knew better than Jim did how necessary it is to keep a company in good spirits, and to keep them from dwelling on the danger that might threaten them.

There was nothing to interrupt our slumbers that night, and we arose refreshed the next morning, ready for the day's journey and whatever was before us.

For the next three days nothing happened to interfere with our journey. The third day brought us to the foot of Look Out mountain, which is a spur of the Sierra Nevada mountains. In the eastern part of what is now the State of Nevada, but which was at that time one of the wildest countries in all the west, this particular portion I am speaking about was inhabited solely by the Ute Indians, which at that time was a very large tribe, and one of the most barbarous tribe that ever inhabited North America.

It is now fifty years ago since the events I am speaking of took place, and after all that Uncle Sam has done for them, they are not civilized yet.

At the time I speak of, this tribe inhabited all of the country from Snake river on the north to the Colorado river on the south and probably four hundred miles east and west, and at that time it was one of the greatest game countries west of the Rocky mountains. Such game as Buffalo, Elk, Antelope and Deer ranged all through that country in countless numbers. The Buffalo traveled much less in that particular portion of the country than they did in the country east of the Rocky mountains. The Buffalo that inhabited this part of the country scarcely ever crossed Snake river on the north or strayed as far as what is now known as the States of Oregon and Idaho, and it was no uncommon sight to see from fifty to two hundred and fifty Elk in one band.

It would seem unreasonable at this period to tell how many Antelope one could see in one day.

But to return to the emigrant train and our camp at the foot of Look Out mountain, just before I got to our intended camping place, I crossed a trail where the Indians had just passed. I followed this trail for some distance, and judging from the signs I decided there was quite a large band, five hundred or more of them.

I went back to the main trail and signaled to my scouts to come to me. I selected one to go with me, gave the others their orders what to do, telling them to be sure and tell Bridger to not look for us until he saw us, for I was going to follow a trail until I found where the Indians went into camp.

Myself and my assistants now took the trail of the Indians, and we had followed it about five miles when we came to a high ridge, and as we looked down into the valley we saw the Indians in camp.

I was now satisfied that the Indians had not seen us and would not see us, so we turned and rode back to the place where we started from. When we reached the camping ground, Jim had just got the train corralled. I reported to him what I had seen and where the Indians were. After listening to my report, Jim said, "That is good. There is no danger from that band anyway."

We passed a quiet night at this camp. The next morning we were up very early and got an early start on the road, for we had a long drive before us that day, as it was all of twenty miles before we could reach water again.

Before we started that morning, Jim said to me, "Keep a sharp look out for Buffalo when you get near the next water, for if there are no Indians there, you will be sure to find Buffalo, and tomorrow being Sunday we will lay over a day and rest up, and if we can have some fresh meat I think everyone will enjoy it."

I answered that if there were any Buffalo in that part of the country, I would surely find them, "for, besides the treat the Buffalo will be to us, we can have another Coyote dance."

Jim clapped his hands and, laughing, replied, "Yes, Will, I'll be dog gorned if we won't, for the Coyotes will howl to beat any band if you can kill a few Buffalos."

I and my scouts pulled out at once, and to my surprise I did not see an Indian track all that day. When I was within three or four miles of the place where we were to camp, I commenced to see signs of Buffalo, so I signaled all the other scouts to come to me. As soon as they came, I showed them the tracks of the Buffalo in the sand, and then I told them that we would scatter out and go in abreast, keeping about a hundred yards apart, and keep a sharp look out, and if either of us see any Buffalo, signal to the rest of us to come, "for, we are going to lay over in this camp tomorrow, and we want some Buffalo meat to feast on."

We saw no Buffalo until we were almost to the camping ground. Then one of the men discovered a herd of perhaps twenty-five cows and calves in a little valley close to the place where we were going to camp.

As soon as he saw them, he signaled to the balance of us, and we got to him as quickly as possible. On examination of the valley, we found that there was only one way the Buffalos could get out, and that was the way they went in, which led down to where our camp would be that night. There were not more than eight or ten acres in the whole valley, and it was almost surrounded by high bluffs, and the only outlet which was not more than thirty paces wide led directly to the spot where we intended to camp over Sunday.

I told the men to dismount and tie their horses to some Sage brush that was near and go down to a little grove of trees that stood at the mouth of the valley.

"I will ride in among them and try to separate the herd so we can get as many of them as possible, and aim to kill the smallest of the band as they pass you. If I am successful in separating the band, and you can get two shots at them, we will get all the meat we want. I will try to hold all the calves until the cows are out of the valley, and when the last cow is out, all you men rush and close the opening, and then we will have lots of sport killing the calves."

As I rode into the valley, all the Buffalos ran to the opposite end, and I saw then that I should have a hard time to separate them. I rode quickly to where they were all in a bunch. As I drew near them, they all broke for the outlet in one body. I took my hat off and, waving it over my head and with a yell, I dashed into the midst of the band and succeeded in separating three cows and ten calves. At one time I thought they would run over me and my horse in spite of all I could do to prevent it. But finally I separated the three cows and ten calves from the rest and turned them back to the head of the valley. I now heard the report of the guns, so I knew the men were getting some meat. I then rode back to them as quickly as I could, and I found they had shot ten Buffalo cows, which all lay dead within a few feet of each other.

I said, "Now boys, we have enough cows, but we want some of the calves, and I will go up and start them down, and you let the cows all pass out but hold the calves inside and shoot all of them you can."

I went back to the other end of the valley, and as luck was on my side the cows separated themselves from the calves, and I had no trouble in running the cows out, which I did at full speed. I then said, "Now boys, you may kill all these calves but one, and that one I am going to have for a pet."

They all commenced to laugh and asked, "How are you going to catch it?"

I answered, "You just watch me," at the same time I was loosening the riata from my saddle. I then rode up near to where the calves were huddled together, and as they started to run I threw my rope at the largest one in the bunch and caught him around the neck, and there was some lively kicking and bucking for a few minutes, but he found it was no use to struggle. After that it took only a few minutes before the men had all the others killed.

The excitement being over, I looked down to the other end of the valley and saw that Bridger had the train corralled. I sent one of the men to tell Jim to send ten or twelve teams up the valley to drag the Buffalos down to camp. The men reported the number of cows and calves we had killed, and Jim sent enough teams to drag them all down to camp in one trip.

As soon as the teams had started with their loads, I asked the boys to help me with my calf. I told them to all get behind him and give him a scare, and he would go to camp in a lively gallop, for I wanted to show the women and children how a wild Buffalo looked when alive.

When we reached the corral, Jim Bridger was the first to meet us. The calf had got pretty wild by this time. No one could get near him. Jim said he had been seeing Buffalo for the last twenty-five years, and this one was the first he had ever seen led into camp, and in a few minutes all the women and children and the majority of the men were gathered in a bunch looking at my calf and laughing at his antics, for he did not submit to captivity very gracefully. After watching him a while, Jim said, "What are you going to do with him, Will?"

I answered that I did intend to eat him, but I thought now I had better turn him loose.

Jim said, "That won't do, Will, for he would kill someone before he cleared himself of the crowd. Tie him up to a tree, and we can kill him and take the meat with us when we leave here."

I tied him up as Jim thought best, although I pitied the little fellow and had rather have let him loose and seen him scamper away over the hills to join his friends in freedom.

The men set to work skinning and getting the meat ready to cook for supper. We now had fresh meat enough to last the entire outfit nearly a week.

After we had finished supper Jim told the women to get ready to dance, "for," he said, "we will have more music tonight than we have had for a long time."

One of the old ladies asked him, how he could tell when the wolves would howl more one night than another, and she said, "every time that you have said they would howl, they have made such a noise that none of us could sleep." Jim answered, "this will be the worst night for them to howl you have ever heard, and I will tell you why. You see, all those Buffalos have been dressed here at the camp, and the Coyotes will smell the blood for miles away from here, and they will follow the scent until they get to us, and as they cannot get to the meat they will vent their disappointment in howling. So you see why I say the ladies will have a plenty of music to dance to." And sure enough, as soon as it commenced growing dark the din commenced, and there was no sleep for anyone in that camp until nearly daylight the next morning. A number of times that night I went out perhaps fifty yards from the wagons and saw them running in every direction. I could have silenced them by firing once among them, but this I did not dare to do, for I did not know how many Indians might be in hearing of the report of my gun, and I thought it the better policy to hear the howling of the wolves than to have a fight with the Indians.

The next morning I called the scouts together and divided them into four squads, and we started out to examine the country in all four directions for Indians or the signs of them, our calculation being to investigate the country for five miles in every direction.

I told the men that if we saw no Indians or the signs of them that day that we would have a chance to sleep that night for I would fire a few shots among the Coyotes and stop their music, for that time at least. I and the men that went with me took a direct western course. After traveling perhaps five miles we struck a fresh Indian trail; the Indians had passed along there the evening before going in a southern direction. We followed it some distance, and I came to the conclusion that there were four or five hundred Indians in the band, and I knew by the direction they were traveling that they would have to go fifteen or twenty miles before they could find water, so I knew we were perfectly safe from this band. So after explaining this to my companions, I said, "Let us go back to camp."

On our arrival there we found that all the scouts had got into camp except the squad that went east, and in a few minutes, they came riding in as fast as their horses could bring them shouting at the top of their voices, "The Indians are after us."

Jim ordered the stock all corralled at once, and the men were not long in obeying orders. While these were attending to the stock, Jim was placing the other men in a position to protect the train, and as good luck, or rather Jim's forethought, had it, he had stuck the scalps we had used for the same purpose before on the wagons the night before, saying as he did it, "We don't ever know when they will be needed."

I with all my scout force rode out to meet the coming Indians. About two hundred yards from the corral there was a little hill which the Indians would have to climb before they came in view of our camp. I told the men that we would meet them at the top of the hill and give them as warm a welcome as we could, and then we would get back to the train as quickly as possible, and I then told them to shoot with their rifles first and then to pull their pistols and to let the savages have all there was in them, and then wheel their horses and make for camp.

We heard them coming before we reached the top of the hill. When we got on the crest, they were not more than thirty or forty yards from us. Every one of my men fired together, and I saw a number of Indians fall from their horses, and after we emptied our pistols among them, we wheeled our horses and sped back to camp.

The Indians just rounded the top of the hill where they could barely see the train, and then they stopped. Seeing the wagons with the scalps on them and all in seeming waiting for them seemed to take them by surprise. Bridger was making arrangements to make an attack on them when they all gave the war whoop and wheeled their horses and went back the way they had come.

Myself and scouts went to the top of the hill to see if the Indians were still in the neighborhood, but finding no signs of them we went back to camp. When I told Jim that there were no Indians in sight, he sprang up and laughed as loud as he could and clapped his hands together and said, "Another battle won by Will's Indian scalps. Didn't I tell you all that them scalps was worth more to us than all the soldiers we could get around us? They have won two good strong battles for us, and we will not have any more trouble here. Them scalps is worth a hundred dollars apiece to this train."

My men and I now went back over the hill to see how many Indians we had shot in our first meeting them, and strange to say we did not find a dead Indian, but there was plenty of blood all around where they were when we fired on them. I knew by the blood that we had killed some of them, but their comrades had taken their bodies on their horses and carried them with them, which the Indian always does if he can.

When we returned to camp the excitement was all over, and everyone was as cheerful as if nothing had happened to disturb them. Jim and I were talking together a short time after I got back when two young girls came to us and said their mother wanted us to eat dinner with them, for they were going to have pie for dinner. Jim said, "Is it calf pie? I do love calf pie above all things."

The girls laughed and said, "No, it is apple pie." Jim said, "All right, I like apple pie too."

When we sat down to dinner, which the reader will understand was not spread on a table, but was spread on the ground, I was surprised to see what was before us to eat. I have paid a dollar many times since then for a meal that would not compare in any way with this dinner that was cooked out in the wilds with no conveniences that women are supposed to require.

There was a stew made of the Buffalo calf, a roast of the same kind of meat, corn bread, fried wild onions, apple pie and as good a cup of coffee as I ever drank.

After we had finished eating, Jim said to the lady, "Are you going to run a boarding house when you get to California?"

She answered, "I don't know what I shall do when we get there. Why do you ask?"

Jim answered, "I wanted to know because if you are, every time I come to California, I am coming to board with you."

Her husband then said, "It don't make any difference whether we keep a boarding house or not. Any time you or Mr. Drannan come near our place we shall expect you to come to us. You both will be perfectly welcome to a seat at our table at any and all times. After what I have seen today, I am more fully convinced that everyone in this train owes their lives to you two men. What would have become of the whole of us this morning if you two men had not been here to guard us? I will tell you what would have happened. Our stock and all we possessed would have been in the hands of the Indians, and our scalps would be hanging at their girdles at this time, and I want to say now that the people that compose this train can never pay you for what you have done for us on this dangerous journey."

Jim answered, "When we undertook to pilot this train across to California, we knew what we would be likely to meet with and that the undertaking was no child's play. We both understood the nature of the Indians thoroughly, and if all you people stick together and obey our orders, we will take you through in safety."

The man answered, "Mr. Bridger, you need not have one uneasy thought about anyone wanting to leave your protection on this trip, for everyone in this company understands that their lives are in the hands of you two men."

By this time there was quite a crowd around us, and Jim said, "We both appreciate the good opinion you have expressed, but after all we have only done our duty by you as we always do, or at least we try to do to everyone who intrust themselves and their property in our care. And now, to change the subject, Will says he is going to stop the wolves howling tonight so you people can get some sleep."

When it had grown dark I took a few of the scouts with me out on the edge of camp perhaps a hundred yards from the corral, and when the Coyotes began their howling, we began firing, and in a few minutes there was not a sound to be heard. We were satisfied that we would not be disturbed that night by the savages or the Coyotes, so we all turned in, and we had a good night's rest.

The next morning we were up and had an early breakfast, and I had not seen the emigrants in such a cheerful mood as they all were this morning, since we left Fort Kerney. Every one was cracking jokes.

As my scouts and I were about to leave the train to take our usual position as guards, one of the young girls came to me and said, "Mr. Drannan, I knew you were a good Indian fighter, but I did not know the Coyotes were so afraid of you. Did you hang up some of their scalps so that they could see them and know they would share the same fate as their comrades if they did not keep away?"

I told her that the report of our guns told the Coyotes what to expect if they came where the bullets would hit them. "But if my shooting interferes with your dancing, I will be careful and not do any thing to spoil the music."

She laughed and said, "Never you mind, Mr. Drannan, we are going to give you a dance before many nights."

I answered that I only knew how to dance one kind of a dance, and that was the scalp dance.

She said she had never seen a scalp dance, and said, "What is it like?"

Jim Bridger said, "When we have the next fight with the Indians, Will and I will show you how it is done, that is providing the Indians don't get our scalps, and if they do they will show you."

Jim said to me, "I don't think we will have any more trouble with the Indians until we get to the sink of the Humboldt; it is about a hundred miles from here. There is quite a strip of country through here that I am afraid we will have a great deal of trouble in, for at this time of the year all the game that is in the country seems to gather there, and as the Indians always follow the game I am afraid there will be plenty of them too. But we could not have a better scare crow than the scalps we have scared the last two bands away with, and I think if we are always successful in getting the train corralled before they come on us we will get through in safety."

I answered, "Jim, if it is possible for me to prevent it, you will never be surprised, for I and my men will keep a sharp look out for any signs of Indians at all times, and if there is any danger, you will know it as soon as we can get the news to you, for all the men under my control seem to be the right stuff, and they want to do what is right and for the best interest of all the train."

Jim answered, "I know I can trust you, Will, to do all in your power to get this train through in safety. I have every confidence in you. If I had not had, I should not have undertaken such a dangerous business as we are engaged in. But it stands us both in hand to be always on the lookout for danger, for we can never tell when the red friends may pounce on us when we are anywhere near them."

Monday morning we were up and ready to take to the road early, feeling in good spirits after our rest over Sunday. I asked Jim if we could make Sand Creek by night. He answered, "Yes, we have got to if we are to reach the sink of the Humboldt tomorrow."

We broke camp and pulled out. Everything worked smoothly until we had nearly reached Sand Creek, where we were to camp that night, when the two scouts that guarded the north side of the train discovered a large band of Indians coming in our direction. They reported their discovery to me at once. I put spurs to my horse and rode out where I could see the Indians myself. After I had gone about two miles or so I came in sight of them, and I saw that the men were right. The Indians were making directly to the spot where I thought the train was, and I realized that there was no time to lose in getting word to Jim.

As soon as I got near the road I signaled all the scouts to come to me, and in a few minutes, they were with me. I sent them all to the train to help Jim, except two which I kept with me. We three rode out to the spot where we could see the Indians. When we got in sight of them, they were within a mile of the train, and I knew that the time for action had come, and wheeling our horses we made for camp at a pace that would surprise the readers of today. I told Jim that the Indians were upon us, but there was no need to tell him this, as he had seen us coming and suspected the news we were bringing and had ordered the train corralled before we reached camp, and I do not think a train was ever got into shape to resist the savages quicker or with less excitement than that train was that day. And we were none too quick, for the Indians were in sight of us as soon as we were ready for them. At this spot our trail led down a little valley. Consequently, when the Indians hove in sight they were not more than a hundred yards from the corral.

I sang out, "What do you say, Jim? Let's form in line and give them a salute."

Jim shouted, "Every man form in a line and shoot, and be sure you hit your mark."

By this time there were as many as two hundred Indians in sight, and every gun seemed to go off at once. At that moment Jim cried, "Every man pull your pistol and shoot as loud as you can, and let us make a dash on them." And every man in the train did as Jim told them to, and it surely had a good effect on the savages, for they wheeled and fled as fast as their legs could carry them in the direction they had come. We found twenty-seven dead Indians all laying close together, and it did not take us long to take their scalps off. When we had finished this job, Jim made the remark that he had scalps enough now to protect the train all the way to California.

As it was yet about three miles to our camping ground, I told my scouts what to do, and then I told Jim that I meant to follow the Indians alone and see where they went to and not to expect me back until he saw me, for I intended to see those Indians go into camp before I left them, if it took me until midnight to do it, for if I did this I could tell whether they meant to give us any more trouble or not.

Jim told me where to look for the camp when I wanted to find it, and I left them, on a mission the danger of which I do not think one of my readers can understand, but which at that time I thought very little about.

I had followed the trail of the Indians but a short distance before I was convinced that there were a great many wounded in the band, for there was so much blood scattered all along the trail. I had followed the trail about five miles when I came to a high ridge, and on looking down on the other side I saw what looked to me like two or three hundred camp fires, and from the noise I heard I thought that many that I had thought to be wounded must be dead, for it was the same sound that I had often heard the squaws make over their dead. I decided by the appearance of the camp that I had discovered the main camping ground of the Indians. On deciding this in my mind, I hurried back as quickly as I could to tell Jim. When I reached camp, supper was just over. After I had looked after my horse, I went into the camp, and a lady met me and invited me to her tent, saying she had kept some supper warm for me and had been on the lookout for me to come back, and the reader may rest assured I was hungry enough to accept the invitation and to do ample justice to the good things the kind lady had saved for me.

While I was eating, Jim came to me and asked what I had discovered. I told him of the big Indian camp I had found at the foot of the ridge, which was probably five or six miles from where we were then in camp, and I told him of the noise the squaws had made too. He said, "Well, I will bet my old hat that we won't have any more trouble with them, for when they come back to get their dead warriors in the morning and find them without their scalps, they won't follow us any farther."

So feeling safe to do so, everyone except the guards turned in for the night. The night passed without anything happening to disturb us. Next morning I got up early and mounted my horse and went to the place where we'd had the fight to see if the dead Indians had been taken away. I found that they had all been taken away during the night. I got back to camp in time for breakfast. I told Jim that I had been to see about the Indians we had killed the day before, but I found no bodies there and supposed the squaws had taken them away in the night.

Jim jumped up and clapped his hands together and said, "Good, good, we will not have any more trouble with these Indians, and I don't believe we will have any more fights with the Indians this side of the Sierra Nevada mountains, for the news of our scalping so many of the Indians will fly from tribe to tribe faster than we can travel, and you may be sure they all will be on the lookout to avoid meeting us."

Everything moved quietly for the next three days, and we made good progress on our journey.

The night before we reached the sink of the Humboldt, while we were at supper about a dozen ladies came to Jim and me. One of them said with a smile, "Mr. Drannan, we have two favors to ask of you."

Jim looked up at them, and seeing that there was mischief in their eyes, he said, "Say, gals, can't I have one of them?"

The lady that had spoken to me said, "I am afraid neither of them would suit you, Mr. Bridger."

I then asked her what I could do for them. She answered that they would like to have some more fresh meat, but that they did not want any more such music as had accompanied all that they had had before, but if I could supply the meat without the music it would be a great favor as well as a treat. I said, "What kind of meat do you prefer, ladies?" She answered that they were not particular, any kind that was good.

Jim said, "Well, how will Coyote do you? That kind of meat will answer a double purpose. I-t will satisfy your hunger, and then you can howl the same as they do."

She answered, "Now Mr. Bridger, you know that Coyotes are not fit to eat. Are they not a species of a dog?"

Jim replied, "Yes, they are, and dog is the Indians' favorite meat, and that is the kind of meat you will have to eat when you go to live with them, so you had better learn to eat it now."

She said she was pretty sure that she didn't want to neighbor with the Indians, and she didn't want any dog meat either.

I told her that I would try and get some kind of fresh meat for them between then and night.

"It may be Elk or it may be Buffalo or it may be Antelope."

She said, "What kind of an animal is an Elk?"

I told her that an Elk was about as large as a cow and equally as good meat, and all the ladies said, "Well, well, wouldn't we like to have some."

I told them that I wouldn't promise for sure, but I thought I could get some fresh meat for supper tomorrow night.

The next morning my scouts and I were off early. I told them before we started that we must keep two objects in view that day. One object was to look out for Indians, and the other was to look for camp.

"We are in a game country, and there is plenty of Elk and Buffalo, and the first man that sees a band of either kind must signal to the others, and we will all get together and see if we can get enough to supply the camp for a day or two at least."

We had gone perhaps five or six miles when I heard a signal from the south. I got to it as quickly as possible, and as pretty a sight awaited me as I ever saw in the way of game. Down in a little valley just below the man that had signaled to the rest of us were about fifty Elk cows feeding, and there were also a few calves running and jumping around their mothers. As soon as all the men got there, I began to plan how we could get to them and kill some of them before they saw us. They were feeding towards the road, and they were not more than a quarter of a mile from it when I first saw them. A little ways from us there was a little ravine which was covered with brush, and it led down to the valley where the Elk were feeding. I told the men that we would hitch our horses and then crawl down the ravine, and I thought we could get a few of them before they could get away from us. All the men were as anxious to get the game as I was. I took the lead, and when we got down to the valley the Elk were only a short distance from us. I said, "Now wait until they feed opposite us, and then they will not be over fifty yards from us, and as I am to the right I will take the leader and each man in rotation as they come to him. In doing this way we will be sure to each get an Elk as not two of us will fire at the same animal, and if they are not too far from us after we have fired our rifles, let us pull our pistols and try to get some more."

When the Elk had got near enough to us, I gave the word to fire, and down came twelve Elk cows, and then we went for them with our pistols, and we got five calves, and so we knew we had plenty of meat to supply the camp for a day or two.

I sent one of the men back to meet the train and to tell Jim what we had done, and told him to send all the help he could so we could get the meat to the train as quickly as possible, and the rest of us commenced to skin the animals. In a short time there were forty or fifty men there, and it did not take long to finish the job, and we had the meat on the way to the wagons. About the time we had got the meat all dressed, several ladies came with sacks in their hands. I asked them what part of the animal they wanted. They said they wanted the livers and the hearts. This was a new idea to me. I asked them what they were going to do with them. One of the women said, "We want you and Mr. Bridger to take supper with us tonight, and we will show you what we have done with them then."

In a short time we had the meat to the train and each family had their share. Jim said he did not think he had lost over twenty-five minutes time in waiting for that meat.

The train proceeded on now without any more stops towards the place where we were to camp that night at the sink of the Humboldt. We reached the camping ground quite a little while before sundown, and we certainly had selected an ideal place to camp. A beautiful pearling stream of water, plenty of wood and any amount of grass met our eyes as we came to the place to stop. In a few minutes we had the stock out to grass and the women were busy cooking supper. Jim and I took a walk down towards the Sink, and as we were coming back we had got near the wagons when a couple of girls came to meet us and said, "We want you two to come and eat supper with us. Our two families got supper together tonight." Jim said, "Have you got something good to eat?"

One said, "You may just bet we have; we have got Elk roasted and fried Elk calf and fried liver. Isn't that something good?"

Jim said it sounded good and we would go and see for ourselves.

When we got to the tent Jim said, "These girls told us that you had invited us to eat supper with you; that you had some stewed dog, and as that is our favorite dish we thought we would accept the invitation."

One of the girls cried, "Oh Mr. Bridger, we didn't tell you any such thing."

Jim answered, "Oh, excuse me, girls. I thought you were going to have something good for supper, so of course all I could think of was dog."

We had a fine supper, and as fried liver was a new dish to Jim and me, we ate heartily of that, and we thought it was beyond the ordinary. It seems to me now in thinking of those days that people had better appetites then for hearty food than they have now; at least it is so in my case. The reason may be that we lived in the open air both day and night, and the air of that western climate was so pure and clear and free from all the different scents that impregnate it now. The amount of food that each person ate at that time would surprise the people of today.

After supper Jim told the girls that they would not get any music to dance to tonight, so they had just as well turn in and have a good night's sleep.

CHAPTER V

The next morning we had an early breakfast and were on our journey in good season. Nothing of interest occurred to us until we reached where the city of Reno now stands, which is in the western part of what is now the state of Nevada.

We were about to go into camp on the bank of the Truckee river when I looked off to the north and saw a band of Indians, and they were heading directly for the train.

They were probably a mile away from us when I saw them. I reported to Jim at once, and he was not long in corralling the train, and he made the largest display of scalps that I had ever seen then or ever have since. It looked as if every wagon had a scalp hanging on it.

Apparently the Indians did not notice the decorations on the wagons until they were within three or four hundred yards of them, and the sight seemed to take them by surprise.

[Illustration: Fishing with the girls.]

All at once the whole band stopped, and of all the actions ever an Indian performed that band did it. Jim said, "Will, do you think you can reach them with your rifle?"

I answered that I thought not at that distance, but I said, "My men and I will get nearer to them and give them a scare anyway."

I called my scouts to follow me out to a little bunch of timber, and we all fired at them at once. Whether we hit any Indians or not I never knew, for they wheeled their horses and fled, and if any of them were killed or wounded the others did not leave them, and we saw no more of that band, but they left three horses laying on the ground, which showed us that our bullets had done a little execution.

We now settled into camp for the night. Jim told the emigrants as it was Saturday evening we would lay over here until Monday morning, and he told them that all who liked to have a good time fishing could enjoy themselves to their hearts' content, for this stream was full of Mountain Trout, and he added, "They are beauties."

Both men and women asked what kind of bait to use to catch them. We told them that grass hoppers or crickets was good bait for Mountain Trout, and both of these insects were numerous around the camp.

It was very amusing to me to see the girls run to their mothers to ask if they could go fishing the next day. They were as excited as if they were asking to go to some great entertainment.

It being Sunday morning and as there was no danger from the Indians, I did not get up very early. Jim and I occupied the same tent together, which was the blue sky above us and the ground beneath us, a bed that I have no doubt the reader will think a not very desirable one, but rolled in our blankets, a bed on the soft moss with the trees waving over us was as good a bed as Jim and I cared to have, and our sleep was as sound and restful as if we were laying on a bed of down.

When Jim arose in the morning, he gave me a shake and said, "Wake up, Will. We are going to have fish, for everyone in the camp is hunting grass hoppers," and it was really an amusing sight to see, for everyone, as Jim had said, was running, trying to catch grass hoppers. Both men and women were racing about like children.

Jim and I had started to go to the river to take a wash when a little girl came running to us saying, "Papa wants you to come and eat breakfast with us, for we have got fish for breakfast."

Jim said, "All right, sissy, but I am afraid you haven't got enough fish to go around."

She said, "Oh yes we have, for papa caught fifteen this morning, and they are all great big ones."

So we did not go to the river but went with the little girl to her father's tent and washed there, and sure enough, there was enough fish for all the family and Jim and me and some left over.

The man laughed and said to Jim, "Mr. Bridger, you made the right remark when you said that the river was full of fish. I have been fishing all my life, and I never saw so many fish at one time as I saw this morning. I went down to the river about daylight, and I caught fifteen fish, and I don't think I was over fifteen minutes in catching them, and I believe they will average two pounds to a fish, and they are as luscious as I ever tasted in the way of fish."

I asked him if this was his first experience in eating Mountain Trout. He said it was, but he hoped it would not be his last, and said, "Can you tell me why they have such an extra flavor?" I said, "Certainly, I can. There is no stream in the world that has purer water than the Truckee river, and do you see that snowcapped mountain yonder?" and I pointed to a mountain at the south west of us which was always covered with snow at the top. "This stream is surrounded with mountains like that, and the water is cold the year around, no matter how hot the weather may be, and that is the secret of the fine flavor of the fish caught in it."

And here I must say that, although I had eaten Mountain Trout many times before that morning, I never enjoyed a meal more than I did this one. As I finished eating, six young girls came to the tent and asked me if I was going fishing. I said I had thought of going. They asked if they could go with me, I said, "Certainly, you can if you wish to, but I shall have to go out and hunt some bait before I can go."

One of them said, "We have enough grass hoppers to last us all day, and we will share them with you for bait."

I answered, "Well, we will go up the river a little ways to those rocks yonder," and I pointed up the stream.

When we got opposite the rocks which were in the middle of the stream, I helped each of the girls to a place by herself and then took a place on a rock myself, but I could not do anything for laughing at the girls. I told them they would scare all the fish out of the river. In a moment one of the girls caught a fish on her hook, but he struggled so hard that she could not pull him out of the water, and she cried for me to come and help her to land him. I got to her as quickly as I could and took the fish out of the water, and it was the largest trout I had ever seen, and I did not wonder the girl could not land him, for he made a brave fight for liberty, and it was all I could do to capture him.

By this time it was a sight to look up and down the stream and see the people that were fishing. Men, women and children, old and young, seeming to be perfectly happy and to be having the time of their lives.

In about an hour they began to realize that more fish were being caught than they could take care of, so everyone gathered their catch and went back to camp. Some of the emigrants estimated that three thousand fish had been caught that day by the entire crowd. I think the most of the people had fish until they were tired of it. For the next two days we had fish for every meal served in every way that fish could be cooked.

Monday morning we pulled out from this camp bright and early for Honey Lake. We made the trip in two days, which was as we considered very good time, and we did not see an Indian on the way or a fresh sign of them.

When we reached Honey Lake and saw that there were no signs of Indians there Jim said to me that there would be no more trouble with the Indians, and if we could convince the emigrants of this fact we need not go further with them.

I told him I did not think it would be best to mention to the emigrants any change in the contract we had made with them when we started on the trip, that we had better go on with the train until we crossed the Sierra Nevada Mountains, as we had engaged to do.

Jim thought it over a few minutes, and then he said, "I guess you are right, Will, for they might think we wanted to shirk our duty in leaving them here, although I am sure there will be no more danger to guard them from."

Everything moved on without anything to interfere with our progress for the next four days, and by that time we had crossed the top of the Sierra Nevada Mountains.

After we had eaten our supper the night after crossing on the other side of the mountains, Jim shouted that he wanted to talk to everybody for just a few minutes, and in a few minutes all the people of the train, men, women, and children, were around us thick.

Jim then said to them, "I wanted to speak to you together to tell you that all danger to this train is passed, there will be no more Indians to molest you, and you are perfectly safe to continue on your journey without fear of being troubled by them. Tomorrow night we will camp in the Sacramento Valley, and being sure that we can leave you in perfect safety, our contract with the people of this train will be closed, and we will leave you the next morning. There is one thing I am sorry for, though, and that is we can't furnish any more music for a farewell dance with the ladies before we leave them."

This joke created a laugh all around and brightened the faces of the older people, for we had shared in and protected them from too many dangers for the thought of separation from us not to sadden the faces of the older members of the train.

Mr. Tullock, one of the committee, got upon a chair and said, "I want to ask if there is a person here in this company can realize what these two men have done for us in the seven weeks they have been with us. I for one know for a certainty that if we had not met them, and they had not accompanied us on the dangerous journey we have almost finished, not one of this large company would have been alive today. I will acknowledge that I have no doubt that all the rest of you thought them to be barbarians when they took the scalps off those first Indians' heads, but the events that followed showed their knowledge of their business and also of our ignorance in Indian warfare for that what we thought barbarism was the means of saving some, if not all our lives. Now I will tell you what I propose doing. I am going to write a recommendation for each one of these men, and I want every one of you to sign it."

It sounded as if every one in the crowd said at once, "I'll sign it."

When Mr. Tullock stepped down, Jim took his place on the chair and said to the people, "I want you all to distinctly understand that Will Drannan and myself do not think we have done anything but our duty to the people of this train, and I want to thank all the men that have helped me to protect the train when the savages were upon us. You all showed that you were brave men and willing to obey orders, which, I will tell you now, is a rare thing among so many men, and Will tells me that he had the best men as scouts to help him that he has ever had, that everyone tried to do his duty. So it seems to me that we have all done our best to make the journey a success. Now let us get away from here early in the morning, for I want to reach our camping ground in good season tomorrow evening. We have quite a long drive before us tomorrow, but as good luck is on our side it is all downhill."

We got an early start in the morning, and we landed at our camping place about four o'clock in the evening, and I think there were as many as twenty invited us to take supper with them that night. The last one was from four young girls, who came to us together. One of them told Jim that she wanted him and Mr. Drannan to come to their tent right away, as supper was waiting. Jim answered that we didn't want any supper but told her that if she would invite us to breakfast next morning and would promise there would be enough to eat to fill us both for three or four days, we would be glad to come and eat.

She answered, "All right, Mr. Bridger, I will get up before day and get to cooking, so I shall be sure and have enough for you at least."

Jim and I now went to the tent of the people who had invited us first, as had been our custom all through the journey. These were elderly people who had one son and one daughter, both grown to man and womanhood. While we were at supper the older woman asked how much bread we could carry with us. Jim said we would like enough to last us three or four days, and he thought three loaves like the ones on the spread would be enough.

She said, "Why, Mr. Bridger, everybody is making bread, and cooking meat for you to take with you."

Jim said, "Why, my good woman, we can kill all the meat we want as we need it, and three loaves of bread is all we can carry on our horses with our other stuff."

The first thing in the morning the girls we had promised to eat breakfast with were after us to come to their tent, and we found a fine meal waiting for us.

Jim said, "Now ladies, you know that in going back, Will and I have to go over a very dangerous road, and we won't have time to cook in the next three or four days, so we calculate to eat enough to last us till we get to the Sink of the Humboldt, and that will take us three or four days, so in our accepting your invitation to take our last breakfast on this trip with you we may make you twice glad."

The elder woman smiled and told the girls they had better be frying some more meat. Jim looked around the spread and told the girls he guessed they had better wait till we had eaten what was before u, before they cooked more, and there certainly was enough food before us for as many more as sat around it, and although it was spread on a cloth laid on the ground, I have never partaken of a breakfast served on the finest table that tasted as good as that one did that morning.

We had almost finished eating when the elder lady said, "Girls, pass that cake around."

Jim said, "Is there cake too? I'm not used to eating cake, only on Sunday mornings, and this is Saturday."

I told the girls that Jim hadn't seen any cake since we left Fort Kerney, and that if she wanted any left for themselves they had better not pass the plate. She answered, "There is aplenty, and I have a great big cake for you to take to eat on the road."

Jim said, "That won't do at all, for Will will want to stay in camp all the time and eat cake until it is all gone."

As soon as breakfast was over, we caught our horses and began packing. We each had two saddle horses, and we had one pack horse between us. When we were leading up our horses, Jim said, "This is the worst job of all, for all these women have a lot of grub cooked for us to take along, and plagued take it, we have no room on the pack horses to put it. What shall we do?"

I said, "We will take what we can pack, Jim, and we can thank the ladies for their kindness, and tell them we are sorry we can't take all they would give us, and then we can mount and be off."

Jim said, "That sounds easy."

When we were packing, sure enough, every one of the elder women and some of the girls brought something for us to take with us to eat. Jim told them that we were a thousand times obliged to them all, but we could not take anything but a few loaves of bread, and then, as was usual, in his joking way he said with a glance at me, "I know, Will feels bad to leave that cake, and he will dream of seeing cakes for a week, but I can't indulge him this time."

When Jim had done speaking, one of the girls, that we had taken breakfast with handed him a small sack, and told him not to open it until we camped that night. At this moment Mr. Tullock, came to us and said, "Here, my friends, is a recommendation, and I think every grown person in the train has signed their name to both of them, and all the company have asked me to say a few words for them. If either or both of you ever come to California, we want you to find some of us and make your home with us as long as you wish, for you will always find a warm welcome with any of this company."

I had been acquainted with Jim Bridger several years and this was the first time I had ever seen him overcome with feeling. His voice shook so he could hardly thank the people for their kind words and when it came to shaking hands and biding them good bye, he almost lost his speech.

But it was over at last and we mounted our horses and left them. For the first ten miles I don't think Jim spoke ten words. Finally he said, "Well they were a good crowd of people, weren't they Will? If I ever go to California and can find any of them, I mean to stay all night with them, for it would be like visiting brother or sister."

We now began to calculate where we should camp that night. I said, "Let's make a dry camp tonight, we can fill our canteen, and water our horses at a stream that crosses the trail, and then we can ride on till dark. In doing this way we will avoid the Indians and will not have to guard against them in the night, for the Indians invariably camp near the water."

We made a long ride that day and picked a nice place to camp that night. As soon as we had unsaddled and unpacked our horses, I said, "Jim, I will stake the horses if you will make a fire." When I came back from attending to the horses, Jim said, "Look here, Will, see what them girls gave me, but I guess they meant it for you."

And he showed me the sack which the girls had given him as we were leaving them that morning. I looked into it and saw two large cakes and a good-sized piece of roasted Elk calf. The reader may imagine how good this nice food looked to two hungry men, and we surely did justice to it. When we were eating, Jim made the remark that it would be many a long day before we met with such a company again as those we had left that morning. He said, "In nearly all large companies there are cranks, either men or women, and sometimes both, but all that outfit were perfect ladies and gentlemen, and they all seemed to want to do what was right, and the men were all brave and the women were sensible."

The next morning we pulled out early, and we made good progress for five days, making dry camps every night. Nothing occurred to disturb us until we reached the Sink of the Humboldt. Here were Indian signs in every direction. We knew we would be in the heart of the Ute country for the next hundred miles, so we decided to do our traveling in the night and lay over and rest in the daytime.

We picked our camping places off the trail, where we thought the Indians would not be likely to discover us. The second night after we left the Sink of the Humboldt, we crossed a little stream called Sand Creek, and just off to the right of the trail we saw what we thought must have been five hundred Indians in camp. Most of them were laying around asleep, but a few were sitting at the fire smoking, and we succeeded in riding past them without their noticing us. After we had got entirely away from their camp fires, Jim said, "Will, we are the luckiest chaps that ever crossed the plains, for if them Indians had seen us, they would have filled our hides full of arrows just to get our horses, and I think we had better keep on traveling in the night until we strike Black's Fork, then we will be pretty near out of the Utes country."

When we got to Lone Tree on Black's Fork we lay over one day to let our horses rest and to get rested ourselves.

It was a little before sunrise that morning when we reached Lone Tree. I said to Jim, "Are you hungry?" He replied that he was too hungry to tell the truth.

I answered, "All right, you take care of the horses, and I will get an Antelope and we will have a fine breakfast."

Jim said, "Well, don't disappoint me, Will, for I am in the right shape to eat a half an Antelope."

I took my gun and went up on a little ridge and looked over, and not a quarter of a mile from me I saw a large band of Antelope, and I saw that they were feeding directly towards me. I hid myself in a little bunch of sage brush and waited until they fed up to within fifty yards of me. I then fired and brought down a little two-year-old buck. I took him up, threw him over my shoulder, and went back to Camp as fast as I could go. When I reached there, Jim had a fire burning, and in a few minutes we had the meat cooking. Jim made the remark that we had enough to do to keep us busy all day, for when we were not eating, we must be sleeping, for he was about as hungry as he ever was and so sleepy that he did not dare to sit down for fear he would fall asleep without his breakfast.

After we had enjoyed a very hearty meal of meat and bread, for we ate the last piece of bread that the ladies had given us that morning, we smoked our pipes a few moments, and then we spread our blankets on the ground under the only tree in ten miles of us, and we were soon lost to everything in a sleep that lasted until near night. I did at least. When I awoke I found Jim cooking meat for supper. When he saw that I was awake, he said, "Come, Will, get up. We have had our sleep. Now we will have our supper."

While we were eating, I asked Jim if we could make Green River tomorrow. He said, "Yes, we must get out of here tomorrow morning by daylight. Our horses will be well rested as we ourselves will be. We want to make Green

River tomorrow night and Rock Springs the next night. I consider it is about eighty miles to Rock Springs from here, and we ought to make it in two days."

The next morning we were up bright and early and were on our journey as soon as we could see the trail. Nothing happened to disturb us, and we reached Green River just before sunset. We crossed the river and went into camp just above the Ford. We had just got our horses staked out when we heard whips snapping and people's voices shouting.

Jim listened a moment and said, "What in thunder does that mean?"

I answered, "I think it is an emigrant train coming." Jim said, "By jove if that is so, we will have to move from here and stake our horses somewhere else, for no doubt they will want to camp right here, and if there is much of a train, they will take all the room in this little valley."

In a few minutes they hove in sight. Jim said, "Now, let's get to one side and see if they have any system about their camping, and then we will know whether it is worth while for us to apply for a job or not."

They did not seem to know that they were near a river by the way they acted. Some of them would leave their wagons and run down to the stream and run back again and talk with the others. Finally they discovered Jim and me, and about twenty of the men came to where we were sitting. We had started a fire and were waiting for it to get hot enough to cook our meat for our supper, and it was certainly very amusing to watch their faces. They looked at us as if they thought us wild men. We learned afterwards that they had never seen anyone dressed in Buck Skin before.

After staring at us a while, one of them, an old man, said, "Where in creation are you two men from?"

Jim answered, "We have just come from Sacramento Valley, California."

And did you come all the way alone?

Jim answered, "Yes sir, we did."

"Did you see any Indians?" he inquired.

Jim said, "Yes, about a thousand, I think."

"Did they try to kill you?"

"Oh, no," Jim said. "They were asleep when we saw them."

"Why, they told us back at Fort Kerney that the Indians never slept day or night," the old man said.

Jim answered that they slept a little at night sometimes, and that was the time we took to travel. We had traveled nearly all the way from California to this place after night, and in some places where we traveled over, the Indians were as thick as jack rabbits.

One of the men then inquired when we went to California.

Jim answered, "We left Fort Kerney about eight weeks ago and piloted the biggest train of emigrants across the plains that has ever gone to California, and we did not lose a person or a head of stock, but we got a good many Indian scalps on the way."

One of the men then said, "Ain't you Jim Bridger and Will Drannan that the commander at the Fort told us about?"

Jim replied, "That is who we are."

One of them then asked if we would pilot another train to California.

Jim answered, "I don't know. The Indians are getting so dog goned thick that there is no fun in the job, but you folks go and get your supper, and let us eat ours. We are dog goned hungry, for we haven't had a bite since day-break this morning. You can come back here after supper, and we will talk to you."

By this time there must have been a hundred men standing around us, but when Jim told them that we wanted to eat our supper, they all scattered. After they had left us, Jim said, "You get supper, Will, and I will go and see whether there is any system about this outfit or not, and if supper is ready before I get back, don't wait for me, for I may not get back in half an hour or more."

I had got my meat on the fire and was just making the coffee when a number of women, I should think about a dozen of them, came near me and stopped and gazed at me. I bid them good evening and asked them to have supper with me. One of them answered, "No, I came to ask you to come and eat supper with us. My father sent me to invite you."

I thanked her and told her that as my own supper was nearly ready, I would eat at my own camp. I had taken my Buck-skin coat off and laid it on our pack. One of the women asked me if she could look at it. I told her that she could if she wished to.

While they were looking at the coat and exclaiming over its beauty (it was heavily embroidered with beads and porcupine quills, and was an odd looking garment to one not accustomed to seeing the clothing of the frontiers men), a couple of girls came running to me, saying, "Father wants you to come and eat supper with us, Mr. Bridger is eating now." So I took the meat and coffee off the fire and put my coat on and went with them. When I got in speaking distance of Jim, I said, "I thought you told me to cook supper." Jim answered, "I know I did Will, but we didn't have any fried onions, and these folks have, so I thought we would eat here and save our supper."

The people all laughed at Jim being so saving, and then the old man asked what we would charge to pilot the train through to California. Jim asked, "How many wagons have you in this outfit?"

He answered that he was not sure, but he thought there were about a hundred and thirty-five.

"How many men are there in the train?" The old man said, "Oh, dog gone it, I can't tell."

Jim said, "Have you got no Captain?"

The old man answered, "Why no, we haven't any use for a Captain."

Jim then said, "Well, I don't suppose they have any use for a commander over at the Fort then. Suppose the Indians should make an attack on them over there, and there was no Commander there, what do you think the soldiers would do? I will tell you what would happen. The most of the soldiers would be scalped, and it is the same way with a train of emigrants if the Indians attack them and they have no leader or what we call a Captain; they will all be scalped and in a mighty short time too. Now you call the men together and come to our camp, and we will talk this matter over, and then we will see if we can make a bargain with the crowd."

In a few minutes it seemed as if all the men and women of the train were standing around our camp.

Jim said to them, "I want some man who is a good reader to read this letter to the company."

And he held up one of the letters of recommendation given us by the people of the train we had left a few days before. A middle-aged man came forward and said, "I reckon I can read it; I am a school teacher by profession, and I am used to reading all kinds of handwriting."

He took the letter, stepped up on a log and in a clear, loud voice read it to the company. After he had finished reading it, the man handed the letter back to Jim with the remark that it was a fine recommendation and gave a character few men could claim.

Jim now told the emigrants that before we took charge of a train he always had the men of the train select a committee from their number, and this committee had the entire charge of the business in making arrangements with us and all other matters that might take place on the trip. "Now if you want us to pilot this train across to California, get together and select your committee, and they can come to us and we will talk business."

It was now nearly eleven o'clock at night, so Jim told the people that we had traveled a long distance that day and were very tired, and he thought we had better not make any bargain that night. We would go to our rest, and in the morning they could tell us what they had decided on. Next morning Jim and I were up very early, and so were the most of the emigrants. We were building a fire to get our breakfast when one of the emigrants came to us and invited us to take breakfast with him. He said there had been a committee selected, that the men talked the matter over after they left us the night before, and they chose five men to make arrangements with us. "But as we did not go to bed until nearly morning, I don't think they are all up yet," he said, smiling.

We went with him and found breakfast waiting for us. After we had finished, two of the men came to us and said they were two of the five who had been appointed to do business with us, and that the other three would meet us at our camp in a few minutes. So Jim and I went back to our camp, and in a very short time the five men were with us. One of them asked us how much we would charge to pilot them to California. Jim said, "How many wagons have you?"

He said, "We have ninety here now, and there will be twenty more here by noon."

Jim asked, "How many men are there in the company?" They said they did not know for certain but thought there would be about a hundred and ninety. Jim said that we would take them across to California for five dollars a day, which would be two dollars and a half for each of us. "Providing you will promise to obey our orders in all things pertaining to the protection of the train and also give us two days to drill the teamsters and the scouts, but we will have to move on one day from here, as there is no ground here that is fit to drill on."

One of the committee said, "We will give you an answer in twenty minutes," and they went back to their camp, which was a hundred yards or more from ours. Jim and I caught our horses and were saddling them when the committee came back to us and told us we could consider ourselves engaged.

I now spoke for the first time, Jim having done all the talking before. I said, "I want you men to select ten good men who own their horses. I prefer young men who are good horsemen, for I want them to assist me in doing scout work."

This seemed to surprise the men. One of them asked, what the young men would have to do. Jim now spoke up in his joking way and said, "They will find enough to do before we get to California. For example I will show you what Will and his scouts have done on our last trip across." At the same time he was untying the sack that held the Indian scalps we had taken on our last trip to California. When he emptied the sack it was amusing to us to see their faces. Their first expression was of surprise, and the next was of horror. Jim took up one of the scalps and shook it out and said, "Taking these is one of the things you young men may have to do," and he continued, "These scalps which seem to give you men the horrors to look at now, will be worth more than money to all the people of this train, for they will save the lives of all of you, and that is more than money could do in an attack by the Indians."

Some of the men wanted to know in what way the scalps would save them. Jim answered, "Let us get on the road to our next camping ground, and I will explain everything in regard to the protection of the train when we get to drilling."

In a short time every thing was on the move, and we reached our place to camp about four o'clock in the afternoon. Jim commenced to put the numbers on the wagons as soon as we landed in camp in order to get to drilling as early as possible in the morning. We had been in camp but a short time when one of the committee men came to me and said, "We have selected your men, Mr. Drannan. Come out, and I will introduce them to you, and you can see if they would suit you, and if they do, you can tell them what you want them to do."

We went outside the corral, and we found the ten men there with their horses. I asked them if they all had rifles and pistols. They said they had. I next asked them if they had ever practiced shooting off their horses' backs, and they all said no, nor had ever heard of such a way of shooting. I then said, "Now boys, it is too late in the evening to commence practicing, but I want you all to meet me here after breakfast in the morning, and have your horses and guns and pistols with you, and you may make up your mind to do a hard day's work tomorrow."

That evening Jim and I had a talk by ourselves in regard to how much time we should take to drill the men. Jim said, "Will, do you think you can drill your men in one day so they will know enough to risk starting out day after tomorrow?"

I answered, "I think I can, Jim."

He thought a moment and then said, "I don't like to hurry you in training your men, Will, but you know it is getting late in the season, and we have a long road to travel after we get these emigrants through to California in order to get back home to Taos before the winter sets in, and I have no doubt Kit will be looking for us long before we get there."

I said, "Jim, this will be my last trip as a pilot for emigrants."

Jim laughed and answered, "I thought this kind of business just suited you, Will, for you are a favorite with the girls, especially when you bring in scalps."

I answered, "The girls are all right, Jim, but there is too much responsibility in such an undertaking, and besides, it is impossible to suit everybody."

Jim answered, "There is a good deal of truth in what you say, Will. It is not an easy job to please so many people all at once. We will hurry this trip through as quick as possible and get them off our hands."

The next morning I was up early and met the men who were to be trained to make scouts. We went to a little grove of timber about a quarter of a mile from camp. I selected a small tree, probably a foot through, dismounted and made a crossmark with my knife. I then asked the boys, if they thought they could hit that cross with their guns or pistols with their horses on the dead run. One of them said, "No, I don't know as I could hit it with my horse standing still."

I answered, "But that is just what I must teach you to do if you are ever to make a scout to guard against Indians or fight them. I will mount my horse and go back to that little bunch of brush," and I pointed to a bunch of brush that was perhaps a little more than a hundred yards from the tree, "and all of you men follow me."

When we reached the brush, I turned my horse's head towards the tree I had marked, and I then said, "Now boys, I am going to put my horse down to his best speed, and I want you all to follow me and keep as close to me as you can, and each man look out for his own horse when I commence to shoot. At the same time keep your eyes on me, for I want each one of you to take his turn in doing as I do, and I want you to repeat the thing until you can hit the mark as I shall do."

I now started my horse at full speed, and before I had got to the tree I had fired my second shot, and both balls struck near the cross, but I was surprised, and I will not deny also amused, to see the way the boys were trying to stop their horses; they were running in every direction and appeared to be nearly frightened to death, and apparently their riders had no control over them, but finally they checked them and rode back to where I stood.

I said, "Boys, you certainly have your horses trained to run from the Indians if you can't stop to fight them."

One of the boys said, "I never saw my horse act the fool as he has done today."

I said, "Now, which one of you are going to try it again first? Don't all speak at once."

It was some minutes before anyone answered. At last one of them said, "I will try it. Shall we all come down together as we did with you?"

I told him, "No, I want you to all to try it single-handed once and then we will try it in groups of three, but if you are afraid you cannot manage your horse, I will ride beside you."

He answered, "No, I have got to break him in to it, and I might as well do it at the start."

So the others got out of his way, and he rode to the brush, wheeled his horse, put the spurs to him and came at full speed. When within fifty feet of the tree he fired his rifle and missed the tree but pulled his pistol and made a good shot, and he did not have much trouble in stopping his horse this time.

When he rode back to us, I showed him the hole where the bullet struck it and told him he had done exceptionally well.

He said, "Can't I give it another trial?"

I said, "Not now. Best let everyone have a try first."

I saw that they were a little encouraged by the first one's success, so I said, "Who comes next?"

One of them said, "I reckon it is me next," and he was on his horse in a twinkle and off for the brush. This man was in a little too much of a hurry; he shot too soon and missed the tree, which scared his horse, and he turned and ran in an opposite direction, and the rider had all he could do to attend to him so he did not fire his pistol at all. When he came back the boys had a laugh on him.

He said, "All right, see that the balance of you does better."

They all gave it a trial, and out of the ten men only three hit the mark with either rifle or pistol. Before we got through practicing, there must have been as many as a hundred men from the camp watching the performance. After each man had tried singly, I formed them in squads of three, and they were more successful that way than they were alone from the fact that their horses were getting used to the report of the guns.

The reader will understand that the drilling was done more for the benefit of the horses than it was for the men, for many times if the horses were unmanageable when in a fight with the Indians, the rider was in a great deal more danger of being killed than he would have if he could manage his horse.

As it was getting near noon I called it off until after dinner. When we were near the corral going back to camp, I pointed to a large log that was laying on the ground and told the boys to meet me there on foot, and I would put them through another kind of a drill, which was more essential for them to know than the one we had been practicing. One of them said, "What can it be?"

I answered, "It is to learn to signal to each other without speaking when you are in danger."

After dinner I had a talk with Jim in regard to how he was succeeding in drilling his teamsters. He said they were doing fine and would be ready to pull out in the morning. He said, "Will, these are not such people to handle as the last train we drilled."

I said, "What makes you think so, Jim?"

He answered, "There are a few in this outfit who do not believe there will be trouble with the Indians."

I answered, "Well, Jim, these are of the class that will not obey orders, and they will get the worst of it, and no one can blame us."

When I went to meet the boys, they were all standing or sitting on the fallen tree, waiting for me. I asked if they had ever heard a Coyote howl. They said not until they heard them on this trip. Then I explained to them, that the Indians were so used to hearing the Coyotes howl that they took no notice of that kind of a noise day or night, so we frontiers-men always used the bark or howl of a Coyote as a signal to call each other together in times of danger. I then gave a howl that the boys said no Coyote could beat, and in a couple of hours I had them all drilled so they could mimic the Coyotes very well.

We went back to camp, got our horses, and put in the afternoon in shooting at targets on horse back. Before we separated that evening, I told the men what position I wanted each one of them to take when the train was ready to move in the morning. I also told them they must always meet me at the head of the train before we started the train every morning to get their instructions for the day. Every one of the ten seemed to be willing and ready to obey everything I asked them to do.

CHAPTER VI.

All was in readiness for the start on the road the next morning, and we pulled out in good season. Every thing worked smoothly for the next three days, and then we were in the Ute country, and there were also a great many Buffalo scattered all through the country. I had seen some signs of Indians, but up to this time I had seen only one small band of them, and they were going in the opposite direction from the one we were going.

The evening of the third day, after we had eaten our supper, about twenty men came to where Jim and I were sitting on a log having a smoke and a private talk together.

One of them who seemed to be the leader said, "We want some Buffalo meat, and we propose to go out and get some tomorrow. Now what do you think about it?"

[Illustration: They raced around us in a circle.]

Jim said, "Which way do you think of going?" Pointing to the south, he said, "We think of going down into those low hills not more than eight or ten miles from the trail."

Jim answered, "I have no doubt you would find Buffalo and maybe kill some, but I have grave doubt of your ever getting back alive."

The man said, "Do you think we would get lost?"

Jim answered, "Yes, I think you would, if the Indians shoot you full of arrows and take your scalp off."

He answered, "We have got to find some Indians before they have a chance to scalp us, and I don't believe there is an Indian out there, and we are going hunting in the morning."

Jim answered, "All right, do just as you darned please, but I will tell you this just here and now. When you go a half a mile from the train without our consent, you will be out from under our protection, and we shall not hold ourselves responsible for your lives."

They turned away from us, saying, "We will take the chances; we want some Buffalo meat, and we are going to get it."

The next morning when the train pulled out twenty-three men left us, mounted on their horses with their guns all in trim for a Buffalo hunt, and four out of the twenty three was all we ever saw again either dead or alive.

We pulled out, and everything moved on nicely all day. I saw a great deal of Indian sign at various places during the day. About the middle of the afternoon one of the scouts reported that he saw a band of Indians off to the south. As soon as he reported this to me, I went with him to the top of a high ridge where we could see all over the country, and sure enough, there was a small band of Indians some two or three miles south of our trail.

After watching them a few minutes, I saw that they were going from us, so I knew that we were in no danger from that band.

We had to make an early camp that evening on account of water. It was one of my duties to ride ahead of the train and look the country over for signs of Indians to select a safe camping ground for each night, although Jim and I always talked over the best place to camp the coming night before we struck out in the morning.

That night I did not get in until Jim had the wagons all corralled. Jim came to me as soon as I rode in and said, "Will, have you seen anything of the men that went hunting this morning?"

I answered, "I neither saw or heard anything of them since I saw them ride away this morning, but I will call my scouts together and ask them if they have seen them during the day."

When I inquired of the men, I learned that they had not seen or heard of them and had not even heard the report of a gun all day.

We had just finished eating supper that night when one of the committee men came to us and said, "Don't you think you had better send out some men to look for the party that went a hunting?"

Jim said, "I told those men not to go away from the train, that there was danger of their losing their scalps if they left us, and I also told them that if they went a half a mile from the train I should not be responsible for them dead or alive. They answered that they did not believe there was an Indian in the country, and that they would take the chances anyway, and more than that, I would not know where to go to hunt for them any more than you would, for the country for miles around is like this, and I would be willing to bet anything that you will never see them all again."

Dusk was settling down, and as the night came on and the hunters did not come in, the excitement grew more intense. About twenty men came to me and inquired if I knew what kind of a country the hunters would be apt to go into. I answered that if they kept the course which they said they intended to go, it would lead them to the Buffalo country and also into the heart of the Indian country. One of them then asked me if I would be willing to try to find the absent men if I had enough men with me to help.

I answered, "Why, my friends, it would be like hunting for a needle in a haystack. You certainly do not understand the ways of the Indians. If the

Indians have killed those men, they will take the bodies with them if they have to carry them a hundred miles. They will take them to their village and spend two or three days in having a scalp dance, so you will see how useless it would be to try to find them, and what is more to be thought of, if we should stay here two or three days we should in all probability be attacked by the Utes ourselves, and there is no knowing how many of the people would be killed, or how much other damage would be done."

It was getting towards bed time when four women came to me with their faces swollen with tears. One of them said, "Mr. Drannan, do you think our husbands have been killed by the Indians?"

I answered, "That is a question I can not answer, but I will say that I hope they have not; they may have lost their course and in that way have escaped the Indians."

While I was talking with the women, I heard the tramp of horses' feet coming towards camp on the trail.

I said, "Listen, perhaps they are coming now." and we went to meet the coming horsemen. There were four of them, and one of them was the husband of the woman I had been talking to. When they came up to us, he jumped off his horse and, clasping his wife in his arms he said, "Oh Mary, I never expected to see you again."

In a few minutes everybody in camp was standing around those four men, and they surely had a dreadful story to tell. They said, they did not know how far they had ridden that morning when they sighted a band of Buffalo in a little valley. They fired at them and killed four; they dismounted and turned their horses loose and went to skinning their Buffalo and had the hides nearly off of them when, without a sound to warn them of danger, the Indians pounced upon them, and of all the yelling and shouting that ever greeted any one's ears, that was the worst they had ever heard, and the arrows flew as thick as hail.

"One of them struck me here," and he pulled up his pants and showed us a ragged wound in the calf of his leg. After we had looked at the wounded leg, he continued his story. He said, "As soon as I heard the first yell, I ran for my horse and was fortunate in catching him. I think the reason of we four being so lucky in getting away was that we were a little distance from the others. We were off at one side, and we four were working on one Buffalo, and lucky for us our horses were feeding close to us. I do not believe that one of the other men caught his horse as their horses were quite a distance from them, and the Indians were between the men and their horses. The last I saw of them was their hopeless struggle against the flying Indians' arrows.

"We had mounted and had run a hundred or two hundred yards when we saw that four or five Indians were after us. They chased us two or three miles. It seemed that our horses could outrun theirs, and they gave up the chase, but in the confusion we had lost our course, and we did not know which direction to take, and we have been all the rest of the day trying to find the train, and we are just about worn but, and we are hungry enough to eat anything, at least I am."

As it happened, Jim Bridger was standing near me when the man was talking. The man turned and said to him, "Mr. Bridger, I hope all the people of this train will listen to your advice from this night until we reach the end of our journey. If we four men had done as you told us to do, we would not have suffered what we have today, and the nineteen, who I have no doubt have been scalped by the savages, would have been alive and well tonight. There is no one to blame but ourselves. You warned us, but we thought we knew more than you did, and the dreadful fate that overtook the most of the company shows how little we knew what we were doing in putting our judgment in opposition to men whose lives have been spent in learning the crafty nature of the Red-men."

Jim answered, "I always know what I am saying when I give advice, and I knew what would be liable to happen to you if you left the protection of the train. This is the third case of this kind which has happened since Will and I have been piloting emigrants across the plains to California, and I hope it will be the last."

There was but little sleep in camp that night. Out of the nineteen men that were killed, twelve of them were the heads of families, and the cries of the widows and orphaned children were very distressing for Jim and me to hear, although we were blameless. The next morning just after breakfast the committee of five men came to Jim and me and said they wanted to have a private talk with us.

Jim said, "All right," and we all went outside the corral. When we were alone by ourselves, one of them said, "I want to have your opinion with regard to hunting for the bodies of the men who are lost. Do you think it possible to find their bodies if they were killed?"

Jim said, "No, I do not. In the first place, we do not know where to look. In the second place, the Indians may have carried them fifty or seventy-five miles from where they killed them. In the third place, we do not know where the Indian village is or in what direction to look for it, and if we should find the Indian camp, they may be so strong that we would not dare to attack them, so you will see at once how useless it would be for us to attempt to do anything in regard to finding their bodies."

One of the committee said, "Well, so you propose to pull out and go on?"

Jim said, "Yes, that is what I propose doing. For the next four hundred miles we shall be in the worst Indian country in the West, and I want to get this train through it as quickly as I possibly can."

The man answered, "It seems cruel to do it, but I suppose we must give orders to get ready to move."

Jim replied, "Yes, we must be moving at once, for I cannot risk the lives of the living to hunt for those who are dead."

We were on the road in less than an hour, the committee having told the friends of the lost men what the consequences would be if they resisted the idea of moving, and also the utter uselessness of trying to find their friends dead or alive.

When the train was already to move, Jim rode down the whole length of the wagons and told each man that he wanted every one of them to have their guns and pistols loaded and ready for immediate action, for, he told them, "We cannot tell at what minute we may be attacked by the Indians, and if your guns were not ready for use, you would have a slim chance of saving your own lives or the lives of those dependent on you."

Everyone seemed to understand the situation better than they ever had before and promised to do as we had asked them to do. Everything moved on satisfactory until about two o'clock in the afternoon, when one of the scouts from the north side reported that a big band of Indians was coming directly towards us. I spurred my horse to a run, and when we reached a little ridge about a half a mile from the trail, I could see them myself, and I could see that they were all warriors, for there were no squaws or children with them, and I thought they would number a thousand strong.

I sent my companion back to tell Jim what was in prospect for a fight, and to be sure and have the Indian scalps hung up in the most conspicuous places. I watched the Indians until they had got within a half a mile of the trail, where they all stopped and huddled together for several minutes. I decided they were planning the attack, for when they started, they went directly for the train, which fact convinced me that the Indians had had a scout out as well as I had, and that he had been a little sharper than I was.

I now signaled for all the scouts to get to the train at once, and the reader can rest assured that not one of them including myself was long in getting there.

We found everything in readiness to receive the Indians. We rode inside the corral of wagons and dismounted. I told my men to follow me. We went to the head of the train, which was but a short distance. I placed eight men under two wagons, four to a wagon, and took the other two with me to the next wagon. I told them to lay flat on the ground, and when I cried "fire" for each one to shoot and to be sure that he got his Indian.

When the savages got in sight of the wagons, they were probably a hundred and fifty yards from them, and to my surprise they all stopped. I had forgotten the scalps that Jim had hung up, but of course the sight of them hanging on the top of the wagons stopped them, but they did not stop longer than a few minutes. Then they began circling around the wagons. I could see that there were two war chiefs with the outfit. I knew this by their dress, for a war Chief always wears what is called a bonnet. It is made of feathers taken from the wings and tails of eagles and reaches from their head almost to their heels.

When they started to circle around the wagons, I said to the boys who were with me under the wagon, "Now you watch that old red sinner who has the lead. I am going to shoot at him, but I do not know as I can hit him, he is so far away, but if I can get him we have won the battle."

They answered, "Fire away, and if you miss we will try our hand at him."

I drew a bead at the top of his head, and when the gun cracked I saw that I had hit him. One of the boys cried, "You have hit him," and at that moment he swayed and tumbled from his horse. The report of my gun seemed to be a signal for the whole train to fire, and for the next minute the noise of the guns was terrific. While they all did not hit an Indian, they did fairly well for men in an Indian battle for the first time. There were forty-two dead Indians left on the ground, and as the report of the last gun died away, the Indians turned their horses and fled in the opposite direction, and I ran to the old Chief to get his scalp.

I had just finished taking his scalp after taking his bonnet off when Jim Bridger and quite a crowd of the other men came running up to me. Jim said, "Did you do that, Will?" I answered, "I did," and then one of the boys who were with me under the wagon said, "Mr. Drannan sure shot him, for he told us to see him get him, and at the report of his gun, Mr. big Chief went to the Indians' happy hunting grounds."

Jim slapped me on the back and said, "That is the best shot you ever made, Will, for that bonnet and that scalp will protect this train from here to California without another shot being fired." I said, "You can have this bonnet to use for a scare crow, Jim, but be sure and take good care of it, for I want to keep it as a memento of this trip."

I then asked Jim if he were going to take the scalps off of the other dead Indians. He said, "No, we have scalps enough now to protect the train, and that is all we want. Besides, we haven't time; we must go on to our camping ground, we have fifty or sixty miles to drive before we can camp for the night."

As we were pulling out, I said to the scouts, "We are in the Buffalo country, and there will be no more trouble with the Indians; let us try to get some fresh meat for supper." I knew that we would camp near a little stream a few miles from where we had the fight, and also that it was a great feeding ground for Buffalo at this time of the year. When we were within a quarter of a mile of the stream, where we were to camp that night, we saw that the valley was covered with Buffalo. I sent all but one of the men down a little ravine to the valley. I told them to dismount and tie their horses just before they got to the valley and to crawl down and each one get behind a tree at the edge of the valley, and I and the other men would go around to the head of the valley and scare the Buffalo, and they would run down to where they were in hiding. I told the men to be sure and not shoot until the Buffalo started to run, and then to shoot all they could get with their guns, and when they had emptied them to use their pistols.

"Let us give the women and children a surprise tonight in giving them all the fresh Buffalo meat they can eat."

Myself and companion rode around to the head of the valley, and when we reached the top of the ridge, we looked down and saw hundreds of Buffalo feeding. We spurred our horses to a run, and in a moment we were in the midst of them, and it certainly was a grand sight to see that immense herd on the stampede, as they all rushed down to the outlet where the boys were waiting for them. In a few moments we heard the report of guns, and we knew that the other boys, were getting the meat for supper. I told my comrade to pick out his Buffalo and I would pick mine, and I said to him, "Now don't shoot until you get near the other boys, and if you want to kill him quick, shoot him through the kidneys." When I had reached the mouth of the valley where the Buffalo had crowded together in one big mass, I chose a two-year-old heifer, rode up to her side and shot her through her kidneys, and she fell at my horse's feet with hardly a struggle. I pulled my pistol and shot another one and broke its neck. My comrade had picked a big cow, and she was the fattest Buffalo I ever saw killed. The other boys had killed twelve, and we got three, making fifteen in all, and what was best of all, the Buffalo all lay near to where Jim had corralled the wagons. As the wagons were corralled, I went to one of the committee and told him that my scouts and I had killed fifteen Buffalo and asked him to send some of the men of the train to help dress them and to divide the meat so all the emigrants could have some fresh meat for their supper, and in a short time I saw men and women with their arms full of meat, hurrying to their camp fires.

Jim and I were sitting on a wagon tongue talking as we usually did every evening when two little girls came running to us and said their papa wanted us to come and eat supper with them. We went with the children to their father's tent, and we found an appetizing meal waiting for us. Jim and I had not tasted any fresh meat since starting out with this train of emigrants at Green river. When we sat down, Jim said, "Lady, I am afraid you will be sorry that you invited Will and me to supper, for you may not have meat enough to go around. We have not had any fresh meat in a dog's age, and we are big meat eaters any time." She answered, "Oh, don't be uneasy. I have two pans full on the fire cooking now. I know how much it takes to fill up hungry men, and you two are not the only hungry men around this camp, and you may be sure we appreciate the feast you planned to surprise us with"; and she turned to me with a smile. "You see, Mr. Drannan, the boys told me all about your suggesting the Buffalo hunt."

I answered that the meal she had set before us would pay for more than I had done. Her husband said, "It has surely been a great benefit to all the people of the train, for we were all suffering for fresh meat, and you don't know how much we appreciate your thoughtfulness in providing it for us."

As I left the tent where I had supper, about a dozen middle-aged ladies came to me and said, "We would like to see that pretty thing you took off that Indian."

I did not know what they meant by "A pretty thing" until Jim said, "Why, Will, they want to see that war bonnet you took with the old chief's scalp."

I went to our pack and got the bonnet and gave it to them, and for the next two hours that Indian adornment was the talk of the camp. It was carried from tent to tent, examined by nearly everyone, old and young, in the whole emigrant train, and it was a curiosity to any white person, and still more so to those not used to the Indians' way of adorning themselves.

Jim explained to the emigrants why this piece of Indian dress in our possession would be a protection to them in case of an attack on us by the Indians; he said, "The Indians have no fear of being killed in battle. Their great dread is of being scalped. They believe that if their scalps are taken off their heads in this world, they will not be revived in the next, or what they call the "Happy Hunting grounds of the Indians," where they will dwell with the great spirit forever, and if they should see this bonnet which none but a great chief can wear they will think we must be powerful to have got it and will keep away from us, fearing they may share the fate themselves."

Jim told the emigrants to be ready for an early start in the morning, and then we separated for the night, the emigrants going to their tents and Jim and I to lay our blankets under a tree.

Next morning after we had a hearty breakfast of cornbread and Buffalo steak, Jim said, "Now, men and women, Will gave you all a treat in Buffalo meat last night, but if all goes well, and we meet with nothing to detain us, in one week from tonight I will give you a treat that will discount his."

An old lady answered, "You must be mistaken, Mr. Bridger, for nothing could taste better then the chunk of meat I broiled over the fire last night."

Jim laughed and said, he would own up to the last night's supper being extra good but asked how she thought Mountain Trout would taste. She said she did not know, as she had never tasted any; Jim said, "Well, you will know in a week from tonight, and you will say that my treat is better than Will's, for Mountain trout is the best fish that ever swam in the water."

We were on the road soon after sunrise the next morning, and everything went well for the next three days. The third day's travel brought us to Humboldt Well. As we were going into camp, I discovered a band of Indians coming directly for the train. I notified Jim at once, and he soon had the train corralled, and the chief's bonnet hung high above the Indian scalps so all the Indians could see it. The savages seemed to discover the bonnet and the scalps as soon as they saw the train, for they stopped and came no nearer, and after gazing at the decorations on the wagons a few moments they wheeled their horses and galloped away in the same direction they had come, and we saw no more of them. As soon as the Indians disappeared Jim slapped his hands and said, "Didn't I tell you the effect that bonnet would have on the Red Skins? And I don't think we will have to shoot another Indian on this trip, for they will not get close enough to us for us to get a show to hit them."

The second day from this camp we reached Truckey river, and it happened to be Saturday, and Jim told the emigrants that this was the place where he proposed to outdo Will in the way of a treat and told them that everyone who could catch a grasshopper could have a mess of fish for supper, as the river was swarming with the speckled beauties, and it was really amusing to see the old of both sexes as well as the children running in every direction, catching the little hopping insects. Everyone seemed to be of one mind, what they were going to have for the evening meal, for they were all on the margin of the river, and Jim and I staid with the wagons and watched the crowd which was great amusement for us, for they were all so excited. But our fun did not last long. In a few minutes the crowd commenced to come back with their bands full of fish; one woman passed us with two little girls. She had about a dozen fish, and the children had their hands full too. She said, "Come, Mr. Bridger, I want you and Mr. Drannan to eat supper with us tonight, and after we get through I will tell you which treat is the best, Buffalo or Mountain Trout."

Jim told her she hadn't got half enough fish for him, not reckoning the members of her own family. She said, "Don't you be uneasy about not having enough. My man will come back in a few minutes, and he will have enough to make out the supper, I reckon."

We went with her to her tent and helped to clean the fish, and it was not long before the appetizing meal was ready. While Jim and I were cleaning the fish that the woman and children had caught, the man came back, and he had fifteen of the handsomest trout I had ever seen on a string. He greeted us with a laugh and said this was the first stream he had ever seen where a man could take a long-handled shovel and pitch out all the fish he had a mind to. "It is wonderful to think of the amount of fish that has been taken out of that stream, and they would not be missed if we wanted more."

Jim said, "If you could stay here and fish a week, they would be just as thick when you got through as they are now, and will be until the spawning season is over."

That night Jim suggested that we get up a party and go over on Truckee Meadows and kill some Antelope tomorrow.

I said, "All right, Jim, that is the greatest feeding ground for Antelope of any I have seen. I will go and speak to my scouts now, and we may get a party so we can start early in the morning."

I hunted my men up and told them what Jim and I thought of doing, and they were delighted with the idea. They said that every man in the outfit that owned a horse and gun would be glad to go with us. I told them to see everyone that they thought would like to or could go and for them to meet us at the head of the corral right after breakfast in the morning.

Next morning Jim and I went to the place agreed upon. We were mounted and had our guns all ready for business, and in a few minutes there were forty-three men all mounted and anxious to go with us on the hunt for Antelope.

Jim told them that the hunting ground was eight or ten miles away from camp, and he said, "I will guarantee that you will see a thousand Antelope today. Now we will all travel together until we begin to see the Antelope."

The place called Truckee Meadows was about twenty miles long and ten miles wide and very level and covered with the tallest sage brush in all the country around and with an abundance of fine grass. We crossed the Truckee river just below where the city of Reno now stands, and then we struck out south east, Jim and I taking the lead and the others following us.

When we were about five miles from camp, I discovered a band of Antelope. They were probably a half a mile from us, and they were feeding in a northeasterly direction. I called Jim's attention to them at once. After he got a good look at them, he said, "I will bet my old hat that there is a thousand Antelope in that band."

We stopped our horses and waited for all the crowd to come up to us, and Jim pointed to the Antelope, saying, "There is your game. Did you ever see a prettier sight? Now my friends, I want every one of you to have an Antelope across your saddle when we go back to camp. It don't make any difference who kills it so we all have an Antelope."

Jim then turned to me and said, "Will, do you see that open ridge yonder?" and he pointed to a low ridge about a mile from us right in the direction towards which the Antelope were feeding. I told him, yes, I saw it. He then said, "I will take all the men but you and two others, and I will station them all along on that little ridge at the edge of sage brush. Now, Will, you pick out your two men and ride clear around the south end of the band, and when they start to run towards us, crowd them as hard as you can, but give us time to locate before you start the band."

My men and I rode probably a mile and a half before we got around the herd, and it looked to us as if the whole valley was covered with Antelope. I told the men not to shoot at first, but to give a whoop or two to get them started and then to crowd them for all they were worth, and when the Antelope got to the open ridge to shoot.

In a few minutes, after we started the herd of Antelope, we heard the guns of Jim and his men, and it sounded as if they kept up a continual fire. When we struck the opening, I told the boys to get all the Antelope they could, and we had a plenty to choose from, for there were hundreds in the herd ahead of us. I fired my rifle and knocked one down, and then I pulled my pistol and got another. Just then I heard someone shouting at the top of his voice just ahead of me. I looked to see who it was and saw Jim Bridger, shaking his hat at me. I held up my horse so I could hear what he said. He cried, "For pity's sake, Will, don't kill any more Antelope, for we have more now than we can carry to camp."

I called my men to me, and we rode to where Jim and his men were waiting for us. Jim said, "Will, I have been in the Antelope country twenty years most of the time, and I never saw so many Antelope together at one time as I saw here this morning; why, there must be fifty or seventy-five laying around here at this minute, that we have shot, and you would not miss them out of the herd."

One of the men said, "It did not need any skill with the rifle, that hunt, for a blind man could not help hitting one of them, for as far as I could see, there was a mass of Antelope."

Every man now went to work skinning and getting the meat ready to carry to camp. My two companions and myself put two Antelopes on each of our horses and started on ahead of the others, and although it was five miles and we walked all the way, we got back to camp a few minutes before they did.

As soon as they saw us, the women came to meet us and wanted to see what we had on our horses. As I threw one of the Antelopes off the horse, a middle aged woman said, "Mr. Drannan, can I have a piece of this one? My little girls have just picked some wild onions, and I can make some hash, and I want you and Mr. Bridger to come and take dinner with us today."

I told her to help herself, that I brought the meat to camp for all of them to eat as far as it would go. Her husband came at that moment with a knife and skinned a portion of the Antelope and cut out what she wanted. By this time the other hunters began coming in, and everyone was getting fresh meat for their dinner, and by the way they acted I thought they enjoyed the Antelope fully as well as they had the Buffalo.

While we ate dinner, I asked Jim how many Antelope were killed by the whole party. He answered. "Why, dog gone it, I forgot to count them, but I know this much. Pretty near all of the men brought two across his saddle, and I will bet that it was the biggest Antelope hunt that was ever in this country before. Why, Will, the Antelope came along so thick at one time that a man could have killed them with rocks."

If the reader will stop to think a moment, I think he will be surprised at the great change that has taken place in that country in fifty years. At that time there was not a white family living within two hundred miles of this place, and if there had been any one brave enough to tell us that in a few years this would be a settled country, we would have thought he was insane. And just think, this very spot where the wild Antelope roamed in countless numbers fifty-five years ago is today Nevada's most prosperous farming country and is worth from fifty to one hundred dollars an acre, and the city of Reno, now a flourishing town of several thousand inhabitants stands on the very spot where we camped and had the Antelope hunt, and I have been told by reliable people that the whole country from the city of Reno to Honey Lake is thickly settled, and that cities and villages and thriving farms now cover the ground where at the time I am speaking of there was nothing but wild animals, and what was worse to contend with, wild savages lurking in the thick sage brush which covered the ground for hundreds of miles, and I am also told that the whole country around Honey Lake is a thriving farming country, but at the time I am speaking of, we did not have an idea that it would ever be settled up with Whites or used for anything but a feeding ground for wild animals. If we had been told at that time that a railroad would pass through the place where the city of Reno now stands, we would have thought the one who told us such a wild, improbable story to be a fit subject for a straight jacket.

We pulled out of there early Monday morning; we took the trail up Long Valley towards Honey Lake, which we reached on the evening of the third day. Nothing occurred to disturb us during this time. As soon as we went into camp that evening the emigrants got out their fishing tackle and went to the lake. Some of them caught some fish, but many of them came back disappointed. None had the luck they'd had at Truckee river. Still, the most of us had some fish for supper that night.

While we were at supper, Jim told the people that they were through catching trout, that the next fish we had would be salmon. They said they had never heard of that kind and asked what it looked like. Jim told them that the meat of some kinds of salmon was as red as beef, while another kind was pink, and still another kind was yellow, and they were considered the finest fish that swim in the water, and he continued, "I have seen them so thick in the spring in some of the streams in California that it was difficult to ride my horse through them without mashing them, and they ran against the horse's legs and frightened him so that he was as eager to get away from them as they were of him."

An old man presently asked how large a salmon usually was, to which Jim answered, "Well, they run in weight from ten to fifty pounds, but I have seldom seen one as small as ten pounds, and they are very fat when they are going upstream to spawn, but when they are coming down they are so poor they can scarcely swim."

We left Honey Lake in the morning, and the third day from there we struck the Sacramento valley, and we now told the emigrants that they had no further use for our services, that their road was perfectly safe from this point to Sacramento city.

Two of the committee came to us and said, "As this is Saturday we will camp here until Monday, and we want you two men to stay with us, for the women want to fix up something for you to eat on your way back."

Jim answered that we would stay with them over Sunday and take a rest, for we had a long and tiresome journey before us, but it must be understood that we did not want the women to go to cooking for us, for all we could take with us was a few loaves of bread, enough to last us a few days. Our meat we could get as we wanted it, which would be our principal food on the trip, as it always was when we were alone.

Sunday was a very pleasant, restful day to us. All the emigrants seemed to vie with each other in being social. Among the company was a man and wife by the name of Dent; these two came to us and said that they were going to make their home in Sacramento city and were going into business there, and they wanted us if we ever came there to come to them and make their home ours as long as we wished to stay, for, said they, "We appreciate what you have done for us on this journey we have passed through. Besides the protection you have given us, the Buffalo and Antelope meat you have shown us how to get and have helped to get has been worth more money to us than all we have paid you to pilot us to California.".

We thanked them for their kind offer and good opinion of us but disclaimed having done anything but our duty by them.

Monday morning Jim and I were about the first to be astir. We caught our horses and had them saddled by the time breakfast was ready, and we accepted the first invitation offered us to eat. While we were eating, our hostess said she had baked two loaves of bread for us to take with us, and that she had roasted the last piece of Antelope that she had and wanted us to take that too. We took the food this lady had prepared for us and went to our horses, but before we reached them we saw the women coming from every direction with bread and cake. Jim said, "Will, let's fill this sack with bread and cake if they insist on giving it to us and then get away as soon as possible."

As Jim made this remark, it was very amusing to see how every woman tried to get her package in the sack first, but it would not begin to hold half that was brought. As soon as the sack was full, Jim said, "Now ladies, we can take no more, so be kind to us in letting us get away."

By the time we had our pack fixed on our pack horses' backs, every man and woman and all the children were around us to bid us farewell and good speed on our journey back to Taos, New Mexico.

We had shaken hands with probably a hundred or more when Jim sprang upon his horse all at once, saying, "Now friends, we will consider we have all shaken hands," and he took off his hat and, waving it to the assembled crowd, gathered up his reins and galloped away, and I followed suit. But as long as we were in hearing distance we could hear, "Good bye, good bye," floating on the wind. As the sight of the train faded in the distance, we waved our hats for the last time.

For the next two days everything went smoothly with Jim and me, which brought us to Honey Lake. The night we reached Honey Lake, we camped in a little grove of timber near a pearling stream of cool, sparkling water about a half a mile south of the trail.

We had eaten our supper and were about to spread our blankets and turn in for the night when we heard a dog bark close to our camp, but it was too dark to see him. Jim said, "Don't that beat any thing you ever heard?"

We listened a moment, and then it was a howl, and then in a moment he barked again. Jim said, "You stay in camp, Will, and I will take my gun and see what is the matter."

In a moment Jim called, "I see him." I waited about an hour before Jim came back and was beginning to feel anxious about him. When I heard his footsteps, he said, "I followed that dog nearly a mile, and then I found the cause of his howling, and what do you think it was?" I answered, "Jim, I have no idea," to which he said, "Well, I will tell you. I found the body of a dead man laying on his blanket just as if he was laying down to rest. I did not get near the dog until I had discovered the body, and then he was very friendly with me, and came and whined, and wagged his tail, as if he knew me. I looked all around, but I could find nothing but the body laying on the blanket. I could not see that there had been a fire, and I saw no signs of a horse or anything else, and the strange part of it is that, although the dog was so friendly with me, I could not coax him away from the body which I suppose was his master."

I asked Jim what he thought it was best to do. He answered, "What can we do, Will? We have no tools to dig a grave with, and the body is laying among the rocks, and I expect that dog will stay beside it and starve to death."

"Wouldn't it be a good idea to go to the place in the morning and pile rocks on the body to keep the wolves and other wild animals from eating it up?" Jim said, "Yes, we will do that, and we will shoot some jack-rabbits and leave them with the dog, so he can have something to eat for a few days anyhow."

On the way over to the place where the body lay, we killed three rabbits and threw them to the dog, and he ate them as if he was nearly starved, and I have always thought that his master died of starvation, as he had no gun or pistol with which to kill anything to eat, and Jim thought that he must have got lost from some emigrant train and wandered around until he was too weak to go farther and lay down and died with no one but his faithful dog to watch over him in his last moments.

We covered him up with stones and brush the best we could and left him and the poor dog together, although we tried every way we could to tempt the animal away. The faithful dog would not leave his master's body. After trying persuasion until we saw it was no use, Jim said, "Let's put a rope around his neck and lead him off." I answered, "No, Jim, if he will not be coaxed away, it would not be right to force him to leave his dead master." Jim said, "It seems too bad to leave him to starve, but you are right, Will," and so we left him, and we never saw him again.

Saddened with the experience of the morning, we mounted our horses and struck for the trail. We had nothing more to disturb us for the next three days. About the middle of the afternoon of the third day we were riding along slowly, talking about where we should camp that night, when Jim happened to look off to the south, and he saw a band of Indians about a mile from us, and they were coming directly towards us, but we could not tell whether they had seen us or not. Jim said, "Let's put spurs to our horses and see if we can get away from them Red devils without a fight with them."

We put our horses to a run and had kept them going this gate for five or six miles when we came to the top of a little ridge, and in looking back we saw the Indians about a half a mile in the rear and coming as fast as their horses could carry them.

Jim said, "Will, we are in for it now, and we must find a place where we can defend ourselves."

At that moment I saw a little bunch of timber a few hundred yards ahead of us. I pointed to it and said to Jim, "Let's get in there and show them our war bonnet and scalps, and maybe that will save us from having a fight with the Red imps."

Jim laughed and said, "Why dog gone it, Will, I forgot all about your war bonnet. Sure, that will be the very thing to do."

We had reached the timber while we talked. We now dismounted and tied our horses, and in less time than one could think we had the war bonnet and scalps dangling from the trees all around our horses. We had scarcely got ready for them when the Red Skins were in sight. They raced around us in a circle but did not come in gun shot of us. They went through this performance a few times and then stopped and took a good look at our decorations, and then they wheeled their horses and left in the direction they had come from, and that was the last we saw of that bunch of Indians.

We waited a few minutes to be sure that all was clear, and then we mounted again and rode about two miles before we found water so we could camp for the night. When we were eating our supper that night, Jim said, "Will, I don't think you realize what a benefit those scalps and that bonnet is to us; if I were you, I would never part with that bonnet as long as you are in the Indian country. This being a Ute bonnet, the Comanches will offer you all kinds of prices for it, but if I were you I would not sell it at any price."

I answered, "Jim, I am going to keep that bonnet for two reasons. One is for the protection of my own scalp and the other is to keep in remembrance my last trip in company with you as a pilot across the plains to California."

Jim looked at me a moment and then said, "Will, you don't pretend to say that you will never take any more trips with me."

I answered, "Yes Jim, I mean what I say. This is my last trip as a pilot for emigrants."

Jim did not answer for a few moments, and then he said, "Who will go with me next year Willie? I thought the pilot business just suited you."

I answered, "In some respects I do like it, and in others I dislike it very much. You know yourself how impossible it is to please everybody. There are so many of the people who come from the east that don't think there is any more danger of the Indians than there is of the Whites, and you know Jim that is the class of people who will always get us into trouble. See what those nineteen smart alecks did for us on this last trip. Do you think if they had known any thing of Indian trickery they would have left our protection to go hunting in the very heart of the Indian country? And if we had not been firm with the rest of those people the whole outfit would have been scalped and then we would have had to bear the blame."

Jim answered, "There is more truth than poetry in all you say Will, but maybe you will change your mind when spring comes."

We had a peaceful night's sleep and pulled out on the road bright and early the next morning. We left the main trail and took a south east course and crossed the extreme southern portion, of what is now the state of Utah. We traveled hundreds of miles in this country without seeing a human being.

A year ago I passed through this same country in a comfortable seat in a railroad car, and it would be difficult for me to make the people of this day understand the feelings that I experienced when in looking from the car window I saw the changes that fifty-five years have made in what was a wild, rough wilderness, inhabited by Buffaloes, Antelopes, Coyotes and savage men.

We kept on through this section of country until we struck the Colorado river, which we crossed just below the mouth of Green river, and a few days' travel brought us into the northwest part of what is now New Mexico.

The country which is now New Mexico was at the time of which I am writing considered perfectly worthless. It is a rolling, hilly country with smooth, level valleys between the hills and is proving to be very fertile and is settling as fast as any part of the west.

There was nothing more to trouble us, and we made good progress on our journey, and in ten days from the time we left the Colorado river we reached Taos, New Mexico, which was the end of our journey, and tired and worn with the long hours in the saddle and the anxiety of mind which we had experienced in all the long months since we left there in the spring, we were glad to get there and rest a few days and to feel that we were free with no responsibility.

[Illustration: The mother bear ran to the dead cub and pawed it with her foot.]

CHAPTER VII.

We found Uncle Kit and his family all well and glad to see us. It was late in the afternoon when we got there, and we spent the remainder of the day and evening in recounting our summer's experience for Uncle Kit's benefit, who was a very interested listener to all that had befallen us since we parted from him in the spring.

While we ate supper, Jim told Uncle Kit of the fight with the Indians in which I killed the old chief and took his scalp and war bonnet, an account which amused Uncle Kit very much, and later in the evening he insisted on my undoing my pack and showing the bonnet to him.

After he had examined it, he said, "Will, I always knew that you would make an Indian fighter since that night when you were not fifteen years old and showed such bravery in showing me the two scalps of the Indians you had killed that morning all by yourself. But little did I think that you would have the honor of killing a Ute Chief and capturing his war bonnet. There will be many times when that bonnet will be as much protection to you as a whole regiment of soldiers would be," and turning to Jim, Carson said, "Bridger, don't you think my Willie must have been an apt pupil and does me great honor for the instruction I gave him?"

Jim answered, "Yes, Kit, I certainly do, and if you had seen him tested as I have the past summer, you would not need to ask me that question."

Uncle Kit patted me on the back and told Jim that he did not need to see his boy's bravery tested, for he always took it for granted that Willie would stand any test.

The next morning, Uncle Kit and Bridger commenced to lay their plans for the winter's trapping. I heard Uncle Kit say, "Bridger, we have got to get down to Bent's Fort right away; here it is in the last days of September, and you know that when the fall of the year comes, them trappers are like a fish out of water, and if we don't get to the Fort soon, Bent and Roubidoux will fit them out and send them out trapping on their own hooks."

Jim answered, "That is true, Kit, and the quicker we go the better it will be for us."

On the fifth day after we arrived at Taos from California, we were on the road to Bent's Fort with twenty-two pack horses besides our saddle horses. Uncle Kit, my old comrade Jonnie West and a Mexican boy by the name of Juan accompanied us.

We reached Bent's Fort in safety without having any trouble on the way. The evening we got to the Fort it seemed to me that there were more trappers than I had ever seen together at one time before, and they all huddled around Carson and Bridger. Uncle Kit told them all that he would talk business with them in the morning. When supper was ready that evening, Col. Bent invited all of us to take supper with him. We accepted the invitation, and while we were at the table, a runner came with a note to Uncle Kit from Capt. McKee, asking Carson to send all the men he could muster to join him at Rocky Ford to escort a government train to Santa Fe, New Mexico.

According to the Capt's. note Carson had only twenty-four hours to gather his men and get to Rocky Ford. When Uncle Kit read the note so unexpectedly brought him, it seemed to upset and confuse him. He said, "My God, I can't go," and then he read the note aloud. When he had finished reading. Col. Bent said, "I will go out and see how many men will volunteer to go." After Col. Bent left the room, Uncle Kit said to me, "Willie, will you take charge of the men if Col. Bent can raise a company? I know you can handle them as well as I could."

I answered, "Yes sir, I will do any thing you think is best."

In a short time Col. Bent came back and said he had found twenty seven men who were willing to go, and that every man had his own horse and a gun and a pistol, "but who will take the command of the company? Do you intend to go yourself Carson?"

Uncle Kit said, "No, I do not, but Willie here," and he touched my shoulder, "will take my place and do as well as I could."

Col. Bent said, "Well, come with me, Will, and I will introduce you to your men."

When we went outside, all the twenty-seven men were there waiting for us. Col. Bent said to them, "Now, gentlemen, I have brought you a leader in Mr. William Drannan. He will have charge of you until you reach Rocky Ford."

I then told the men to furnish themselves with four day's ration and also to take blankets to use at night, and to be ready to take the trail at sun rise in the morning. They all promised to be ready at the time I specified, and we separated for the night.

I found Uncle Kit in the dining room writing a letter to Capt. McKee. He gave the letter to me, saying, "Give this letter to Capt. McKee, and if you want to go to Santa Fe with him, do so, or if you had rather be with me, you will find Jim and me on the Cache-La-Poudre; just suit yourself, Willie, in regard to this matter, and I shall be satisfied."

The next morning we were up and on the road by the time the sun was up. We rode hard until about eleven o'clock, when we dismounted, staked our horses out to grass and ate our luncheon. We let our horses feed about an hour, and then we mounted and were on the road again. A little before sunset we came in sight of Rocky Ford. As soon as I saw where we were, I pointed it out to the boys, and said, "There is Rocky Ford, and we are ahead of time."

We had ridden but a short distance when one of the boys remarked, "We are not much in the lead, for there comes Capt. McKee's company just across the river," and as we reached the Ford, Capt. McKee and his men were crossing. So we both met on time. I had never met Capt. McKee but knew him from the fact that he was in the lead of his men.

I rode up to him and saluted and asked if this was Capt. McKee. He said it was. I told my name at the same time I gave him Carson's letter.

He read the letter and then said, "Let us go into camp. My men and horses are tired, and we will talk business after we have had supper."

We rode perhaps a quarter of a mile from the Ford, where we could get plenty of sage brush to make fires, dismounted and staked our horses out to grass, and it was not long until our meal was ready to eat. As soon as the meal was over, the Captain came to me and inquired if I had ever been over this country before. I told him I had a number of times. He said, "I am a stranger in this country; will you please tell me where the main body of the Comanches are at this time of the year?"

I told him that the main body of the Comanche tribe was at least a hundred miles down the river.

"They go down there to shoot the Buffalo as they cross the river on their winter's feeding ground. You will find the Indians very numerous all through that part of the country. Sometimes there are from two to three hundred wigwams in one village, and the Indians will stay there for nearly a month yet before they go farther south."

The Capt. then asked if I was acquainted with any of the Comanche Chiefs. I told him that I was, and that I had traded with pretty near all of them.

"The Comanches are all great friends with Kit Carson, and as I have visited them and traded with them in company with him, they extend their friendship to me."

The Capt. thought a moment and then said, "I am mighty afraid that we are going to have trouble with the Comanches from the fact that that Government train is at least two hundred miles from here, and there are forty wagons in it, and they have no escort, only their drivers and herders, and I am weak myself; you see, I have only twenty men with me. Five days before I received this order, I sent all of my men, except the twenty with me, to Fort Worth, Texas to protect the settlers in that country as the Comanches are on the war path there, and the few men we have with us now will not be as much as a drop in a bucket as far as protecting the train is concerned if the Comanches attack it."

I answered, "Captain, if we can reach the train before the Indians do, I believe we can get the train through to Santa Fe without firing a gun."

This seemed to surprise him, for he looked at me as though I was insane in making such a remark and said, "What do you mean, young man?"

I answered: "Capt. McKee, all the Comanche tribe know me, and they also know that I have for several years been closely associated with Kit Carson, and they think that all Kit Carson does or says is right, for they both love him and fear him, and they have the same feeling for the boy Carson raised, and furthermore I have in this pack," and I pointed to my pack which was laying on the ground near me, "more protection, in my estimation, than a hundred soldiers would be to the train."

He said, "Explain what you mean, for I do not understand."

I then unrolled my pack and, taking out the Indian scalps and the Ute Chief's war bonnet, I showed them to him and told him how I had used them to protect an emigrant train when I only had twelve men to help me that were of any use in a fight with the Indians.

I said, "Now, Captain, you must know that the Indians have no fear of death, but they do dread to lose their scalps after they are killed, as they think there will be no chance for a scalpless Indian to enter the Happy Hunting ground. So if we reach the train before the Indians get there and fear they will attack it when they do, all we have to do is to hang these scalps up in a prominent place and put the Chief's war bonnet high above them all, and there will be no need of a fight or chance for one, for the Indians will not come near enough to be shot at, for they will fear that they will share the same fate that befell the Indians that these scalps belonged to."

Capt. McKee then asked me if I were willing to go on and assist him in this way until the train reached Santa Fe, and he said, "I am quite sure your plan in using the scalps and bonnet for protection with the Indians will prove a success, for I know how superstitious the Indians are about being scalped, and I am also sure that we have not sufficient men to save the train from the Indians without some other means is used."

I then asked the Capt. who would pay me and my men for our time if we went with him. His answer was "The Government pays me and will pay you and the men with you, and if we have a chance to test your plan and it proves a success, I will see that you have double pay."

Everything being understood and arranged to the satisfaction of all hands, we separated and turned in for the night.

Next morning we were all up in good season and got an early start on the road.

Late that evening just before we went into camp we saw a few Buffalo feeding near the river. I asked the Capt. where he was going to camp that night. He pointed to a little ravine about a half a mile from us, and answered, "We will camp on that ravine." I said, "Take my pack on your saddle in front of you, and I will kill a calf for supper."

He took my pack, saying, "All right, we surely will enjoy some fresh meat," and the company moved on, and I struck out to kill the Buffalo. I rode around the herd so if they became frightened they would run towards the place where we were to camp. They saw me before I had got in gun shot of them and started to run directly towards where the Capt. had gone into camp.

As soon as I saw the direction they were taking, I commenced to shout to the men at the camp to look out, for the Buffalo were coming, and they did not get the news any too quick before the Buffalos were there. The men grabbed their guns and commenced shooting, and that was all that saved the camp from being overrun with Buffalo. They shot down three calves and two heifers right in camp.

The boys had the laugh on me for several days. When anything was said about getting fresh meat, some of them would say, "Will can go and drive it into camp, and we will shoot it," and the Capt. would laugh and say he reckoned that was a good way to save me from packing it.

I do not think I ever saw men enjoy a meal more than these did that night. We had all ridden hard that day and had only a light lunch at midday, so we were all very hungry and young and hearty and just at the time of life when food tastes best, and every one of us knew how to broil Buffalo meat over sage brush fire.

The next morning the Capt. told the men to all cut enough meat from the Buffalos to last until the next day and to put it in their packs, for, he said, "We may not meet with as good luck again as we did today, and if we take the meat with us we will be provided for anyway."

We were on the road early in the morning and traveled without stopping until noon, and we saw numerous small bands of Buffalo all along the way. We stopped on the bank of a little pearling stream of cold water, where there was plenty of grass for the horses, and ate our luncheon and rested about an hour. We were about ready to continue our journey when I discovered a small band of Indians coming up the trail.

I sang out to the Capt., "There come some of our neighbors." He looked at them and said, "Boys, mount your horses and be ready, for we are going to have fun right here." I said, "Hold on, Capt., and let me see if I can't settle this thing without a fight." He said, "How will you do it?" I said, "I believe I know all those Indians, but I will ride down and meet them and see, and if I am acquainted with them we will have no trouble with them."

Capt. McKee said, "Won't you be taking a desperate chance, Mr. Drannan, in going to meet those savages when you are not sure whether you know them or not?" I said, "I am not afraid to go to meet them, but if anything is wrong, I will signal to you by raising my hat, and if I do so you must charge at once, but if I give no signal you may be sure everything is all right."

I started my horse at full speed down the narrow valley to meet the approaching Indian band. When I was within a hundred yards of them, they recognized me, and they all began crying, "Hi-yar-hi-yar," which translated into English means, "How do-yo-do," and in a few minutes, they were all swarming around me, each one trying to shake my hand first. I shook hands with all, and I then asked them where they were going. The Chief told me that they were going to their village, which was on the opposite side of the river. We had passed their village a few hours before, but owing to the timber being so thick we did not notice it. They wanted to know when I was coming to trade for Buffalo robes with them. I told them I would come in four months. This seemed to please them well, and they said they would have a plenty of robes to trade for knives and rings and beads.

I rode back with my Indian friends to the camp. On the way I told the chief where I was going, and that the white men he saw in the camp were my friends and were going with me. Not knowing any of the men in the camp, the Indians passed on without stopping, as is their custom when they are not on the war path.

When the last Indian had passed the camp, Capt. McKee ordered the men to mount, and we continued our journey.

When we were under way the Capt. rode to my side and said, "Mr. Drannan, will you tell me how it is that you have such a control over those Indians? Why, I would not have ridden to meet that savage band for anything that you could have offered me, for I should have considered doing such a thing equal to committing suicide, and I know I should not have come out alive."

I said, "Very true, Capt. I don't think you would. But there is this difference between your going to meet them and my doing so. You are a stranger to them, and a member of the white race, which they hate. They, not knowing who you are, are suspicious of your being on their hunting grounds, but in my case I have known them all for years and have accompanied them many times to their village. Whom they trust, although he be a "pale face," they have confidence in, as they have in me. So they are all my friends, and when

I told the Chief that you and all the company were my friends and were going with me, he or any of his braves had no wish to trouble you."

Capt. McKee looked at me as if he thought me something hardly human while I explained why I was not afraid of the Indians who had just passed, and in a moment after I had ceased speaking he said, "Can you control all of the Comanche tribe the same as you did the band which has just passed us?" I answered, "I certainly think I can if I have my way about it." He answered, "If that is so, the United States Government will be under great obligation to you." "The obligation is nothing to me Capt., but if the men will obey my instruction I think I can pilot the train through to Santa Fe without their having to fire a shot," I replied. The Capt. said, "I am not acquainted with the wagon master, so I can not say what he will do, but I will give you my word that my men will do as you instruct them, and as soon as we meet the train I will have a talk with the wagon master and try to influence him to submit to being directed by you."

The third day from this place we met the train at a place called Horse Shoe Bend. We saw a number of bands of Indians and passed several Indian villages on the way, but we did not come into contact with any of them. The train was just corralling for the night when we met them, and the most discouraged-acting men I ever saw were in that train. The wagon master told us that the Indians had attacked the train the day before and killed five of his men, and he said, "If this had been anything but a Government train, I should have turned around and gone back, and Capt., you haven't half men enough to protect this train through the Comanche country; we have just struck the edge of it, and the Comanches are the largest and most hostile tribe in the west, and you see that I lost five of my herders in the Kiawah country, and they are a small tribe beside the Comanches."

Capt. McKee then told the wagon master what he had seen me do with a band of Comanche warriors, and also told him what I said I could do for the train if I had the control of the men and they would obey me.

The wagon master turned and looked at me a moment as if he was measuring me and then said, "Young man, do you pretend to say that you know all of the Comanche tribe?"

I answered, "No, sir, I do not know them all, but they all know me, and there are hundreds of them that are particular friends of mine, and if you are acquainted with the Indian character, you know that when an Indian professes to be a friend he is a friend indeed, and there is no limit to what he will do for you."

He then asked how I proposed to handle the train and the men. I answered, "I want the men to ride beside the wagons, and in the rear of them with a half a dozen just a little ahead of the teams, and I will ride alone from a quarter to a half a mile ahead, and if the men in the rear or those on the side see any Indians advancing on the train, I want them to notify me at once, for I want to talk with the Indians before they get to the train, no matter whether there are a few or many of them."

The wagon master said, "I don't see anything to find fault with your plans," and turning to McKee he asked what he thought of the arrangement. Capt. McKee answered, "All that I find fault with is the desperate chances Mr. Drannan will take in going out to meet the savages all by himself." I said, "Capt., there is where you make a mistake. My safety lies in my going out to meet the Indians alone, and I will assure you and the other gentlemen that there will not be a gun fired if I can get to the Indians before they get to the train."

At this moment the cook said supper was ready, and it did not take long for me at least to get to eating it, for I was very hungry.

The wagon master, the Capt. and I messed together. The Capt. asked me what I thought about putting out picket guards that night. I told him that I did not think it necessary tonight, but further on the road it might be advisable.

We had a quiet night's rest, and everybody seemed cheerful in the morning, and we were on the road quite early. Before we started, I asked the wagon master how many miles he traveled in a day, and if he stopped at noon. He answered that he was four or five days behind time now and would like to make twenty miles a day if he could, and he thought it would not be advisable to stop at noon while we were in the Comanche country, but when we got clear of the Indians probably he would lay over a day or two, and let the teams have a rest.

Everything moved on pleasantly all that day. We did not see an Indian, but towards evening we saw large bands of Buffalo all going south. That night when we had got settled into camp, I told the Capt. that I would take a ride five or six miles up the valley and see if I could find any Indians' village or see any Indians and for them not to be uneasy about me or look for me until they saw me.

I had ridden perhaps three miles when I saw a large band of Indians just going into camp. They were about a half a mile from our trail right on the bank of the Arkansas river. I knew that they were a hunting party because their squaws and papooses were with them, which is never the case if the warriors are on the war path.

I rode down among them, and as soon as the squaws saw me they commenced to cry, "Hi-yar-hi-yar," and ran to me with extended hands, and they all asked together if I had come to trade rings and beads. When I told them that I would come again in four months and trade with them, they laughed and said in their own language that they would have many Buffalo robes ready to trade with me. As I was talking with the squaws, an Indian came to me, one that I had known for quite a while, and invited me to his wigwam to take supper with him and stay all night. I explained to him that I could not accept his invitation that time and told him what I was doing, and where I was going, but that I would return in four months and would bring a plenty of knives and rings and beads to trade for Buffalo robes.

This seemed to please him very much.

I bid them all good bye and went back to camp. It was rather late and supper was over, but the cook had saved some for me. While I was eating, Capt. McKee and the wagon master came to see me. The Capt. asked what I had seen while I was gone. I said, "Capt., I saw enough Indian squaws to keep me shaking hands for twenty minutes, and besides the squaws I saw four or five hundred warriors and shook hands with a good many of them and was invited to eat supper and pass the night with one of the Chiefs, but I declined to do either, although I would have been more than welcome."

The Capt. asked where the Indians were, and I told him. He asked how far from our trail their village was. I told him between half and a quarter of a mile. He said, "Have we got to pass in full view of that Indian village?" I answered, "Yes, sir, that is the only road that leads from here to Santa Fe." "And do you believe that we can pass them in the morning without being attacked by them?" he asked. I said, "Capt., if the men will obey my instructions, there will be no danger when we strike out in the morning. We will all travel in the same order as we did today, except that I shall not ride so far in advance of the train, and if the Indians start to come towards the train, I will ride out and meet them, and the train must keep right on, as if nothing had occurred, and I will hold the Indians until the train is out of sight, and then I will leave them and overtake you."

The Capt. said, "All right, Mr. Drannan, we will do as you have directed, and if you succeed in this venture, I shall know that you have the control over the Indians that you thought you had."

The wagon master said that he would not feel very easy until we had passed and were out of sight of the Indians and their village, and I believe he spoke the truth, for he was up and had everything ready. We were on the road by sunrise. When we were nearly opposite the Indian village, the squaws discovered us and came running towards us in droves. I rode out and met them and had a general hand-shaking with them, and they wanted me to assure them that I was coming in four months to trade with them and wanted me to go and look at some of the robes they had dressed, which I did, and in doing so, I saw something that I had never seen before nor have I since. It was a white Buffalo skin, and the animal must have been a half-grown cow judging from the size of the skin. It was the prettiest thing of the kind that I had ever seen, or ever have since. When I was looking at the beautiful thing, I asked the Indian that I thought it belonged to how much he would take for it. He said it was not his, that it was his squaw's. I asked her what her price would be, and she answered, "One string of beads." I told her to save it for me and in four months I would come back and bring the beads to her and take the robe. I was so interested in looking at the robes and talking with the Indians that time passed without notice, and the first thing I thought about it, in looking at my watch I found it was nearly noon. I now bid the Indians good bye, mounted my horse and started to overtake the train. When I caught up with them, I found that the Capt. was feeling very uneasy about me, and the wagon master thought the Indians had taken me captive.

When I rode to the Capt's. side, he said, "This settles it. I have been fighting the Indians for several years, and I must admit now that I don't know anything about them, and I will confess that I was like "the Missouri"; I had to be shown before I believed. But having seen like them, I am satisfied that you knew what you were talking about. After the experience of this morning, I cannot doubt that through your friendship with the Red skins we shall get through to Santa Fe in safety without having any trouble with them."

That evening when we went into camp, the Capt. and the wagon master came to me. The Capt. said, "Mr. Drannan, you are so well acquainted with the Comanche Indians, perhaps you can tell us where we shall pass their main village and where the Indians are likely to be the most numerous." I answered, "This is an unusually late fall, and the Buffalo are as a consequence unusually late in going south and are more scattered than they would be earlier in the season, and I do not think we will pass the Comanches' main village under forty miles from here. You must understand that the Comanches' main village is always near where the largest herd of Buffalo cross the river, and from this on we will travel as we have been doing; I will take the lead five or six miles in advance of the train so that if we come on to a band of Indians or a small village I can meet them and have a talk with them before the train gets up to them, and Capt., I want you and the other men to keep a close look out, and if any of you see any Indians coming towards the train from any direction, send a runner after me at once, for I want to meet the Indians before they get to the train."

The next morning we pulled out early, and we traveled without interruption all day, and we did not see an Indian and but very few Buffalo.

That night we camped on a little stream called Cotton Wood Creek. There was fine water and the best of grass for the stock. That evening I told the

Capt. and the wagon boss that the three main Buffalo crossings were within thirty miles of us, and we would probably have more trouble with the Buffalos than we would with the Indians. "At this time of the year it is no uncommon thing to see a herd of Buffalo from eight to ten miles long, and from a half to a mile wide, and if we meet with such a herd, all we can do is to stop and wait until they pass, for we could no more get through them than we could fly over them, and, Capt., we now have two dangers to avoid. The Indians and Buffalos. If you see a band of Buffalo coming and I am not with you, have the wagon master corral the train as quickly as possible, and as close as he can get them together. I have considerable influence with the Indians, but I have none with the Buffalos, so we must give the latter their own way and a plenty of room, or they will tramp the train under their feet and us with it."

We were on the road in good season the next morning, and every thing went smoothly until about eleven o'clock in the morning, when I saw a large band of Buffalo coming from the north and heading directly for the river. I rode back and met the train and told the wagon master that he must corral the train at once, and he did not have time to get it corralled too soon before the herd was near us, and I will say I had seen a great many large herds of Buffalo before and have since that time but never saw anything that equaled this herd. We waited until three o'clock in the afternoon before we could move on our journey, and after they had all passed us, one could see nothing but a black moving mass as far as the eyes could see.

I asked the Capt. how many Buffalos he thought there were in that band. He answered, "I think the number would run into millions. How many Buffalos would it take to cover a half a mile square?"

I thought a moment and answered, "That is a difficult question to answer, Capt. The way they were crowded together here I believe there would be a hundred thousand on every half a mile square."

Capt. McKee said, "Yes, and on some of the half a mile square there would be more than that number. I was in Texas nine years, and I saw a great many bands of Buffalo in that time, but I had no idea that they ever traveled in such immense bodies as the one that passed us today."

We proceeded but a short distance that afternoon but made an early camp on account of water. While we were at supper, I was amused at some of the remarks made by the teamsters. One of them said, "Boys, if I live to get home, you will never catch me any farther west than the state of Missouri again. Who would live in such a country as this is? Good for nothing but Indians, Buffalos, and Coyotes, and any of the three is liable to kill you if you get out among them." And another said, "How in creation are we going to get home? If this train don't go back, we are sure in for it."

The wagon boss said, "Boys, I should not think you would want to go back over this country again." One of them said, "How would we live?" He answered, "Why, you could go and live with the Indians, and then you could have Buffalo meat to eat and hear the Coyotes howl all the time."

This remark made a laugh, but I noticed one of the teamsters wiped his eyes on his coat sleeve and got up and left the crowd, and I saw the tears running down his cheeks. After he had gone, one of the other drivers said, "I pity John, for he thinks he will never see his sweetheart again. It was to get money to settle down with that brought him out here, and now he is afraid that he will never get back, and I believe he will go crazy if he don't get to see his girl in a few months."

The boss said, "It is too bad, and I will go and see if I can console him."

When we were ready to strike the trail the next morning, I told the Capt. that I thought we would pass the Comanches' main village that day. Said I, "If it is late in the afternoon when we pass the Indian camp, it will be best to drive on four or five miles before you stop for the night, and do not pay any attention to me, for very likely I shall be in the middle of the camp, talking with the Chief."

I struck out, and I had not ridden more than eight miles when in looking off to the south I saw the Indian village. It was about a mile from the trail on the bank of the Arkansas river. I turned my horse and went for the village. When I was about halfway there, I met a number of young bucks, and they all knew me. After I had shaken hands with them, I asked where the old Chief's wigwam was, and they all went with me and showed me where it was. As soon as I struck the edge of the village, every buck and squaw commenced to shout and shake their hands at me. When I got to the Chief's wigwam I dismounted, and as he came out to meet me I offered my hand, which is always customary when one visits an Indian, be he Chief or warrior.

After we had talked a few minutes, he told me in his own language that I had come too soon. He supposed I had come to trade with the Indians for Buffalo robes. I told him that I had not come to trade this time but would come all prepared to trade in four months.

Then I told him what I was doing and where I was going, and I told him that if he would tell all his Warriors to let us pass without disturbing or molesting us in any way, I would make him a present of two butcher knives when I came in four months to trade with them.

This promise seemed to please him, for he said I and the pale faces with me could go through his country and none of his Warriors would disturb us. I told him I would want to come back with the same wagons in about one month, and he answered, "It is well," which meant "It is all right."

By this time there were hundreds of bucks and squaws and papooses around the Chief's wigwam. They all thought I had come with knives and rings and beads to trade with them. When the Chief told them that I was only making him a visit, and that I would return in four months to trade, they all wanted to shake hands with me, and while I was shaking their hands, I saw the train pass along the trail, and by the time I had shaken hands with them all it was out of sight.

I was now about to mount my horse to follow the train when the Chief said, "No go now, stay eat dinner."

I knew that it would be considered an insult to refuse, so I said, "Wa to," which means "All right."

I staked my horse out by tying him to a sage brush and accompanied the Chief to his wigwam, and it was not long before the squaws had a plenty of juicy Buffalo steak broiled and ready to eat, and I have no doubt the reader will think me a very strange person when I say that I enjoyed that meal, which was of broiled Buffalo meat alone without even bread, more than I would now the most sumptuous dinner that could be cooked and spread on the finest mahogany table, and that meal was spread on the ground in an Indian wigwam with wild Indians for companions.

After a while, which seemed short to me, I looked at my watch and was surprised to find that it was two o'clock in the afternoon. I bid the Chief and his squaws good by and mounted my horse and was off in pursuit of the train.

I overtook them just as they were corralling for the night. As I rode into camp, Capt. McKee met me and said, "Mr. Drannan, you must bear a charmed life. I never expected to see you again, either alive or dead."

I laughed and answered, "Did you think I was going to marry a squaw and settle down in the Indian village, Capt? I thought you had a better opinion of me than that. I will confess that I like the Indians pretty well, but not well enough to be a squaw man."

This answer made a general laugh and upset the gravity that was settling on all their faces. Capt McKee then said, "Where have you been all day, Mr. Drannan?"

I told him I went to the Indian village which he passed and was invited to eat dinner with the head Chief, and they made such a spread that I like to not got away today. He said, "What could you have had for dinner that it took all day to eat it?" I answered, "Buffalo steak straight cooked in the most approved style."

This answer made such a laugh that the Capt. did not ask any more questions until he and I were alone that evening. The wagon master and Capt. McKee asked me to take a walk with them. After we had strolled along a while, the Capt. said, "Mr. Drannan, how is it that you can go into those Indian villages be they large or small? It seems to make no difference to you, and the Indians do not molest you. Have you no hesitation at all in going among the Indians?"

I answered, "Yes sir, I would hesitate a long time before I went into the village of some tribes of Indians, but I have no fear of the Comanches in small bands or when they are all together, for they are all friendly to me, and instead of hurting me they would protect me from harm, and there is something else I can guarantee, and that is that this train will not be molested by the Comanche Indians, either going or coming on this trip."

Capt. McKee said, "Where in the world could you get that guarantee, Mr. Drannan?"

I replied, "Capt. McKee, I got it from the head Chief of the Comanche tribe, and his word is law with all his warriors."

Then the wagon master spoke for the first time since we started on our walk. He said, "In that case there is no need of all these men as an escort, is there?"

I answered, "That is none of my business; it is nothing to me how many men the Government employs to escort the trains. All I have to do with it is to do my duty."

The Capt. inquired how I came to make such an arrangement with the Chief. I told him that I had the idea in my mind from the beginning, and that was the reason I wanted to go to the main village in advance of the train, so I could arrange everything to suit myself before the train came in sight.

The Capt. inquired how much it cost me to get the guarantee. I said, "The cost was considerable, but I think the teamsters will be willing to make it up to me, considering the trouble and perhaps loss of life I have saved them."

The wagon boss said, "I reckon we all will want to take a hand in that payment. Tell me what it costs, and be it ever so much, you shall not be out a cent. I will go and see the boys right away and see if we can make it up. How much shall I tell them?"

I answered, "I promised the Chief two butcher knives for the safety of this train's passage through the Comanche country, both going to Santa Fe and coming back."

They both stared at me as if they were amazed, and finally the Capt. said, "What are you giving us? Are you joking or in earnest, Mr. Drannan?"

I answered, "I have told just what I promised to give the Chief. We did not call it 'paying,' and I have over three months to pay it in."

Capt. McKee said, "Two butcher knives for the safety of all our lives and all the property in our care? How in the name of common sense could you make such a bargain as that?"

I answered, "There is nothing very wonderful about the transaction, Capt. I told the Chief that I would give him two butcher knives if he would tell his warriors not to molest the train either going or coming back, and he accepted my offer and seemed to think himself well paid. I told him that I would come to trade with his tribe in four months and that I would give the knives to him then."

Capt. McKee asked how many more villages we would have to pass through. I told him that there were two more small villages. One was about ten miles, and the other one about fifteen or twenty miles above us.

He inquired if I intended to visit each of those in advance of the train as I had the ones we had passed; I replied, "I certainly do, for they would think themselves greatly insulted if I should visit the other villages and pass them by without paying them a visit too. The Indians are very much like children. If you notice one, you must pay the same attention to the others or there will be jealousy, and that is very much to be avoided in this case. Besides, I expect to trade with those Indians next spring, and I want to keep on the good side of all of them. If one gets the ill will of one Indian, the whole tribe is against one, and if you have the Chief on your side there is no danger from the others."

When we returned to camp from our walk, the wagon master said, "Boys, Mr. Drannan has hired the Chief of the Comanches to forbid his warriors interfering with this train going to Santa Fe or when it is coming back. Now I want to know how much money each one of you are willing to chip in towards helping him out. You must remember that the contract he made with the Indian Chief has not only saved the destruction of the train, but more than likely some of us would have lost our lives if the Indians had resented our passing through their country."

Three drivers, all from Missouri, came forward at once and said, "Mr. Drannan, we haven't any money now, but as soon as we draw our pay, we will give you twenty dollars apiece as our share."

Another man cried out, "I will give twenty-five."

Capt. McKee frowned and said, "Don't you think your lives worth more than twenty-five dollars, men?"

This remark seemed to stir them up, and in less than ten minutes they had subscribed four hundred and forty dollars.

The Capt. clapped his hands and said, "Mr. Drannan, you are safe," and then told the men what the real expense would be to me. The Missouri men answered, "Don't make any difference to us what he is to pay. The bargain he made to save our lives is what we want to pay for as far as we can."

I said, "Now boys, I believe that I have been instrumental in saving some of your lives and probably the whole train, but you don't owe me a cent of money for what I have done, and I want to say to you all that if there should be any Indians come near the train while we are passing through the Comanche country do not interfere with them in any way, and you may rest assured they will not with you."

The Capt. now turned to the wagon master and said, "How much further do you want me and my men to accompany you?" He answered, "I will leave that for you and Mr. Drannan to decide."

I said, "Capt. McKee, I think you had better stay with the train until we cross the river at Rocky Ford, which will take the train nearly out of the Comanche country at this season of the year, and we ought to reach Rocky Ford day after to morrow night, and as far as having an escort is concerned, I do not think there will be any more need of one after we cross Rocky Ford. I think the train will be perfectly safe to go on alone under the present circumstances."

To this neither the Capt. or the wagon master would agree, for Capt. McKee said, "You, Mr. Drannan, have been really the only protection the train has had, and it is no more than right that you should accompany it through to Santa Fe. I with my men will go on to Santa Fe, and I will report that all is well with the train, and I will also report what you have done in protecting the lives of the men as well as the Government property on this trip."

The next morning we broke camp early and hit the trail in good season. Everything went along smoothly until about two o'clock, when we came in sight of a little Indian village. It was on the opposite side of the Arkansas river.

I rode to the bank of the river where I saw a number of squaws on the other side. I waved my hand at them, and they recognized me at once and began crying, "Hy-ar-hy-ar," and they came to the brink of the river and waved their hands at me. I called to them that in four months I would come with a plenty of beads and rings and knives to trade with them. They clapped their hands and answered, "Good-good," and I turned my horse and rode back to meet the train.

I will here explain that all this conversation had been carried on in the Comanches' language, as the Indians, neither bucks or squaws, could understand a word of the English language at that time, and if I could not have talked with them in their language, I would not have had the influence over them that I had now.

That night when we went into camp, Capt. McKee got off a good joke on me.

While we were eating supper, he said, "Mr. Drannan, I have caught on to your tricks with the Indians. First you make love to the squaws, and then you get the good will of the bucks by giving them knives to scalp the white men with. I saw how you made love to the squaws today when you were flirting with them across the river, and I saw them throwing kisses at you too."

I answered, "Capt., you ought to be with me when I come down here to trade with them. You would then see the real thing. I will acknowledge that I get all the hand-shaking that I can stand up to, but as far as kissing and hugging is concerned, that the squaws save for their own if they give them to anyone."

The Capt. laughed and answered, "Well putting joking aside, Mr. Drannan, I think the Indians of the Comanche tribe are all your friends, and no mistake, and I see that you have a wonderful influence over them."

I answered, "Capt. McKee, I have been trading with those Indians four years, and I have always done just as I agreed to do with them, which is the secret of what you call my wonderful influence over them, and I certainly have never had any trouble with one of the Comanche Indians yet, and I will tell you furthermore, Capt., that I intend, if I go back with this train, to carry the knives with me and stop at the main village and give them to the old Chief, for I do not know how soon I may have occasion to ask another favor of him, and I feel confident that as long as I keep his good will he will never refuse to do me a favor."

We left this camp quite early in the morning, and all things worked satisfactory throughout the day. We did not see an Indian and but very few Buffalos. We reached Rocky Ford and crossed the river just before night and went into camp, and Capt. McKee began to make preparations to leave the train, as with his twenty men and also the twenty-seven men who went with me from Bent's Fort he intended to strike out in the morning for Santa Fe, where he could make his report, and the men could receive their pay from the Government for their services on this trip.

Before he left us in the morning, I said, "Now Capt., there is a part of the route between here and Santa Fe which I am not familiar with, and as the country is strange to the wagon master also, can you tell me about the water and also tell me how many days it will take the train to reach Santa Fe from this place?" The Capt. answered, "As for water and grass, you will find a plenty all along the way; there is not more than four or five miles from one stream to another, and for the time it will take to reach Santa Fe, I figure that it will take fourteen days if everything moves as smoothly in the future as it has done the last few days, and now, Mr. Drannan, have you any word you would like to send to Bent's Fort to Mr. Bent or Roubidoux? I intend to go back that way, and I will take any message to anyone there that you would like to send."

I said, "Tell Mr. Bent and Mr. Roubidoux that I will be at Bent's Fort as soon as I finish this job and can get there, and that if they want me to go and trade with the Comanches, I have everything cut and dried for business, for I have visited all the main villages on this trip, and the Indians are expecting to see me back in four months to trade with them."

The men all mounted now, and we shook hands and bid each other good bye, and the Capt. and forty-seven others struck out back across the Arkansas river for Santa Fe by the way of Bent's Fort, while the train kept on up the old Santa Fe trail by the picket-wire route.

From this place I had a jolly time all the way to Santa Fe; we were in a wild country where game was plentiful, such as Deer, Antelope, and black Bear, and after the first day's travel there was never a night on the trip but I had fresh meat for supper.

I traveled along with the train until the middle of the afternoon. Then I always asked the wagon boss what kind of meat he wanted for supper. Sometimes he would say Antelope, and at other times he said he would like a piece of black tail Deer, and I invariably got what he mentioned.

We got up into the foot hills where Trinidad, Colorado now stands. The wagon boss and I were riding along together one afternoon. I looked at my watch and saw that it was about time to be looking for some meat for supper. I asked him in a joking way what he would like best for supper if he could get it. He replied that he would like a Cub Bear for a roast tonight. Up to this time I had not seen a bear, although I had seen some signs of them, and I had no more idea of killing a bear that evening than I had of flying when I started out to get something for supper.

I struck out on a low ridge that ran almost parallel with the trail. I had gone but a short distance when I came on a patch of huckleberries, and they certainly looked as if they might be delicious. They were the first I had seen that year. I jumped off my horse and went to picking and eating as fast as I could. In a few minutes my horse gave a little snort. When I turned to see what was the matter, I saw that something had frightened him. I went to him at once, and not over fifty yards from him was an old she bear, and she had two cubs with her, and I thought they, like myself, were so taken with eating berries that they had not noticed the horse or me either.

I took my rifle, dropped down on one knee, fired and broke one of the cubs' necks. The mother bear ran to the dead cub and pawed it with her foot. While she was thus engaged, I mounted my horse drew my pistol, rode up to where the mother bear and her two cubs were in a bunch and shot the other cub and broke this one's back, and it looked for a few minutes as if I must run from the mother, as I did not want to kill her for the reason that I had no use for so much meat. So I rode away a short distance and watched her a few minutes. She pawed them over a few times and seemed to think that they were no more good and with a few low growls she trotted off into the brush, and I saw no more of her.

I then rode to the dead cubs and dismounted from my horse. I picked them up and strapped them both on the back of my saddle and struck out to overtake the train, which I did just as they were going into camp.

When the wagon master saw me coming, he came to meet me, and when he saw the load on my horse's back, he exclaimed, "Mr. Drannan, I would like to know if there is anything that you can't do that you take a notion to do. I had no idea that you would bring in a bear this evening than I had of doing so myself. I was only joking when I suggested bear meat for supper."

I answered, "Well, you had your joke, and you and the rest of us can have Bear's Foot roasted for supper, and as I have wanted some bear meat for several days, I can please you and myself at the same time."

The whole outfit was amazed when I spoke about roasting the bears' feet. They had never heard of such a thing before. When I got all the feet roasted, I took one from the coals and told the men to help themselves. They all gathered around me to see how I fixed it so I could eat it. When I had it ready to eat, the wagon boss said, "Well, who ever thought of eating Bears' Feet? But it does look nice."

He watched me eat a few minutes and then made the remark that, as I seemed to like it so well, he guessed he would try one, and it was not long before the boys all had a taste of Bear's Foot.

After he had demolished a whole foot, the wagon boss said, "I have tasted almost all kinds of meat, but I must say that I never ate any meat as good as Bear's Foot."

Some of the boys asked me if I could get some more Bears' Feet for supper the next night, and one said he would give me a dollar if I would get a big foot for him.

We got an early start on the road the next morning, and we traveled along all day without anything of interest taking place.

Along in the middle of the afternoon I told the boss that I guessed I would go and hunt some more huckleberries. He said, "I would not exert myself to get any more meat today if I were you. We have enough for supper that was left over from last night."

"Yes, but I want some huckleberries, and I will pick enough for your and my supper if I can find them."

I struck out and rode a mile or more, but I was not at any time more than a half a mile from the train. I came to a little ridge. When I had ridden to the top of it, I saw something in the way of game that was a great surprise to me, as I had not seen any of that kind in several years. It was a large flock of wild turkeys. I saw that they had not discovered me as yet. I looked all around and could see no place where they could roost except a little bunch of timber about a quarter of a mile from where they were feeding. I got back out of sight and rode back to the train as quickly as I could. When I overtook the train, the boss was looking for a place to corral, and it was not long before all was in shape for the night.

I asked the boss if he would like to go turkey hunting that night. His answer was that he always went turkey hunting in the daytime, when he could see to shoot them. I asked him if he had never hunted them at night, and he said no, and had never heard of any one else doing such a thing.

I said, "All right, I will go to the boys from Missouri and ask them, for I have found a flock of wild turkeys, and I know where they roost."

When I told the Missouri boys of my find, they were wild for the hunt. One said, "Do I know how to hunt turkeys by night? You bet I do, and I have a shotgun that will fetch one every pop."

I said, "All right, you can have a chance to try your gun tonight, for the moon will be bright tonight, and we will start right after supper, and I think we will have some fun and all the turkeys we want besides, for the flock was a large one that I saw this afternoon."

When I was ready, I found eight of the boys had their guns all ready and were waiting for me. It was not over a half a mile from camp to the grove where I felt sure we should find the turkeys. When we reached the edge of the timber, I said, "Now, boys, I think we had better split up and two go together, and when any of you see a turkey, shoot him."

In a few minutes all I could hear was "bang, bang" all around me, and once in a while the cry "I've got one" as the hunter captured one he had wounded.

I spent most of my time laying at the foot of a tree, laughing and watching the other fellows shoot and chase the turkeys, but the fun did not last long. In a few minutes it was all over, and when the boys gathered up their game, there were eleven turkeys, and I had not killed a one, but I had my share of the sport in watching the others.

We struck back for camp, all the hunters feeling proud of what they had done. When we reached camp, we found the cook waiting for us with everything that would hold water and stand the fire that he could get hold of full of steaming hot water, ready to scald the turkeys, and all the men pitched in and helped to dress them.

When we were picking the turkeys, the boss said to the cook, "Say, John, can't you preserve one of these birds, so it will keep until we get to Santa Fe, and we will present it to Capt. McKee?"

John answered, "I am afraid it would not keep, Boss. There are too many of us in this crowd that like turkey fried in bear's grease, and after you have had breakfast in the morning, you won't say anything more about preserving turkeys for somebody else to eat."

But notwithstanding this remark John kept two turkeys until we got to Santa Fe the third day after the turkey hunt. We made the trip from Rocky Ford to Santa Fe in thirteen days. We met Capt. McKee coming to meet us about two miles before we reached our journey's end, and with him was Col. Chivington, the commander of the Government Post at Santa Fe. I was riding alone just a little ahead of the train. When I met them, I saluted the Capt. and after we had shaken hands he introduced me to the Col. whom I had never met before, although I had heard of him, and he had heard of me also.

The Col. said, "Mr. Drannan, I have been acquainted with Capt. McKee for several years, and have known him to have been a great Indian fighter, but he tells me that you can do more with the Comanches alone than he could do if he had five hundred soldiers to help him. Now, there must be some secret about this, and I would like to be initiated into it. The Capt. tells me that you went into the Comanches' main village alone, and I presume there were several thousand warriors there at that time, and what seems more wonderful to me," he said, "that you staid and ate dinner with the head Chief. Now my friend, there must be something in this unusual transaction. Will you tell me the secret of your influence with the red men?"

I answered, "Col., if you were a member of a secret organization, would you think it right to give away the secret to outsiders?"

At this answer the Capt. laughed and slapped the Col. on the back, and said, "Col., I reckon, you have got your match in Mr. Drannan, for I have never asked him a question that he did not find a way to answer me without giving me the information that I was seeking."

Col. Chivington smiled but made no answer to the Capt. or me.

We rode in silence a few minutes, and then turning to me the Col. said, "Mr. Drannan, I want you to come to my quarters tonight. I have a little business that I would like to talk with you."

We soon got to headquarters, and as soon as the train was corralled, I saw cook John coming to where the Col. the Capt. and I were standing, and he had a turkey in each of his hands.

As soon as he reached us, he handed Capt. McKee one of the turkeys, with the remark, "Here is your supper, Capt., and yours also, Col." and he gave the other turkey to that Col.

They both looked at John in amazement, and the Col. said, "Thank you very much, but where in creation did you get them?"

John answered, "I did not get them. You must give that honor to Mr. Drannan, and I will say that he has provided every thing good to eat, from turkey to bear feet, since we left Rocky Ford."

I went to Col. Chivington's quarters that evening, and as soon as we were seated, he asked me if I intended to return with the train to Bent's Fort.

I answered. "I have sent word to Mr. Bent that I was coming back to the Fort as soon as I finished my business with the train here, but I have not asked Capt. McKee whether Col. Bent wants my services or not."

At this moment Capt. McKee came in. I said, "Capt., what answer did Col. Bent give to the message that I sent by you?"

He answered, "He said he wanted you to get back to the Fort as quickly as you can, that they want you to go to the Comanche village on a trading trip for them."

I turned to the Col. and said, "You see the position I am in, Col. You must bear in mind that the train does not need an escort back to Bent's Fort, for there are no Comanches between here and there, and I do not see where there is anything to hinder the train in going back in perfect safety."

The Col. then said, "Now Mr. Drannan, what do you expect for your trouble in piloting the train here?"

I answered, "Col., I will leave that matter with you and Capt. McKee. He knows what my services have been and what they were worth."

The Capt. said, "Col., it will be impossible to ever pay Mr. Drannan the worth of what he has done to protect the train through the Comanche country, in not only protecting the Government property, but the lives of the men that were with the train. So Col., you will readily understand what a difficult matter it is to put an estimate on what his services calls for in money."

Col. Chivington sat in thought a few minutes and then said to me, "Mr. Drannan, will two hundred and fifty dollars be a sufficient amount to offer you?"

"That will be owing to circumstances, Col. If I drop the train here it will, but if I am required to pilot the train back through the Comanche country, I would not think of accepting so small an amount."

He then said, "Mr. Drannan, providing we employ you to take the train back through the Comanche country, will there be need of any other escort but yourself?"

I answered, "No sir, I would much prefer to handle the Indians by myself than to have a crowd with me." I then said, "Col., you have the control of this train. Why don't you make a contract with Col. Bent and Mr. Roubidoux to load the train with Buffalo robes to freight back to the Missouri river? I believe that if you could do so, it would nearly if not quite pay the expense of the whole trip."

He answered, "That is something I had not thought of, but it looks as if it might be a good scheme," and turning to the Capt. he said, "Capt. McKee, will you return with Mr. Drannan to Bent's Fort and see if such an arrangement can be made with Col. Bent and Mr. Roubidoux and report to me as quickly as possible?"

The Capt. answered, "Yes, if you think it best, and we want to be on the road early in the morning if I am to make such an arrangement."

Col. Chivington said, "Very well, I will hold the train here until I get your report, and, Mr. Drannan, come to me in the morning, and I will settle with you."

The Capt. and I now left the Col's, quarters, and on the way to our own quarters the Capt. said, "Mr. Drannan, I think you were very unwise in accepting so small an amount as two hundred and fifty dollars for your efforts to save the lives, and more than that, think of what an expense it would have been to the Government to fit out another train to take the place of the one destroyed if the Indians had attacked it, which I have no doubt they would if you had not been there to control them. A thousand dollars is the least you ought to have accepted."

I answered, "Capt., I thank you for your interest in me, and I will profit by it. I have another chance with the Col. if he employs me to take the train back through the Comanche country, which I feel confident he will."

The next morning we were up very early and ready to leave Santa Fe. I went and bid the wagon boss and the other men of the train good bye and told them of the arrangement now pending between the Col. and the people at Bent's Fort. This news seemed to please the boys very much, especially if I were to be their escort through the Indian country. The wagon boss was anxious to know how soon we would know what we were going to do. I told him we would know in eighteen or twenty days at the outside.

Capt. McKee and I now went to the Col's. quarters, and he paid me the two hundred and fifty dollars I had agreed to take. As we were leaving, the Col. said, "Mr. Drannan, if the Capt. makes the arrangement in regard to the freighting of the Buffalo robes, where can I find you?"

I answered, "I shall make Bent's Fort my headquarters from now on until next spring."

Capt. McKee and I now pulled out for Bent's Fort. He being well acquainted with the country, we did not take any road or trail, but took our way across the country by the most direct route, and we made good time all the way. As well as I can remember, it was called in the neighborhood of three hundred miles from Santa Fe to Bent's Fort, and we covered it in seven days on this trip.

When we landed at the Fort, Col. Bent and Mr. Roubedoux were both there. Capt. McKee informed them what he had come for at once, and they were more than anxious to close the deal with him, but they did not have robes enough on hand to load the train. They then inquired how long it would take the train to get there. The Capt. said he thought it would take about twenty-five days; Col. Bent then turned to me and said, "Mr. Drannan, will you take a pack train and go among the Indians and trade for robes for us?"

I said, "Yes, I will." He asked how many days it would take to go to the Indian village and get back. I answered, "To go to the main Indian village and do the trading and get back here will take fourteen or fifteen days."

Col. Bent asked me if I thought I could take twenty pack horses and go to the Indian village and trade for and load them up with the help of two men and get back to the Fort in fifteen days. I told him I thought I could and was willing to try it anyway. "But, Col., I want you to send the quickest and best packers in your employ to help me." He answered, "I have two men that are number one packers, and you can rely on them in every particular." I said, "All right, we will be off tomorrow morning."

We commenced to pack the goods that I was to trade for the Buffalo robes which consisted of knives, rings and beads. We put each kind in boxes by themselves. When I thought we had enough packed to trade for what robes the horses could carry, Col. Bent said, "Here, Will, take some more," and he threw several knives and some rings, and a bunch of beads into one of the boxes. "Maybe you will want a few to give some of the squaws that are such friends to you down there. Such little gifts are never lost among the Indians, you know, Will."

Col. Bent then sent some of his men out to gather up the pack horses so he could pick out enough for a train.

The next morning Capt. McKee said he wanted to have a talk with me when I was at leisure. I said, "Now is your time, Capt." So we started out for a walk. We walked in silence. The Capt. seemed to be thinking. At last he said, "Mr. Drannan, have you made any definite arrangements with Col. Chivington regarding taking the train through the Comanche country?" I answered, "No sir, I have not."

"What will you charge him if you take the job?"

I said, "Capt., I am not anxious to take the job, but if I take it, I shall charge five hundred dollars for my services this time, and I would like you to tell the Col. so when you go back to Santa Fe. I think this amount will be very reasonable from the fact that there will be no more expense. If he had to feed forty or fifty men and pay them wages besides, he would find quite a difference, and after all, they would be no protection to the train, and they and the drivers also would be scalped before they had passed one Indian village. So taking all things into consideration I think that Col. Chivington acted rather close with me, more close than I shall allow him to do again." Capt. McKee said that he thought my charges were very modest, and he continued, "There is another thing I want to talk to you about, provided you go with this train. What do you propose doing when you come back?"

I answered, "I am open for anything that is honorable and has enough money in it to pay me."

He said, "I intended to make up a company soon to go down on the Pan Handle country in Texas, and I expect to go down as far as Fort Worth. I would like you to join me. What do you think of the idea, Mr. Drannan?"

"What is your object in going down there, Capt.?" I asked. He said, "Western Texas is settling up very fast, and the Apache Indians are very bad there. They are murdering the white people every day, and something must be done to protect them from the Red fiends. I have seen enough of your methods with the Indians to satisfy me that you understand them and how to manage them better than anyone I have ever met with, and I am sure you would suit me better than anyone that I know. If you will join me in this undertaking, the state of Texas will pay us well for what we do towards protecting the settlers. I believe the Apache Indians are the most vicious as well as the most treacherous of any tribe of Indians that ever infested the frontier from the fact that they are so mixed with the Mexicans and never have been conquered."

I said, "Capt. McKee, if I take the train back and you are not gone when I come back here, I will join you in this trip to Texas, or if you will leave word where I can find you, if it is within two or three hundred miles of here, I will come to you."

We turned back to the Fort with the understanding that, in case he left the Fort without me, he would leave word where I could come to him.

CHAPTER VIII

The next morning my packers and myself were up early and ready to be off for the Indian village. I told the boys to be sure and take a plenty of rope as all the hides would have to be baled before they could be packed on the horses. One man said, "I have four sacks full of rope, and I reckon that will be enough."

Col. Bent asked me how many hides I thought I could pack on the horses. I told him I could put twenty hides on each horse, and that would make four hundred and forty hides in all. He said, "That would be a big load, and I am afraid you cannot do it. Besides, it is early in the season for the Indians to have so many robes. But do the best you can, and I shall be satisfied." I bid the Col. and Capt. McKee good bye, and we were off.

The second night out we camped near a little village. I told the boys to get supper, and I would go over to the village, and have a talk with the Indians. As soon as the Indians saw me, they thought I had come to trade with them. I told them that I was on the way to the main village and for them to come there tomorrow, and I would be ready to trade with them.

[Illustration: The next morning we struck the trail for Bent's Fort.]

We landed at the main village about noon the next day, making the trip in a half a day less than I had planned to do. We camped near the old Chief's lodge. The boys commenced to get dinner, and I took the two knives that I had promised the Chief and went to his wigwam. I greeted him with a handshake and handed him the knives wrapped in a paper. He opened the package, and I never saw such a smile on a face before as the one that beamed on that Indian's. He examined the knives carefully, and then he told me how proud he was of them and said in his own language he would always be white brother's friend.

I told him that I would be ready to trade with his people the next morning and asked him to inform them of the fact.

The boys had dinner ready when I went back to our camp. I told the boys when I would commence to trade with the Indians, and that I wanted them to be in readiness to begin packing the robes as soon as the Indians gave them to me.

That afternoon I went around among the wigwams and visited the Indians, and they seemed as pleased to see me as children are with a new toy. I showed the squaws the rings and beads I had with me, and I showed the knives to the braves also, and they could hardly wait until morning to trade their Buffalo robes for them.

The squaws showed me the robes they had dressed since I was there the last time, and I saw that they were in a fine condition.

The next morning they commenced coming very early, hardly giving me time to eat my breakfast, and I fixed my price when I bought the first robe, which was one string of beads for one robe, or two rings or one butcher knife, and the reader can rest assured that the Indians kept me busy handing out my goods and taking the robes in payment for them.

About noon one of the packers came to me and said, "Will, I think you have all the robes the horses can carry." I told him to count them, and then we would know, and in a short time he came back with the report that we had bought four hundred and eighty-nine robes. I said, "That is a few more than we can find a place for, isn't it?"

He said, "I reckon we can get them all on, and we will finish baling as soon as we can, but don't trade for any more," and the boys certainly did prove themselves to be expert balers as well as packers.

The next morning as they finished packing a horse, I had to hold him, and so on until the horses were all packed. It was my job to take care of them, and when the horses were all ready for the trail, they surely were a sight to look at. Each horse was completely covered. All there was to be seen of him was his head and his tail.

The next morning amidst the lamentations of the Indians because we could not exchange more of our goods for robes, we struck the trail for Bent's Fort, and we had the extraordinary good luck to cover the distance in three days, and Col. Bent, and Mr. Roubidoux were very much surprised to see us, as well as pleased.

They did not expect to see us in four days more, and when I told them how many hides we had brought, they were more than pleased. Col. Bent said, "Did you have any goods left over?"

I answered, "Yes sir, almost enough to have loaded another pack train."

He said, "Well, well, Will, you can have all our trading to do whenever you want it."

I asked the Col. when he expected the train from Santa Fe. "I don't think it will be here under four or five days," he answered, "and I want you to make yourself at home and be easy until the train comes. You have done enough to lay over awhile, and the rest won't hurt you."

The fourth morning after this I was saddling my horse to ride out on the trail and see if I could see anything of the Government train when Col. Bent asked me where I was going. I told him I was going to see if the train was in sight, "and what is more important to me, I want to find out whether I am going to escort the train through the Comanche country or not."

Col. Bent said, "I thought that was understood. If I thought you were not going to be the escort, I certainly would not trust my freight with the train."

I said, "Col. Bent, I have not made any positive bargain with Col. Chivington, and after Capt. McKee tells him what I said about the price I intend to charge him for my services this trip, he may decide not to employ me."

Col. Bent said, "Would you be offended if I asked you how much money Col. Chivington paid you for that work, Will?"

I said I would not, and I then told Col. Bent the whole transaction, and I also told him what I would charge to escort the train back through the Comanche country, and that I would take the whole responsibility myself without any helpers. Col. Bent said, "Col. Chivington was not fair to you in offering you so small a sum for what you done to protect the Government property, not speaking of the lives you probably saved from the savages' arrows or tomahawks, and I think you charge a very reasonable price if you undertake the job over again and you don't want any one to help you, for they might upset all of your plans by doing something to anger the Indians."

I answered, "Well, Col. I will soon settle the matter if I meet the train."

I then struck out and had ridden perhaps ten miles when I met Capt. McKee and the wagon master coming just ahead of the train.

Capt. McKee said, "Why, Mr. Drannan, I thought you were at the Indian villages trading for Buffalo robes."

I told him that I had been to the Indian village and bought all the robes we could pack back to Bent's Fort and had been waiting for the train to come four days.

Capt. McKee said, "And I expected to have to wait for you four days." I said, "Now tell me what Col. Chivington had to say about my escorting the train."

The Capt. laughed and said, "After the Col. had studied the matter over for about twenty-four hours, he came to the conclusion that he could do no better than employ you. So the job is yours, and Mr. Drannan, can you tell me just about how long you will be gone so I can lay my plans to meet you here at Bent's Fort?"

I said, "Capt., I want about twenty-five days to complete the trip, and as soon as I return, Capt, I will be ready to join you in the expedition to Texas, and Capt., I would like for you to bring my pay here so I shall not have to go to Santa Fe after it when I come back from escorting the train."

He answered, "I will arrange the matter so Col. Bent will settle with you here."

The next morning Col. Bent had his men commenced to load the train, and they put the entire day in this business. That evening the Col. said to me, "Will, if you had a half a dozen more hides, we could not have put them on the wagons."

When we were all ready to pull out, Col. Bent said, "Now Will, I want to give you some presents to give to the squaws."

We went into the store room, and he gave me a dozen butcher knives, saying, "The bucks will be jealous if they don't have something too," and he gave me a dozen rings, and a hand full of strings of beads and said, "Now, Will, you can give these trinkets where you think best and the knives too. I know the Comanche Indians are all friendly to you, but these little trifles will cement their friendship."

I bid everybody at the Fort good bye, and we were off on the journey east.

Everything passed along smoothly for the next two days. We did not see an Indian, and nothing happened to interfere with our progress. The third evening we went into camp near a small Indian village. I rode over to see the Indians and took a couple of knives and a few rings and strings of beads with me. When I entered the village, I inquired where the Chief's wigwam was. A couple of young bucks showed me where it was.

As soon as I saw the Chief, I knew him at once. He was "White Bird," and he had not met me in a year, but he recognized me as quickly as I did him. He invited me into his wigwam and asked me to eat supper with him, which was ready in a short time. As we sat eating, two young squaws came into the wigwam, and White Bird said they were his sisters. I took out a butcher knife and gave it to him, and I gave a string of beads to his squaw and one to each of his sisters. They all jumped up and commenced to dance, and I think they kept it up for half an hour. Then White Bird said in the language of his race, "White Bird and all the Indians of the Comanche tribe always be pale face brother friend."

His sisters said they had some skins of the young dog which they would tan and give to me so I could make some new clothes for myself.

The train pulled out from there, and the third day we came to the main village. Before the train went into camp for the night, I told the wagon boss that I was going to the Indian village and that he need not expect to see me before midnight as I was going to have a good time with the Indians.

I gave my horse into the herders' care and struck out on foot for the Indian village, which was about a half a mile from our camp. Before I reached the Chief's wigwam, I met several Indians, and they accompanied me to the

Chief's lodge. Chief Light Foot saw me before I did him and commenced to shout at the top of his voice, and as I reached his wigwam the Indians were coming from every quarter.

As soon as Light Foot and I had shaken hands, he said, "Stay to supper, and we have a peace smoke and peace dance tonight."

By the time we had finished that meal there was a dozen or more of his uncle Chiefs at the wigwam, and we took our places for the peace smoke.

I will explain to the reader what the peace smoke is. We all took seats in a circle around the head Chief. He lighted the peace pipe, which is a special pipe kept to use on these occasions alone. He took the first whiff himself, blowing it up into the air, and the second whiff he blew into my face. I being his guest of honor, I sat at the right of him. The third whiff he blew into the face of the Chief who sat on his left, and then he passed the pipe to me. I went through the same performance and passed the pipe to the next, and so the pipe went around the circle until all had smoked, and in all the time this smoking was going on there was not a smile or a grunt or a word spoken. Every motion was in the most solemn way throughout the whole performance. As the last one finished smoking, he passed the pipe to the head Chief, and all of the Chiefs sprang to their feet and shook hands with me, from the head Chief down, and the peace smoke was over.

I will say here for the instruction of the reader that the Indians never held a peace smoke with others than the members of their own tribe, without they had perfect confidence in the outsider, who always occupied the seat of honor at the right side of the head Chief of the tribe.

After the peace smoke was over, everybody left the wigwam and everyone, Chief, warriors, and squaws, all joined in the peace dance, I of course taking a part with the rest. I never knew how many took a part in the dance that night, which is always danced in a circle, and every Indian has his or her own way of dancing, and all, old and young, male and female, that take a part are singing.

It would be impossible to explain to the people of this age so they would understand just what a peace dance is and how the people who took part in it looked with the camp fires throwing their lurid light through the darkness of the forest, lighting up the savage faces of the red men, and the not-much-less wild faces of the squaws. It was a strange sight then. How much more strange it would look to the people of this later civilization.

The dance lasted half an hour or more, and all the Indians of both sexes then shook hands with me. I shook the Chief's hand last of all, and as I did so, I gave him the other knife I had brought with me. He took it and, brandishing it over his head, he shouted as loud as he could yell, which was a signal for all the others to yell too and shake their hands towards me. By my giving these knives to the head Chief of the tribe, I cemented the friendship of him and through him of the whole tribe more than I should if I had presented each one of his warriors with a knife.

Amidst the yells of the warriors and their squaws, I left them and walked back to camp, well satisfied with what I had done towards protecting the train as it passed through the Comanche country, for I knew we would not have any trouble with the Indians of that tribe.

The wagon boss and several of the drivers were sitting at the fire waiting for me. As I came up to the fire, the wagon boss said, "What in the name of common sense was the racket about? Why, some of the time this evening there was such a noise over there that we could not hear ourselves think, much less talk."

I answered, "Why, I was just having a good dance with the squaws, and as they all wanted to dance with me first, they made a little noise over it."

He asked, "How many squaws were there in the dance?" and I told him I reckoned there were about a thousand in the crowd.

"And did you dance with a thousand squaws?" he inquired.

I answered, "Why, I certainly could not show any partiality there, could I?"

He said, "Well, if you have danced with that many squaws, I guess you are tired enough to sleep sound."

So we bid each other good night and turned in, and in a few moments silence reigned over the camp.

We pulled out of this camp the next morning and did not see an Indian for the next three days. On the third evening, as we were getting ready to camp for the night, I discovered a small band of Indians coming directly towards us. I told the wagon master where to corral the train, and I then left him and rode on to meet the Indians. As I drew near them, I saw that I knew them all. They were a small band of Comanches, and when I met them they told me that they had been on a visit to the Kiawah tribe and were hurrying to get back to the main Comanche village. I told them of the peace dance I had taken a part in at the main village a few nights before, and they expressed much regret that they had missed the fun.

I asked them if there were many more of their tribe down the country they had come from. They answered, "No more Comanches that way, all gone to village," which proved to be a fact, for we did not see another Comanche Indian on this trip.

I remained with the train four days after this, and, seeing that my services were no longer needed, I told the wagon master that the train was out of danger, as we had passed through the Comanche country, and there would be nothing to interfere with their progress, so I would leave them the next morning.

In the morning, when the wagon boss told the men that I was going to leave them, a number of them came to me and insisted on my taking at least ten dollars from each of them in payment for the bargain I had made with the Comanche Chief regarding the passage of the train on its way to Santa Fe.

Of course, I did not accept their hard-earned money. I told them that I was glad of the privilege of saving their lives. And besides, the Government would pay me for my services.

Cook John had a nice sack of bread ready for me, and I accepted his gift gladly. I bid them all good bye and struck out for Bent's Fort, and it was about as lonesome a journey as I ever made in my life. I avoided the Indian villages when I could, for I knew that the Indians would take more of my time than I could spare if I stopped at all.

I made a rule with myself when I first left the train to ride eight hours and then stop and let my horse rest and feed four hours. This rule I followed day and night, except a few times I overslept, but I gave my horse his feed and rest just the same, and I was back at Bent's Fort on the twenty-third day after leaving there with the train.

The next morning after I got there, Capt. McKee arrived, and he was very much surprised to find me there before him. He had made arrangements for Col. Bent to pay me for piloting the train through the Comanche country, and Col. Bent settled with me that day. The next morning Capt. McKee and I began our preparations for our journey to Texas. He had thirty-two men with him when he came to the fort, and eight more joined us there, making forty in all. Each man had two saddle horses, and there was one pack horse to every four men. Everything being ready, we left Bent's Fort on what would be considered in these days of rapid transit a long and tiresome journey on horse back, over trackless mountains and plains, through valleys, across rivers, in danger of attacks from wild animals and still wilder red men.

I think we traveled between four and five hundred miles without seeing a white person. We camped and lay over one day to give our horses rest where the thriving little city of Amarillo now stands. At that time we had no idea that vast prairie would ever be inhabited by the white race. That part of Texas was the greatest country for Antelope at the time I am speaking of that I had ever seen. Some days we saw a thousand or more Antelope in one drove.

We now began to see plenty of Indian signs all along where we traveled. There were no roads or trails to guide us. We had traveled down what is now called the Pan Handle country, to where the city of Bowie now stands, before we saw a white person after we left Bent's Fort. We met three men there. They were going around through the country hunting for men to assist them to look after a settlement that had been attacked by the Indians the night before. They did not know what tribe had made the attack. Capt. McKee said, "We will go with you and assist you if you will lead us to the place."

We all struck out with the men, and after riding perhaps five miles, we came to the settlement and found that one man had been killed and all the horses and cattle belonging to the people had been driven off.

Capt. McKee asked if they knew what tribe of Indians had made the attack. They answered that they did not know, as it was very dark when the Indians first came, and they could not see them, but they had a skirmish with them, and one man was killed, and the Indians drove the horses and cattle off in a southerly direction. The Capt. asked me if I thought it would be best to follow the savages and try to take the horses and cattle away from them.

I said, "Capt., these people have lost everything they had to depend on to get a living, and what will they do if someone does not do something to help them? And all the way to do that is to get their horses and cattle and return them to the owners."

He answered, "Well, if you will take the lead and do the scout work, we will strike the trail of the Red devils at once."

I said, "All right, Capt., you pick out two good men to assist me, and we will be off at once, for the sooner we are after them the quicker we may overhaul the Red murdering thieves."

In a few minutes the Capt. came to me, and with him were two men. He said, "These men say they are willing to do all they can to help." I said, "I will take the lead, and don't you pay any attention to my movements. You take the trail and follow it as long as you can see it, and when it is too dark to see, go into camp, and if I locate the Indians, whether they are in camp or on the move, I will inform you at once."

It was in the middle of the afternoon when we pulled out on the trail of the Indians. After following them eight or ten miles, I decided in my mind that there were not more than forty Indians in the band we were after.

I said, "Now boys, if we catch these Indians in camp, we can wipe them out and not leave one of them to tell the tale. We have a bright moon tonight, and their trail is so fresh and plain there will be no trouble in following it."

One man asked if I thought we could overtake the Indians in their first camp. I answered, "I think we can, for the Indians will have no fear of being followed and will not be in a hurry and will be off their guard."

We pushed on until about eleven o'clock in the night when we rode up on a little ridge, and, on looking down in the valley beyond, we saw several camp fires, but they were burning very dimly.

I said, "Boys, there are your Indians, and I want one of you to stay here and hold the horses, and the other to go with me, and we will investigate the matter," and said to the man that we left with the horses, "If you hear the report of a gun, mount your horse and lead ours to us at once, for the gun shot will be a signal that we are in trouble and want you to assist us."

My companion and I crawled down near the camp fires, and we saw that all the Indians were lying around the fires asleep, but they were scattered about so that I could not count them.

I whispered to my companion, "Now let us find the stock."

We crept down a little further and found the horses and cattle all feeding quietly, and they were all bunched up together. We went back to the man who had the horses. I told him to mount his horse and take the trail back until he met Capt. McKee and to tell him what we had found, and if it was possible for him to get here by daybreak to do so, "for if we can all be together before daylight, I think we can capture the whole outfit without losing a man."

He mounted his horse and was off at once. He had been gone perhaps an hour, and my comrade and I were sitting talking, when he raised his hand and said, "Hush, I hear something."

"What did it sound like?" I said.

"Like a horse snorting," and he pointed up the trail the way the Capt. should come. We sprang to our feet and listened, and in a minute more we heard the tramp of the horses' feet. We quickly mounted our horses and went to meet them. I told the Capt. what we had found and what position the Indians were in.

He said, "Mr. Drannan, what do you think is the best way to attack them?" I answered, "It is the easiest thing to do imaginable Capt., if we only work the thing right. Dismount all but ten of the men, and we will crawl down and surround the Indians and not fire a shot until daybreak or till they commence getting up, and when we that are on foot commence firing, the ten on horseback must charge down the hill, and if any of the Indians escape our bullets, the mounted men must follow them and shoot them down. When the Indians find that the Whites are after them, they will make a rush for their horses, and that is the time for the mounted men to get their work in."

The Capt. thought a few minutes and then said, "I believe your plan is a grand idea, and we will follow it."

He selected the ten men and then asked me where he should place them. I showed him where I thought was the best place for them to stand. I then pointed to the place where the stock was still feeding and said, "Now boys, when you make your charge on the Indians, charge down between the stock and the fires, and by doing so you will catch the Indians as they run for their horses, and be sure and get every one of them. Don't let one get away."

Everything being understood, we that were on foot commenced to crawl down towards the sleeping Indians' camp. The day was just beginning to break when we got fixed in our positions around them, and it was nearly sunrise before any of the savages crawled out of their blankets. As soon as the first one got out, we shot him down, and we continued to shoot as long as an Indian remained alive. The men on horseback gave a yell and made the charge. When they reached Capt. McKee, one of the horsemen said, "Where is our part of the fight? We didn't get any chance to fire a shot."

The Capt. answered, "It is all over, boys. You will have to wait for the next time for your shot, for I do not think one of this band is alive for you to shoot at. It was one of the quickest-won battles I was ever engaged in," and turning to me the Capt. said, "Mr. Drannan, you ought to join the army, for you would make a first-class General, and I am sure would always lead your men to victory in Indian warfare any way."

We now led our horses down to the Indian camp and staked them out to get their breakfast from the juicy grass that was very abundant in the valley, and then we began to think that we were very hungry ourselves. We had not had a bite to eat since the morning before, and the hard day's ride and no supper and the all-night vigil had about used us up.

Capt. McKee said, "Come, boys let's get some breakfast, for I for one am nearly starved, and we will lay over here until tomorrow morning and let our horses rest and get a little rest ourselves."

After we had satisfied our hunger with a slice of Antelope broiled over the fire and some bread and a cup of coffee, Capt. McKee said to me, "Let us look around and see how many dead Indians we can find."

We struck out together, and we counted thirty-eight, and not one of them had got ten feet from where he had slept, and all their blankets lay just as they had crawled out of them.

I said at the time, and I think now, that that was the most accurate shooting and with the least excitement of any Indian fight I was ever in. It seemed as if every man was as cool as if he was shooting at prairie dogs, and every shot hit the mark. We did not touch the dead Indians but left them as a warning to others who might come that way. We next looked after the stock. By examining the horses, we found that they tallied with the number of Indians, for every horse that belonged to the Indians had a hair rope around his neck, which was a custom followed by all the Western Indians at that time, as by marking a half hitch around the horse's nose he made a bridle of it.

We found twenty-two horses and thirty-two head of cattle that the Indians had stolen from the white settlers. Capt. McKee looked the horses over that had belonged to the Indians and said, "Those are the most valuable horses that I ever saw in the possession of the Indians. They are all good stock, and we will get a good price for them if we take them to Fort Worth, for good horses bring good money there."

When we returned to camp, we saw that two of the young men had their horses saddled. The Capt. asked them where they were going. One of them answered that, as they did not earn any of the honor that morning in killing Indians, they would try to kill some deer for supper, as they knew they would enjoy a piece of good, fat venison and thought the others would, and they believed there was plenty of deer all around there.

Capt. McKee and I spread our blankets and laid down to try and make up for some of the sleep we had lost while in pursuit of the Indians.

About three o'clock one of the boys came and woke us up, saying they had some fine venison all cooked and ready for supper, and that was one of the times that I enjoyed a venison roast. It was as fat and tender as a young chicken.

The next morning we pulled out of there bright and early, and it took us two days to make it back to the settlement that the Indians had robbed and in whose behalf Capt. McKee and I had gone out to punish the thieves, with what success the reader already knows.

As soon as we landed, we sent word to all that had been robbed to come and get their stock. Each owner came and claimed what belonged to him, and when all had taken what they said belonged to them, there were still four horses left unclaimed. These horses we never found an owner for, so we kept them ourselves. The settlers whose property we had returned to them now met and came to find out how much we intended to charge them for what we had done for them. We knew that these people were all poor, and we told them that they might give us what they could afford to pay without distressing themselves. They made up one hundred and forty-four dollars and gave it to us, which was a much larger sum than we expected to receive. After thanking them for their generous payment and refusing their invitation to stay with them longer, we bid them all good bye and continued on our journey to Fort Worth, which had been interrupted by the Indian raid on the settlement.

We had ridden to within ten miles or so of Fort Worth when we met an old acquaintance of Capt. McKee. His name was Reese. There were two other men with him, and they all three wanted to purchase horses. They examined all the horses we had, and then they asked Capt. McKee what we would take for the entire lot. The Capt. asked me what I thought would be a fair price. I answered, "Let the men make an offer before we set a price."

When the Capt asked them what they would give for them, they said they would give a hundred dollars apiece for them if we would help them drive the horses to Dallas.

I told the men that we would let them have the whole bunch and help drive them to Dallas for a hundred and ten dollars apiece. The three men rode off a few yards and consulted together a few minutes. When they came back, they said they would take the horses on my terms.

Capt McKee then told his men to go on to Fort Worth and go into camp, and he told them where to camp and to wait for us and we would come to them as soon as we could. The Capt. then told Mr. Reese to lead on and we would follow.

We drove the horses to Dallas without any trouble and delivered them at Mr. Reese's stable. He paid us the money for them, and we lost no time in pulling out for Fort Worth. It was thirty-two miles from Dallas to Fort Worth, and we passed two houses on the way from there to Fort Worth at the time of which I am writing. I think there were about fifty houses in Fort Worth. I do not know the number there were at Dallas. The place was somewhat larger, but it was a small town.

[Illustration: I took the lead.]

CHAPTER IX.

When we reached Fort Worth, the news met us that the Indians were on the war path in western Texas and were raiding all the white settlements, killing the people and driving off their stock throughout all that part of the state.

We laid in a supply of provisions and tobacco, enough to last three months, and struck the trail for western Texas. The fourth day after we left Fort Worth, we came to a settlement, and all the people were natives of Tennessee, and as that was my native state, I soon made many friends.

The people of the settlement had met together that morning to try to plan some way to stop the depredations of the Indians, but they did not know what to do or where to commence, and they were glad to see the Capt., he being well known as an Indian fighter all over Texas.

When they asked him what he thought best to be done, he said that he could not advise them what to do, but he had come to that part of the State to protect the settlements from the outrages of the savages for the next six months.

We rode to the edge of the settlement and went into camp, thinking we would stay there until towards evening. We had just eaten our dinner when two of the settlers came to our camp and in a very excited manner told us that a small band of Indians had just gone into camp a few miles from the settlement.

We asked them how they got the news. They said that two of the men had been out hunting and saw the Indians when they went into camp.

We told these men to go and bring the men who'd seen the Indians' camp so we could get all the particulars from them. In a few moments the hunters were with us. I asked them how far the Indians' camp was from the settlement.

"Not over five miles," one of them said. I asked which way the Indians had come from and if there were any squaws with them. The answer was that the Indians had come from an eastern direction and there were no squaws with them, and they were driving quite a large band of horses.

Capt. McKee said to me, "What do you think of it?"

I said, "Capt., I am afraid they will move again before night, but I want one of these men to go and show me where the Indians are, and I will locate their camp tonight, and we can get every one of them and the horses too."

Capt. McKee said, "That is a good idea. How many men do you want to go with you?"

I said, "Give me the two men that went with me on the other Indian hunt."

In a little while my men and I were off. I told the Capt. to stay in that camp until he heard from me, which would be before dark.

We had ridden between four and five miles when we came to a little ridge, and, stopping and pointing to a little bunch of timber, my guard said, "The Indians' camp is there."

We dismounted, and, taking one man with me, I crawled to the top of the hill and looked over, and sure enough, there was a small band of Indians squatted around their camp fire, smoking and talking and apparently not fearing any danger.

I told my companion to count them, and I would count too, and we might find out how many there were. I crawled around in the brush keeping out of sight, and I counted forty-eight, and my men made out fifty-one. We crept along on the ridge to see if we could find out how many horses the Indians had with them, but we could not count them, although I was satisfied that there were at least a hundred horses feeding in the valley. Some few of them were staked out, but the most of them were feeding where they chose.

We went back to our horses, and I told the boys to take the horses to a little ravine which was a short distance from us and to find a place where they could not be seen and to stay with them until they heard from me, for I intended to watch the Indians, and if they did not move before sundown I would send one of them to the Capt.

I went back to the edge of the ridge where I could see the savages and watch their movements. They sat and lay around on the grass until nearly sunset when a few of them went to the horses that were staked out and commenced to move them to fresh places to feed, which convinced me that they intended to stay where they were that night. I crept down the ridge to the ravine where the boys were with our horses and told one of them to go back to Capt. McKee and tell him we had found the Indian camp, and that the Indians intended to stay the night where they were, and that I wanted him and the rest of the men to come to me, but not before ten or eleven o'clock that night.

The other man and I led our horses further up the ridge and hitched them, and we then crawled to the top, where we could watch the Indians and not be seen by them. It was not nine o'clock before all the savages had turned in for the night. Seeing that we could now leave the Indians to their slumbers in safety, my companion and I now mounted our horses and struck out to meet the Capt. and his men. We had ridden perhaps a mile when we met the company. I told Capt. McKee how many Indians there were in the band and how many horses they had with them. He said, "Can we take as good advantage of this outfit as we did of the other one?"

I said, "I think we can, only there are more of them to fight in this band, but as far as the ground is concerned we have all the advantage, and we had better station ourselves around them just as we did before and wait for daybreak, or until the Indians begin getting up."

"Shall we have a reserve on horseback as we did before?" he asked.

I told him I did not think it would be necessary in this case. We could get between the Indians and their horses, and if they started to run for their horses as they surely would, they would put themselves into our clutches. And besides, this way would be more pleasing to the men, as they all would have the same chance to shoot Indians alike and could find no grounds to murmur, as they had the last fight.

We rode to within a quarter of a mile of the Indian camp, dismounted and hitched our horses, and we all got near together, and I explained to all the boys the position that all the Indians were in, and also where the horses were.

I took the lead, and we crawled down and took our stations around the sleeping Indians' camp. When every man was stationed and ready for the Capt's. word to proceed to business, Capt. McKee crawled to the place where I was waiting and whispered, "Why not make the charge at once? I will go around and tell the boys, and we will begin the attack with knives. I could kill a half a dozen Indians before the others are aroused, and when the others begin getting up, pull our pistols and finish them before they are fairly awake, and don't let any of them get away. When you see me in among them it will be your time to begin."

He left me as silently as he had come, and I waited, hardly breathing, till I saw his form outlined among the shadows, as the full moon flickered through the branches of the trees.

As soon as the Capt. reached the Indians, every man sprang for the nearest one, and it was a lively little fight for me at least. The first two Indians I struck never gave a grunt, for I nearly severed their head from their bodies. The third one, as I made for him, shouted, "Woughe," and sprang to his feet. I hit him on the back of the neck, but I gave him the third blow before he went down. Just as he doubled up, I saw another coming directly for me, running at full speed. I jerked my pistol, and when he was in a few feet of me I fired, and he fell, and now I could hear the pistols firing thick, and fast, but no more Indians came near me, and the fight lasted but a few minutes longer. One of our men had a hand-to-hand fight with an Indian. They both fought with knives. I did not see the fight, although they must have been near me, and he was the only man that was wounded in the fight, and he was only slightly wounded. He told me that the first he saw of the Indian he was right before him brandishing his long knife, and he said, "I had to work lively for a little bit, you may rest assured, but I finally got a lick at his short ribs, and then I gave him another on the back of the neck and that got him."

As soon as the pistols ceased firing, Capt. McKee came to me and said, "I think we have got them all."

I said, "Now Capt., call the boys together and see if any are wounded."

He stepped out a little ways and called to the men. "If anyone is hurt, report to me at once, so we can attend to you."

No one came to us but the one I have spoken about. He was cut on one arm and had a slight cut on one shoulder. The Capt. said, "Now boys, go around to every dead Indian and take every knife and anything else that you can find that is of any value and bring them here and lay them in a pile," and then he gave me a title when he said, "The scout and I will go and see about the horses."

Capt. McKee gave me this title in fun that night, but he little thought that years after that night I would win the right to not only be called a scout but would have the honor conferred on me of "Capt., Chief of scouts."

We went to where the horses were feeding, but they were so mixed that we could not count them. After we had looked at some of them, the Capt., said, "I wonder where the Indians stole them. Such fine horses are not found every where. Perhaps after daylight we may discover some brand that will show whom they belong to."

We went back to the Indians' camp and saw that the boys had gathered up all that belonged to them. Each one of them had had a nice blanket and nearly all of them had butcher knives. The Capt., said, "Now we will get our horses and stake them out so they can feed, and we will get to our blankets and try to get a few hours rest, for I am dead tired, and I reckon the rest of you boys don't feel any better."

It was nearly sunrise when I opened my eyes in the morning, and there were only a few others stirring, and I was not long in getting something to eat, for I had not broken my fast since noon the day before. In a short time all the men were cooking their breakfast and as soon as the meal was over Capt. McKee asked me what we should do with those horses. I told him, we could not fight Indians and care for a band of horses at the same time. We must drive the horses some where and sell them, and I think we had better go back to Fort Worth, and if we can not dispose of them there we can take them to Dallas.

The Capt. then called four of the men to us and told them to go out where the horses were and count them and to be sure and get the right number. They were gone about an hour, and when they came back they said there were one hundred and twenty horses out there, and one of the men said, "Some of those horses are of the finest breed that I ever saw, and nearly all of them have been broke to the harness, for I could see the marks where the collars have rubbed the hair off their shoulders, and I bet those Indians drove those horses hundreds of miles, maybe from Kansas or Arkansas, and they and the horses being so tired was the reason that the Indians stopped here to rest."

Capt. McKee and I went back and took another look at the horses, and we found them to be much better horses than we had thought them to be, but we could find no brand on them or any thing that would show whom they belonged to. This convinced us that they had been stolen from farmers. As the horses showed that they had been driven hard and we thought a long distance, we decided to stay over one day as the grass was plentiful and a stream of pure, cool water ran a few feet from where they were feeding.

Three of the other men and myself went hunting, and we killed six Antelope and were back in time to cook some for dinner. Capt. McKee and I cooked dinner together that day, and while we ate he told me the conditions he had hired the men to work under. He said he had guaranteed them twenty-five dollars a month, and each man was to pay his portion of the grub bill. "So you can see that the men have no share in these horses, and what we can make out of the sale Of them belongs to you and me alone. And I think we had better pull out for Fort Worth in the morning, and try to dispose of them there."

So the next morning we pulled out, the Capt. and I taking the lead, and the men driving the horses after us.

The evening of the fourth day we reached Fort Worth.

That night we camped a little south of where the Union depot now stands.

The next morning Capt. McKee and I rode into the town to see if we could find a purchaser for our horses. We found a number of men who wanted horses, but each man only wanted a few. Of course, the first question was what price we asked for them. The Capt. and I had set the price at one hundred and twenty-five dollars apiece, which we considered very cheap for such fine stock.

We talked with a number of men, and a few of them said they would come to our camp and look at the horses. So we rode back, and by noon we had sold half of our horses. I heard one man say as he rode off leading four horses that he had paid one hundred and twenty-five dollars apiece for, that he had made a bargain, as he would not take two hundred dollars for the worst-looking one.

After dinner that day a man came and looked at the horses we had left and said, "You are selling your horses too cheap. If you can stay here a few days and let your horses rest, and the people have time to find out what good stock you have for sale, it would pay you well, and you will have no trouble in selling your horses for a much higher price than you have been asking."

The Capt. answered that we had other business to look after, and it was very necessary for us to get rid of the horses as quickly as possible, even if we had to sell them at a disadvantage. The man said, "Well, I will send some men to you this afternoon, and perhaps you can make a bargain with them."

Before the next night we had sold all of our horses at our own price. Capt McKee said, "I think I will settle up with the boys, and then we will see how we stand."

I said, "I think you had better lay in enough provisions to last three months, Capt., for we do not know where we shall be or whether we can get any as good as we can here. And besides, we may not always have such good luck as we have been having the last few weeks."

Capt. McKee bought the grub and then settled with the boys, and then he came to me and said, "Now we will settle between ourselves."

We walked a few yards away from camp and sat down under a large tree, and he showed me a little book where he had everything set down in black and white, and when all was reckoned up there were twenty two hundred and eighty dollars to divide between us two.

As soon as we had divided the money, he said, "Now, are you willing to do the scout work and take the lead of this company? You are the only one in the outfit who understands the duties of a scout. I know this work will very often place you in positions that will be anything but pleasant, but someone must take the chances, and your knowledge of the Indians and his ways of fighting makes you more suitable than any one else in the company."

I said, "I will accept the position, Capt., if I can have the two men that have been with me in the last two hunts, and one more man. And another thing I want understood is that we four men will be exempt from all camp duty and have the privilege of going and coming any time we please without being interfered with."

He said, "All that suits me, and I will see that you are also exempt from cooking. Your meals will be prepared for you from this on."

Capt. McKee now called the men I had selected, and one of the others to come to him, and when they came, he told them of the arrangements we had made and told them they must look to me for their instructions in the future if they were willing to accept the positions as assistants. They all said they were willing to undertake the job if I was willing to teach them what I wanted them to do. One of them said, "Mr. Drannan, when I make a mistake, I want you to tell me of it at once, for I want to do right in everything as much as you will want me to."

I answered that we would commence by learning the private signals to be used when in the Indian country, which I would teach them tomorrow night.

After we went into camp the next morning, just as we were getting ready to pull out, two men came and told us that the Indians were doing a great deal of damage about seventy-five miles in a southwestern direction from Fort Worth. He said they had been making raids on the settlements every few days for several weeks and had killed several people, and the settlers were kept in a constant fear day and night.

As the Capt. was well acquainted all over the country, he knew just where to direct our course, and we pulled out in that direction making as good time on the way as possible.

The second night after we left Fort Worth, we camped on the edge of one of the settlements where the Indians had been making so much trouble. As soon as we were settled in camp, I rode to a house that was perhaps a half a mile from us to get some information regarding the Indians. The man of the house said that the Indians had come every ten days and sometimes oftener, and, said he, "The Indians do not try to kill the people as much as they did to steal the stock or anything else that they could get their hands on."

I asked him what direction the Indians came from, and he answered that they invariably came from the west. I asked whether they were in large or small bands. He said there were seldom more than thirty in a band, and they always came up that river, and he pointed to a small stream not far from us.

I rode back to camp and told Capt. McKee what I had learned. He said, "The Indians must be very sure that no one will be after them now. What do you think is the best plan to adopt?"

I told him that I thought we had better travel down the stream that the Indians seemed to make a pathway of, for one day at least, and go into camp at night, and I would scout around the country and find their main trails, for I was satisfied that only a part of the band came to this settlement. "And what we want to do, Capt., is to cripple them so they would let this settlement alone, and we can do it if we can catch the main band."

We pulled down this little stream and traveled in that direction.

All day we saw lots of Indian sign all the way, but none of them was fresh. As we were going into camp that evening, I told Capt. McKee that my scouts and I would take a circle around the camp and see if there were any Indian camp fires to be seen.

We rode about three miles on top of a high ridge, and looking off to the west we saw a large Indian camp. I knew this by the number of fires they had burning. I pointed to the fires and said to the boys, "There they are. We have found the main camp. But now the difficulty will be to get to them without being discovered by them."

As the darkness was coming on, I could not see well enough to tell how far the Indian camp was from where we stood, but we struck out towards the fires. I told the boys to ride carefully and keep close together, and for each man to keep a close watch in every direction.

We rode about two miles, and almost before we were aware of it, we were close to the Indian camp. I tried my best to count them, but I could not make out the number of Indians there were in the camp. Their horses were staked all around them, and I could not count them either.

I said, "Now boys, we will go back and report to Capt. McKee and see what he thinks is best to do."

It was late when we got back to camp, and they were awaiting our return. Before turning in for the night, I told the Capt. what we had found, and the position of the Indian camp, and that I thought they were about five miles from us.

He sat in thought a few minutes and, turning to me, said, "What plan have you in your mind about making an attack on that camp, Mr. Drannan?"

I said, "They are so scattered that in my opinion it would be impossible to get them all, and I think the best way to make an attack on them would be at daybreak, and for us all to be mounted on our horses. You and your men make the attack, and me and my scouts make a dash for their horses and cut them loose and run them off out of the Indians' reach. Now Capt., I am satisfied that this fight will be no child's play, but will be a nasty little fight, but if we can get the Indians on a stampede and keep them from getting to their horses, I think we can run them down and get the most of them."

The Capt. told the men that they had better not go to sleep that night.

"If we sit around the fire here until three or four o'clock in the morning, you will all get over your scare and feel more like fighting."

One of the boys laughed and said, "It don't affect me in that way, Capt. The more I study about a bad scrape that I expect to get into, the more nervous it makes me."

Capt. McKee answered, "Perhaps you will fight better when you are nervous than you would if you were cool. Anyway, we will take the chances."

We sat around the fire and told stories and smoked until about one o'clock in the morning, and then we saddled our horses and pulled out for the Indian camp and arrived there in good time to look around and see if we could take any advantage of the Indians in the coming fight.

The Capt. selected the place to make the attack and told his men that he and they would sit on their horses and watch for the first Indian to get up, and as soon as the first Indian attempted to get up, they must make the charge, and every man must do all the shouting he could, "for," said the Capt. "if we can get the Indians stampeded once, we will have as good a thing as we want."

I told my scouts, that we would cut the horses loose and turn them in the opposite direction from the one the Capt. was making the charge, and I told the men to cut the horses loose as fast as they came to them, and to pay no attention to the Indians unless they saw them coming towards the horses, but if the Indians, one or many, seemed likely to get to the horses, to pull their pistols and shoot them down before they caught the horses, "for," I said, "every horse we drive away will be equal to killing an Indian, for it will be putting him in the way of the other boy's bullets."

We did not have to wait long before the sound of the guns and the yells of the men as they made the attack on the half-awake Indians reached us, and the din that the two noises made was something dreadful to listen to as it broke on the stillness of the early morning, but my men and I had too much to attend to to pay much attention to what the others were doing.

After the fight had been going on a little while, one of my scouts came to me and said, "I think we have got all the horses loose."

I answered, "Well, we will drive them all to the top of the hill, and then they will be safe from their Indian masters."

We were not long in driving them there. I told one of the boys to stay and look out for the horses, and I and the other two would go back and see if any of the horses had been overlooked in our hurry.

When we reached the village again, we could only hear a shot once in a while, and the yelling had ceased altogether.

We sat on our horses and waited for the pursuers to come back, and in a half an hour the Capt. and all his men were back to the Indian camp.

I asked the Capt. if he got them all. He answered, "I think we did, and I saw the bravest Indian that I ever saw before. After he had been shot three times, he still fought and wounded two of my men."

While the Capt. was speaking, one of the men came near us and raising his right arm said, "Look at that," and I saw where he had been shot through the fleshy part of his arm with an arrow, and calling one of the other men by name, he said, "And the same Indian shot him through the leg, after he had shot the Indian twice, and then I got a hit at him, and as he fell he gave me this wound in the arm. Either one of the three shots we hit him with would have killed any ordinary man."

Capt. McKee now said, "Come, boys, we will scatter all over this little valley and look carefully into every bunch of brush and see if there are any of the Red skins left."

After they had searched a half an hour, all the men returned without finding an Indian. The Capt. said to me, "Where shall we make our camp? For we are very tired and need some sleep."

I answered, "Why not camp here? There is plenty of grass for the horses, and that stream of water that we can hear gurgling through the stones is as cool as I ever drank, and my men and I can go and drive the horses down the hill again and relieve the man that is watching them."

Capt. McKee said, "All right, and the men can get breakfast while you and I go and count the horses."

We counted them three times and made sixty-six each time.

The Capt. said, "I don't believe there were that many Indians in the band. If there were that number and only two men wounded, and all the Indians killed, it will be a wonderful story to tell.

"After we have had our breakfast, we will look around and find and count all the dead Indians and see if the number tallies with the number of horses they had."

In a few minutes the boys that were cooking called out that breakfast was ready, and I was one of the crowd that was ready to eat it.

While we were eating I was amused at one of the boys who was telling of the shines an Indian cut up after he had shot him.

He said he thought he had given the Indian a dead shot, but after he was hit, the Indian rolled over just like a dog that had been whipped, and that he did not think the Indian stopped rolling as long as the breath was in him.

As soon as we had eaten our breakfast the Capt. and I and four others started out to search for and count the dead Indians. We looked around about an hour and a half, and we found forty-two Indian bodies, and they were nearly all armed with bows and arrows, only a few having knives.

Capt. McKee said he thought that we were the luckiest men that ever hunted Indians.

"Just think," said he, "what we have done in the last month, and we have not lost a man. If we keep this kind of warfare up all summer, there will be no Apache Indians left to bother the settlers. Besides, when these warriors do not return, the rest of the tribe will think that something is wrong, and they will take the hint, and we will be rid of them in two or three months."

We now went back to camp, and we all turned in for a day's sleep. As we were laying down, Capt. McKee said, "The first of you that is awake go out and kill some deer, for we want some fresh meat to eat."

When I awoke it was near night, and the boys were cooking venison around the fire. I inquired who had been hunting. They said no one, that the deer came and hunted them, that when they awoke they saw a band of deer out feeding near the horses, and they got four deer out of the band.

I went and found the Capt. fast asleep. I woke him, and we had supper.

I asked him what course we would take next. He said, "There are some settlements up on the Colorado river that we have not heard from in quite a while, and we will go and look after them."

I asked, "On what part of the Colorado river?" and he said, "At Austin."

We had a good night's sleep, and we were astir very early in the morning and pulled out in the direction of Austin, Capt. McKee and I taking the lead, and the boys following driving the horses we had captured from the Indians.

Late that afternoon we struck the trail of a small band of Indians. I did not go far before I saw that it was quite fresh. I told the Capt. that he had better camp there, for there was plenty of grass and a nice stream of water, and let my scouts and me follow the trail and see if we could find them, to which he consented. My men and I left the main party and started on the trail of the Indians. After trailing them four or five miles in an almost eastern direction, the trail turned to the southwest. We kept on for four or five miles more, and then we came to where the Indians were in camp. I had kept the lay of the country and the direction of our camp in my mind, and when I saw the Indians, I knew that their camp was near ours.

They had a fire and were cooking meat around it. We counted them and found that there were thirteen Indians in the band.

I said, "Now boys, we will go back to our own camp and report to the Capt. at once," and I was really surprised to find it was so short a distance between the Indians' camp and ours. It was not more than a mile from one to the other.

When we reached camp, we found the Capt. and the men waiting for us and very anxious to hear what we had found. I reported to the Capt., and he asked when I thought it best to go after the Red wretches. I told him there was so small a bunch of them I did not think it mattered, but as his favorite time for an attack seemed to be at break of day, I supposed we could wait until then for this one.

He laughed and said, "The break of day has been your time, not mine, Mr. Drannan. You have done all the planning and led all the fights in this campaign, but I am glad to admit that it has been a grand success, and so far you have come out with flying colors."

I said, "Well, Capt., I think in this case we can take a little nap and be up in time to take that outfit before they have time to wake up, for it is no more than a mile from here to their camp."

Capt. McKee answered, "I reckon you are right. There are so few of them that we shall not have to delay breakfast to get them."

We all turned in, and, although we knew that Indians were so near us, we were not afraid to sleep without placing a guard over the camp.

When I awoke, I looked at my watch and saw it was two o'clock. I called the Capt. and told him that it was time we were moving. He asked whether we should go on horseback or on foot. I said, "We can walk there while we would be saddling the horses, it is so short a distance." He said, "All right, we will take twelve men with us," and in a few minutes we were on the road. When we came in sight of the dimly burning campfires of the Indians, I pointed to them and told the Capt. that was the place, and I said, "We will be very careful and not make any noise, and I think we can send them to the Happy hunting grounds while they sleep." But the reader may imagine our surprise when we crept to the Indian camp to find that there was not an Indian there. We looked around the camp where the Indians had cooked their supper, and then we looked for their horses, but they too had disappeared with their masters. Capt. McKee said, "Doesn't this beat you? What do you suppose caused those Indians to leave?"

I said, "This is one of the times that the Indians were smarter than we and have out-generaled us. Probably they too had a scout out, and he saw us before we discovered their trail and reported the fact to the others, and they made themselves scarce, which was a very wise proceeding on their part."

We turned and walked back to our own camp and found the boys we had left there still asleep. I said, "Capt., I think you had better stay here with your men and my scouts, and I will find the trail of those Indians and see where they have gone. It may be that they are a part of a large band and have gone to inform the main tribe of our being here. If this is the case, we will be sure to have some trouble with them."

The Capt. woke the men, and they cooked breakfast from some of the deer that was left over the night before, and in a short time my men and I were off on the trail of the Indians. I told my men they had better take something for a lunch, as it was no telling when we should come back.

We went to where the Indians had camped and soon found their trail leading from it. It led us in a southwestern direction, and we followed it until about twelve o'clock when all at once we came on the Indians laying around a camp fire sound asleep.

I said, "Now boys, there are only two ways to choose from. We have either got to tackle this outfit ourselves alone, or we must give up the idea of getting them at all. Now I will leave it to you to choose which to do."

They were all more than anxious to make the attack. I said, "Now boys, ride slowly and easy until you get in the midst of them, and then don't wait for each other, but turn loose, and each do our best, and let us get every one of them if we possibly can," and it was surprising to me to see how cool the whole three men were in attempting to kill these Indians while they slept. There was not a sound until we were in the midst of the sleeping Indians, and then it seemed as if every man shot at once and aimed to kill, and there were only five Indians out of the thirteen that had time to spring to their feet, and these did not try to defend themselves, but made for their horses with the attempt to get away. Only one of them reached his horse, and as he sprang on his horse's back, I gave him a cut with my knife across the small of his back and almost cut him in two. He tumbled to the ground without a word, and as he did so, one of the boys shouted, "We have got them all. That was the last one, and that was the easiest little fight that I was ever in."

I asked if either of them was hurt. One man said, "Hurt? No, why durn their shadows, they were not awake enough to hurt a fly if it had been in their mouths."

I could not help laughing at his droll way of expressing his contempt for the easily won battle if such it could be called when all the fighting had been on our side.

We staked our horses out to let them eat the sweet grass that was so abundant there, and we sat down and ate our own luncheon beneath a large tree, and after we had satisfied our hunger, we laid around and rested a while, and then we mounted our horses, I taking the lead and the boys driving the Indians' horses after me.

We struck out for camp and reached the place where Capt. McKee and his men were in camp a little after dark.

The Capt. was surprised indeed when we rode into camp with the band of strange horses, and the men commenced to cheer us as soon as they saw what we had with us.

One of my scouts said, "We don't want to go with you any more, Capt. McKee, for you do your work at night and our boss does his work in the daytime."

We dismounted and gave our horses to the man who had the care of the horses and sat down to a supper of fried fish, and we surely did justice to that meal, as we were very hungry.

After we had finished the meal, I told the Capt. all about our day's work in trailing the Indians and surprising them as they slept, and how we wiped the whole band out before they were awake.

The Capt. said, "Tomorrow morning we will keep on down toward the southwestern settlements."

I asked him how far it was to the first settlement, and he answered, "We will make it by tomorrow night."

CHAPTER X.

The next morning we were on the road very early, and we traveled nearly all day before we reached the first settlement.

There was a little cluster of houses there, perhaps fifty all together, and they were as prosperous farmers as I had seen in Texas.

They were all acquainted with the Capt. and were glad to see us.

We staid at this place a couple of days to let our horses rest, and we sold twelve of the horses that we'd captured from the Indians to the farmers.

The people there told us that it was three months since the Indians had made a raid on them, and there had not been any Indians through that neighborhood since the raid, but they had been told that the Indians were doing a great deal of damage to the settlement forty or fifty miles west of there.

Capt. McKee said, "Well, we will go down and investigate."

As we were leaving the village, an old acquaintance of the Capt. said, "Let us know when you are coming back, and we will have a banquet and a dance while you and your men are here."

Capt. McKee answered, "We will not come back until you have another visit from the Indians, and I don't believe you will want to dance then."

We pulled out for the settlements where the Indians had been making the trouble.

In the middle of the afternoon of that day we struck the trail of what appeared to be quite a large band of Indians, and after following it a short distance I concluded it was a fresh trail. Capt. McKee said, "What do you think is best to do? The whole company to follow their trail, or my men and I stop here and you and your scouts keep on after them and locate them if you can?"

I answered, "Judging from the appearance of the trail, I think we would be running a great risk for the whole company to keep on, and I think it would be the safest plan for you to stop here and let my scouts and me trail the Indians until they camp for the night, and, Capt., as you are acquainted with the country, can you tell me how far they will be likely to travel until they strike good water and grass again?"

He said, "I don't believe they will find a good place to camp in five miles from here and maybe further."

I said, "Well, Capt., go into camp here, and if you do not hear from me by dark, have everything in readiness for an immediate start."

My men and I now took the trail of the Indians. We traveled with great caution for several miles, and as it was just beginning to grow dark we came in sight of the Indian camp fire. I left two of my men with the horses, and taking one man with me I crawled near enough to count the Indians, and I was surprised when I saw how few there were sitting around the fires. I could only make twenty-five, and I counted them over several times, and they had made a trail big enough for a hundred Indians. I was satisfied that they must have a large number of horses with them. So we crawled down where they had left the horses to feed, and I saw that I was right. There was a large band of horses, feeding. I could not count them they were so scattered, and the darkness hid them, but I thought there were from a hundred to a hundred and twenty-five horses in the bunch.

We went back to our comrades and mounted and took the back trail to where the Capt. was waiting for our return. As soon as we arrived, I reported to Capt. McKee what we had found. After I had told him the number of Indians in the band, and the number of horses I thought there were, he asked me when I thought was the best time to make the attack.

I answered that any time between that moment and daylight would do, for we had a soft snap before us. He said, "Well, you boys get something to eat, and we will saddle the horses and go for them and have it over with."

In a very short time we were all ready and off for the Indian camp.

When we could see the fires, the Capt. asked, "Which way we shall make the attack, on our horses or on foot?"

I told him that was for him to decide, but that there were so few of them that I thought it would be to his advantage to make the attack on foot.

"It will be impossible for them to get away, for my scouts and I will be between them and their horses, and if any of them should get away from you, we will attend to them before they can get to their horses."

The whole company dismounted, and without making the least noise they crept down to the Indian camp, and in a few moments the firing commenced. But it was only a short time before we knew that it was over, as we heard the boys shouting, and in a moment more we were with them at the Indian camp. I asked them what they made such a racket about, and they said that they were shouting for more Indians to come, that there were not enough of them to go around.

One of the boys said that every time he drew a bead on an Indian, someone else had got in before him, and that he did not get a chance to shoot one Indian in the whole fight.

The Capt. and his men now went and got their horses and unsaddled them and staked them out, and we all turned in for the night.

The next morning the Capt. was up before I was awake, and he and his men had counted the horses that the Indians had. He came back as I was just getting up and said, "Guess how many horses there are in the bunch we have taken?"

"I counted a hundred and twenty-five last night," I answered.

He said, "You are a pretty close guesser. There are just one hundred and thirty-two in the band, and some of them are as fine work horses as I ever saw in Texas. It is a mystery to me where the Indians get such nice horses. Do you think it possible that these wretches have been into Kansas and robbed the people there?"

I said, "It would be hard to tell, Capt., where they got them, for they go anywhere that they think there is anything to steal."

After we had eaten breakfast, Capt. McKee proposed that he and I go to the settlement alone and leave the men in camp until we came back. He said that the settlement was no more than five or six miles from where we then were in camp, and perhaps we could get some information in regard to where the Indians had been stealing stock and doing other depradations to the settlers.

When the Capt. told the men what we proposed doing, one of them said, "That just suits me for one, for we are out of meat, and while you are gone we can go hunting and have a new supply when you get back."

The Capt. said, "All right, but take care of the horses and not let any of them get away, and don't look for us until we come back."

We mounted our horses and struck out for the settlement. A two-hours ride brought us there, and we found that Capt. McKee was acquainted with most of the settlers, and they welcomed us gladly, for at that time when everyone had to travel on horseback or walk. There was not so much visiting, and the sight of a friendly face was very pleasing to the people who lived at those isolated settlements.

When we inquired if the Indians troubled them, they said the Indians had not raided that place in three months, but about three weeks before someone saw a band of about twenty-five Indians going towards the east, and they were the last Indians that had been seen in that neighborhood, but they had heard that the Apache Indians had been doing considerable mischief fifty miles or so further south, but they did not know whether the report was true or not, and they of this settlement had been careful to have their stock cared for by herders through the day, and at night they were put in the corral.

The Captain asked if we could make arrangements with them to take charge of over a hundred head of horses for a month or so, and if so to care for the same as their own by day and at night. The man we were talking to said that his son had charge of the stock in the daytime and would be at the house for dinner, and that we had better stay and have a talk with him.

It was not long before the young man came in, and the Captain asked him what he would charge to herd a few more than a hundred horses for a month, or longer. The young man said that he would take them at twenty-five dollars a hundred, and we could leave them with him as long as we pleased at that price, and that they should have the best of care while he had the charge of them.

At this moment the lady of the house came on the porch where we were sitting and invited us in to eat dinner, and she told the Captain she had prepared a special dinner for him.

The Captain laughed and said: "Well, my good woman, here is my comrade, Mr. Drannan; what shall we do with him? I expect he is hungry, too."

She said: "Well, Captain, you may invite him in. Maybe you can spare enough for him to have a taste. I have only got a gallon of green peas and a ham of venison roasted and four squash pies and a pan of corn bread cooked for you, so I reckon you can spare Mr. Drannan a little bite."

As we went into the house the man said, "My wife must think you are a pretty good eater Capt." to which the lady replied, "I tried him a year ago, and I have not forgotten how much it took to fill him up then."

We sat down to the table amidst the laughter that followed this remark, and I can safely say that I never ate a meal that I enjoyed more than I did that dinner, and I thought that the Capt. had not lost the appetite the lady gave him credit for having the year before. And what made the meal more enjoyable was the Texas style of cracking jokes from the time we sat down until we left the table, and I will say this for Texas that of all the states I have ever visited from that time until this day Texas was then and is now the most hospitable.

It is fifty years ago that I ate that meal in the little settlement that was miles away from the busy cities, and I can with safety say that I have found in the state of Texas more large hearted people than I have found in all the other states put together that I have visited.

When we were leaving the house we told the young man that we would come back the next day and bring the horses for him, to take care of.

We left the settlement and struck the trail for our camp, and we found that the boys had good success in hunting. They had four deer all dressed and hanging to the limbs of trees.

That evening I asked the Capt. what course he intended to pursue now. He said, "We have the horses off our hands for a time at least, and we will pull south for a month or six weeks, and then if all is well we will come back and get our horses and pull for Dallas. By that time the farmers will have disposed of their crops and will have money more plenty, and I think we can do better in selling our horses than we ever have done. I think we have crippled the Apache tribe so much that some of the settlements will not be troubled with them again, and if we are as successful in our fights with them the balance of the season, they will be pretty well down, and what a great blessing it will be to the people of this country that we came to their relief."

The next morning Capt. McKee and I and the whole company broke camp and struck the trail for the settlement, driving the captured horses before us. We met the herder coming to meet us. He assisted us to drive them to his corral and helped us to count them, and there were one hundred and thirty-eight horses in the band. Nearly everyone in the settlement was at the corral when we got there. The people had heard that we were coming, and everybody wanted to see the horses we had fallen heir to when we killed the Indians.

When we told them what we would sell the horses for, some of the men said that they wanted horses and would have the money to pay for them when they disposed of their crops in the fall.

The horses being off our mind, we started for the south, and as we were passing the house where we dined the day before, the lady came to the door and called to Capt. McKee, saying, "Captain, when you get ready to come back this fall, send a runner on ahead, and I will have a square meal all cooked for you."

All the boys heard this, and thinking it must be a joke on the Captain, they all cheered and clapped their hands. The Captain took off his hat and made a bow and thanked the lady, and we all rode on, but the Captain did not hear the last of this joke all summer. Whenever he complained of being hungry, some of us would remind him of the square meal that was waiting for him at the settlement.

We traveled four days, passing through several settlements before we heard of any Indians. As we were going into camp on the evening of the fourth day, two men rode in and said that they had seen a band of Indians a couple of hours before, and there were as many as twenty or more in the band, and that four of the Indians had chased them several miles, and that the Indians seemed to be traveling in an easterly direction.

I said to the Captain, "Let's have the men take supper with us and then go back and show us where they saw the Indians."

He asked them if they were willing to go and show us, and they said they would.

We struck out as quickly as we could, and I think it was all of ten miles before we struck the Indian trail. As soon as we found the trail the Indians had left, Captain McKee thanked the men and told them he would not trouble them to go any further. They inquired if he intended to follow the Indians up and make an attack on them. He told them that was what he expected to do if we found them. They said, "Why, can't we go with you and help to fight the wretches? We both have guns and pistols too, and we would like to get even with them for the run they made us take against our will."

The Capt. said, "I am willing for you to accompany us, but you must watch my men and do as they do, if you are sure you want to put yourselves in the same danger of being killed that we do."

They both said together, "That is just what we want to do, Capt. We want to learn how to fight the Red devils, and this will be a grand chance for us to learn to do it in style."

Myself and my scouts took the lead on the Indian trail. I told the Capt. to ride on slowly, and as soon as I came up with the Indians I would inform him of it.

We three followed the Indian trail until the day was breaking, and when we first saw their camp fires, we were only a short distance from them, as they were down in a little narrow valley, and we were almost over them before we saw them.

We dismounted, and I sent one man back to tell the Capt., and one I left to care for the horses, and the other I took with me, and we crawled down the hill through the thick brush to try to see what position the Indians were in and find out what the best way would be to attack them.

When we had got to within a hundred yards of their camp, I saw an Indian crawl out of his blanket and go to one of the fires and put more wood on it. I whispered to my comrade to stop, and I told him we could not go any nearer now, and in another moment two more Indians got up.

I said, "Now let us get back to our horses as quickly as we can."

As we reached the edge of the brush, I looked around to see where their horses were, but there was not a horse in sight. We kept on until we reached our horses.

I said, "Now boys, you both stay here, and I will ride down the ridge a little way and maybe I can see their horses, and be sure to keep a close watch on the Indians' movements, and if they appear to be excited, signal to me at once."

I discovered their horses feeding quietly about a quarter of a mile below their camp. This seemed very strange to me, and that the horses were not staked out but allowed to run loose seemed still more strange.

I turned and rode back to my two scouts, and after I had told them what I had seen, I said, "Boys, I am tempted to make a proposition."

They asked what it was. I said, "It may not work, but I have a mind for us to go down where the Indians' horses are and get around them and stampede them and drive them to meet the Capt. and the men with him."

Just as I finished speaking, one of the men said, "Hark, it is too late. The Capt. and his men are here now," and sure enough there they were in sight.

When I told the Capt. about the Indians and their horses being so far from them and running loose, he said, "There is something up you may be sure, for it is a very unusual thing for an Indian to do to leave himself so unprotected by letting his horses run at large."

He then asked if I had any idea how many there were in the camp below us. I told him that I had not counted them and could not do so the way the camp was situated and the fires so dim.

He then asked if I wanted any more help to run the horses off. I answered, "No sir, if you and your men will attend to the Indians, I and my scouts will attend to the horses, and you need have no concern but we will get them away all right. We will run them up on this open ridge and hold them until you finish the Indians, and you will know where to find the horses and us."

The Capt. and his men struck out for the Indian camp, and my men and I to get the Indians' horses. We had not reached the horses when we heard the sound of the guns. We had just succeeded in getting the horses on a lope when we heard someone shouting behind us, and turning in my saddle I saw two Indians coming on a run, and they were running for all they were worth.

I said, "Boys, let us wheel our horses and get those Indians," and I had hardly turned my horse when the report of their guns rang out, and both of the Indians dropped in their tracks.

In a moment more a cry came from one of the others, and looking in another direction I saw one of the Capt's. men in full pursuit of two Indians, and he was shouting at the top of his voice, "Lookout, boys, we are coming."

I said, "Now boys, let us get these horses away from here quick, for the Indians are coming in every direction, and in a few minutes they will be upon us, and we will have to fight them and perhaps lose half of the horses, and some of us may get hurt besides."

We spurred our horses and soon had the Indian horses on the dead run up the hill, and on the prairie where we had told the Capt. to come and look for us.

When we had got control of the frightened horses and had time to listen, we could hear the cracking of the guns in every direction, and we knew that it was a desperate fight that was being fought.

I said, "Boys, let us count the horses, and we can then have some idea how many Indians the other men have to contend with."

We found that there were fifty-eight in the band, and we knew that they had all been ridden by the Indians, for each one had a hair rope around his neck, so we decided that there must have been fifty Indians in the camp when the Capt. and his men made the attack on them.

It must have been an hour or more before the Capt. and his men began coming back. When Capt. McKee came back to the hill, he said, "This has been the hardest fight that I have had with the Indians in years. They were nearly all up when I struck their camp, and they were all on the fight. Five of my men are badly wounded, and I don't believe we got near all of the Indians. We must attend to the wounded men first, and then we must take a scout around and see if we can find any more of the Red fiends."

He asked where I thought was the best place to make our camp. I answered that there was a level spot a little below where I'd found the Indians' horses that would make a good camping ground.

He said. "I will go and find the place, and you and your men drive the horses down where you found them."

We had got about half way down to the valley with the horses when one of my men said, "Look out. See what is coming."

I looked where he pointed and saw an Indian running from the brush and making for the horses as fast as he could run. I said, "Let's go for him, boys, and don't get too close to him before you shoot, for he has his bow and arrow ready to shoot you if you don't get him first."

I raised my gun as we went for him and fired and broke his leg, and one of the other boys got close to him and shot him with his pistol and finished him.

We now rushed the horses down to the village in a hurry. When we had got them there, I told the boys that we must watch the horses all the time and change herders every two hours. I went to where the Capt. had established his camp, and I found that five of the men were badly wounded. One was wounded in the hip, and it was the worst arrow wound I ever saw.

I asked the Capt. what he was going to do with those wounded men. "I don't see how you are going to get them to a doctor, and I don't believe they will get well without one. So what are you going to do?"

He said if we could get them back to the settlement where we had left the horses, they could have a doctor's care.

I said, "Well, but let's get them something to eat as well as ourselves, for they must be faint for the lack of food and losing so much blood, and if they are no better by evening, I think you had better send for the doctor to come here and not try to send the men to him for treatment." The Capt. agreed to this, and as soon as we had something to eat, I went to where the wounded men were laying and examined their wounds myself and was surprised to find the men so cheerful. They were laughing and talking just as if they were well.

I asked the one that was so badly wounded if he thought we had better send for a doctor to dress the wound. He said, "No, I don't want any doctor. If you will get me a plenty of the balsam of fir to put on it, it will be well in a week." I answered, "If that is all you want, my friend, I will see that you get all you want of that, for there is plenty of it all around us."

I will say for the instruction of the reader that this birch taken from the fir trees as it saps out of cracks in the bark was the only liniment that the frontiersman had to heal his wounds at that time, and it was one of the best liniments that I have ever seen applied to a sore of any kind.

I now hunted up the Capt. to have a talk with him. I asked him what he proposed doing until those men were able to travel, as they didn't want any doctor and said they could cure their wounds themselves with balsam of fir.

The Capt. said, "Well, we will leave enough men to guard the wounded men and the horses, and we will take the others with us and go and search for more Indians."

Capt. McKee left ten men to guard the camp, and the balance of us struck out on a hunt for stray Indians.

We were gone from camp two or three hours, and we only found one Indian, and he was wounded, but we found a number of dead Indians scattered all through the timber where the men had shot them down as they ran, or as they met them in hand-to-hand combat.

After we got back to camp, I asked the Capt. what he was going to do with those horses.

He said he thought it would be the best plan to stay where we were until the men were able to travel and then to go back to the settlement and get our other horses and then pull for Dallas. "For," said he, "I do not believe that the Indians will make any more raids through this part of the country until next spring, and they may never come back, for we have crippled them so that they will shun a place where they have met such disaster. There has never been a company through here that has had the success in killing Indians and capturing their horses as we have had this spring. Just think what we have done, and not one of our men has been killed."

We remained in this camp two weeks, and everyone had a good time with the exception of the wounded men, and even they were more cheerful than one in health could have thought possible.

Game was plentiful and easy to get, and we had all the fresh meat we wanted, and it was an ideal place to lay around and rest when we were tired hunting, and there was a plenty of grass for the horses and a cool spring of water to quench the thirst of man and beast.

After the first week, the wounded men took more or less exercise every day, and so kept their strength, and it was surprising how fast their wounds healed.

The day before the one set to start for the settlement, I asked the man that had the wounded hip if he thought he could ride on horseback. He answered, "Yes, if I had a gentle horse so I could ride sideways, I could stand it to ride a half a day without stopping to rest."

I told him that I had a horse that was very gentle and would just suit his case.

That evening the Capt. and I talked the matter over together. He said he thought we had better pull out in the morning and travel slowly so as not to tire the wounded men too much, for the farmers would have sold their crops by the time we got to Dallas, and we could do as well with our horses as we could at any time of the year.

In the morning we left the camp that we had grown to almost love, the Capt. and I taking the lead with the wounded men at our side, and the other men brought up the rear, driving the horses who had grown fat and glossy in the weeks of rest.

When we were mounted, the Capt. said to the wounded men, "Now boys, when you begin to feel tired, say so, and we will stop and camp at once."

I never heard a word of complaint from one of them, and we had ridden ten miles or so, when we came to a cool stream of water and a plenty of grass, and the Capt. said, "This is a good place to stop and give our sick boys a rest."

So we dismounted and went into camp. After we had our dinner, several of the men came and asked the Capt. if he was going any further that night, and he replied that he was not. The boys said, "All right, we will catch some fish then."

In about two hours they came from the stream, and each man had a string of good-sized catfish, and the reader may be sure that we all enjoyed that fish supper.

From the time we left the camp in the valley until we reached the settlement, we only traveled ten miles a day.

We traveled this way for the benefit of the wounded men, and they reached the settlement not worse for the journey, but they were much stronger than when we started.

The morning before we reached the settlement, as we were about to mount our horses, one of the men said to the Capt., "Say, Cap, haven't you forgotten to do something?"

The Capt. looked around in a surprised way and said, "I do not remember anything that I could have forgotten to do. What is it?"

The man said, "Didn't you agree to send a runner on ahead to notify that lady that you were coming so she could have the grub cooked for your dinner?"

But the Capt. never answered the question, for before he could speak, there was such a clapping of hands and laughter from all the men that it would have been impossible to have heard him if he had tried.

After the boys had stopped cheering, the Capt. said, "You have the laugh on me now boys, but you wait, and I will get even with you, and he that laughs last laughs best."

We reached the settlement about the middle of the afternoon and we found our horses in much better condition than we expected to.

We staid here all the next day as we were told that several of the farmers near there wanted to purchase horses from us and would come as soon as they heard that we were there.

Before night we had sold thirty-one horses at a fair price. About noon of that day the Capt. and I were sitting under a tree having a smoke when a little girl came to us and said, "Capt., mama says you and Mr. Drannan come and take dinner with us."

As neither of us knew her, the Capt. asked where she lived and who her mama was.

She said, "Come on, and I'll show you," and when we went with her, it proved to be the same place where we had dined the last time we were at the settlement.

Their name was "Jones." The man and his wife met us on the porch and shook hands with us, and the lady said, "Capt., you have been very lucky in killing Indians and pretty lucky in getting something to eat with us. You had some of our first picking of peas last spring, and you will have some of our first turnips today."

The Capt. told her that of all vegetables, he liked young turnips best. She said that she had enough for dinner and supper too, and that we might consider ourselves invited to supper too.

We ate dinner with this hospitable family, and then we went back to the corral and the selling of our horses, which commenced soon after we got there, as the farmers came early in the day.

That night we paid the herder for his care of the horses, and then we pulled out for Dallas.

CHAPTER XI.

I do not remember how many days it took us to reach Dallas, but it was in the middle of October when we rode into that city.

This was in the fall of fifty-eight, and the news had just reached Dallas that gold had been discovered on Cherry creek in the territory of Colorado, and the excitement was intense. All over the city people talked of nothing else but gold, and of all the exaggeration stories about gold mines that I had ever heard, the ones told there were the most incredible. The parties who brought the news to Dallas had not been to the mines themselves, but had been told these wonderful stories at Bent's Fort.

Capt. McKee caught the gold fever right away, and he said to me, "I am going to get up a company in the spring and go to those new gold mines. Don't you want to go with me?"

I answered, "No, Capt. I do not, for I know that Cherry creek country, and I do not believe that there is a pound of gold in all that country. It is nothing but a desert."

He said, "Have you been to Cherry creek?"

I answered, "Yes sir, a number of times."

"Where is Cherry creek?" he asked. I told him that Cherry creek headed in the divide between the Arkansas river and the South Platte river, and emptied into the South Platte river about twenty miles below where the Platte leaves the Rocky mountains and near the center of the territory of Colorado. Capt. McKee said, "Well, I am going anyhow. I did not go to California when I ought to have gone, and maybe this will prove as rich a country for getting gold as that did."

I laughed and answered, "There may be lots of gold in Colorado, Capt., but you or anyone else will never find enough gold in Cherry creek to make you rich."

He said, "Well, the way to find it is to go there and look for it. We surely never will if we stay away."

From the way the people talked, one would have thought that everybody in Dallas was going to the gold fields.

After it was known that I had been through the country where the gold mines were reported to be, a great many men came to me to make inquiries about the country, and some of them seemed surprised because I took the news so coolly and did not seem anxious to go there.

The excitement did not last more than a week before it commenced to die away.

By this time we had about disposed of our horses, and the wounded men were able to go to their homes.

The Capt. settled up with the men, and he and I divided the remainder of the money.

After we were square, the Capt. asked what I was going to do. I told him that I was going back to Bent's Fort. He said, "Well, won't you wait a few days until I can organize a company to go with me to Colorado, and we will go with you as far as Bent's Fort?"

I said I certainly would, for the journey would be very lonely for me to go alone, and I liked company, and besides I was in no hurry to get there.

The Capt. worked steadily to get recruits for his company for two weeks, and he succeeded in getting ten men in all that time.

He said, "This beats anything I ever undertook. When we first came to Dallas, the whole town talked as if they were crazy to go, and now I can't get anybody to join me, but I will make the effort with the ten men that will go, and if this is a success and we make fortunes, we will come back and surprise the city."

I said, "Alright, Capt., but if the people of Dallas are ever surprised, it will not be from hearing of the great amount of gold you and your companions took from Cherry creek."

The Capt. now commenced to get ready for the journey to Colorado, the land of reported gold. Each of his men had to have two saddle horses, and one pack horse for every two men, and each man had three months provisions, consisting of flour, coffee, salt and tobacco.

The question of getting meat was never thought of as one could get a plenty of that anywhere on the journey, and the streams were teaming with the most delicious fish.

The evening before we were to set out in the morning the Capt said, "Which way shall we go?"

I said, "Although it is getting late, and we may have some cold weather to contend with I think our best and most direct route will be by what is called the Panhandle route. There will be no rivers to cross, and there is a plenty of grass for the horses, and also there is nice drinking water in abundance all the way for ourselves as well as the hordes, and there will be days when we will be in sight of Deer and Antelope from morning until night."

There were a few scattering settlements along the trail. The place which is now the city of Childress being the largest, and also the last settlement we passed through, and the last sign of civilization we saw until we struck Bent's Fort which was on the Arkansas river below what is now the city of Pueblo in the state of Colorado which was at that time a territory just a little north of what is now the city of Amarillo.

We killed our first Buffalo on that trip.

It is surprising to the people who saw that country at that early day when they travel through it now and see what civilization has done. There is Amarillo, which has several thousand inhabitants today, and at the time I am speaking of there was not a house or sign of a living person there, and a number of other places I could mention that are thriving cities now were at that time inhabited by wild animals alone.

In the year of forty-eight when Kit Carson and I went across the Rocky mountains with Col. Freemont, we camped three days where the city of Pueblo, Colorado, now stands.

Our camp was under a very large pine tree, one of the largest in that country.

Five years ago I visited the city of Pueblo again, the first time I had been there since that time.

I imagined I could go right to the spot where our camp was located, and the morning after I arrived there I took a walk on the main business street, which I thought was about where our camp had stood. But search as long as I might, there was nothing to show me a sign of the old landmarks.

I went to the river, thinking that must look the same, but no, even the channel of that had been changed.

Amazed at the change civilization had wrought in obliterating everything that I had thought would be a guide to the old places I sought, I spoke to a police officer and asked him if be could tell me whether a very large tree had stood in that neighborhood or not before that street was laid out.

He answered, "Yes, that tree stood right under that brick building," and he pointed to a large building near where we stood, and he continued. "As long as the tree stood there, it was called 'Freemont's camping ground.'"

That particular spot is no exception, for every place I have visited in late years all through the western country has met with the same change, and the places that I was familiar with in my youth are strange to me now.

The place that is now called the city of Denver I will take for an example. At the time I am speaking of, the year of forty-eight, and for several years later, it was one of the greatest Antelope countries in all the west, and I think I am safe in saying that there were not fifty white men in all what is now called the state of Colorado.

I visited several cities in that state a year ago, and it would be difficult for the people of this time to understand the feeling of surprise that I experienced when I saw what civilization had done to every place I visited.

On the Platte river in the eastern part of the city of Denver where the large machine shops now stand is the spot where the largest bands of Antelope were to be found, and it was there that we used to go to get them every morning as they came down to the river to drink.

From the site where Amarillo is now we had all the Buffalo meat we wanted, and when we struck what is now the city of Trinidad, Colorado, we followed the stream known as and called the "Picket Wire," down to the Arkansas river, and as we were in the heart of the Buffalo country, we were not out of the sight of herds of Buffalo all the way down to that river.

It would be an impossibility to make this generation understand the numbers of herds that roamed the western country. While the Buffalo was the most numerous game of the plains, they were the most strange in their habits. They made the round trip from Texas to the head of the Missouri river in Dakota and back again every year. As soon as they reached one end of their journey, they invariably turned around and began their journey back. Another peculiarity of this animal was that the calves never followed their mother, but always preceded her, and in case of fright, or when she thought them in danger when the herd started on the run, if the calves could not keep up with the others the mother would push her calf forward with her nose.

I think I have seen a mother Buffalo throw her calf at least ten feet in one push, and it would always alight on its feet and not break its run.

When we reached Bent's Fort, Capt. McKee asked Col. Bent how the gold mines were on Cherry creek. The Col. laughed and said, he had not heard from them in about three months, and the last news he had from there were that Cherry creek was deserted, so by that he thought the amount of gold there must be rather limited, and then Capt. McKee told him that he had fitted up a company and had come all the way from Texas to dig gold from Cherry creek.

Col. Bent said, "Well, Capt., there has been another discovery made on what is called Russel's gulch which is a tributary of Clear creek, and I have no doubt but there is gold to be found there."

Capt. McKee asked where Clear creek was.

Col. Bent said, "Ask Will. He can tell you better than I can, for he has trapped all over that country."

I told the Capt. that Clear creek was about ten miles north of Cherry creek on the north side of Platte river and I said, "Capt., if Russel's gulch is up on the head of Clear creek, you could not get there this winter with horses, for at this time in the year the snow is from two to ten feet deep, and it is the coldest country you ever struck, and your Texas boys and yourself too would freeze to death before you got half way to the mines."

The Capt. asked Col. Bent if he had any idea how many miners there were up in the Russel's gulch mines.

He answered, "Yes, I saw them when they started on their prospecting trip, and there are six of them. There were seven, but one came back and went back to his home in Georgia.

"Green Russel was the leader, and the mine was given his name. I expect there will be a great stampede from the east especially from Georgia next spring, for the gold excitement always spreads like fire in dry grass."

Capt. McKee said, "Well, I believe I will go there anyway and see what there is in it. I can live there as cheaply as I can anywhere. There is plenty of game there, is there not?" he said, turning to me.

I said, "Yes, there is plenty of game all around the Platte river and Cherry creek, but if you go there, I advise you not to go further than the mouth of Cherry creek this winter. There is a grove of timber there that you can make your camp in, and you could put up a shack to protect you from the weather."

The Capt. and his company pulled out the second day after this talk, but it was very plain to be seen that the whole company was much discouraged in regard to the gold mines.

As they were leaving the Fort, I said to Capt. McKee, "When you come back in the spring, Capt., I hope I shall hear you tell about the grand success you have had in panning gold on Cherry creek this winter."

He said, "If there is any gold to be found in that country, I shall find it. That is what I came out here to do."

As soon as the mining company had gone, Col. Bent said to me, "Will, do you want to go and trade with the Indians for me now, or have you caught the gold fever too?"

I answered, "Col. I have not had the gold fever as yet, and I do not think there is any danger of my catching it, so I am ready to go to work for you trading with the Indians."

Col. Bent laughed and said, "If you haven't got the fever now, Will, I will bet your best hors, that you will catch it bad when the rush for the mines comes in the spring."

At that time I had no idea there would be any rush for the gold mines, for I thought the excitement would die out before spring, because so many had been disappointed in the fall, but in this I was mistaken, for by the first of May they commenced to come to the Fort on their way to the mines, and by the first of June one could see the trains stringing along for miles, and what was very amusing to me, when I asked them where they were going, they invariably answered, "Pike's Peak."

I remember one train that I met that spring down on the Arkansas river, below Bent's Fort. One of the men asked me, if I could tell them how far it was from there to Pike's Peak. I said, "No sir, I can't tell you how far it is, but I can show it to you. There is Pike's Peak right before you," and I pointed to the snowcapped mountain that could be seen for hundreds of miles.

He said, "Oh, I don't mean that. I want to find out where the Pike's Peak gold mine is."

I told him that I had never heard of such a mine. This seemed to surprise him, and in a few minutes the whole outfit was crowding around me, inquiring about Pike's Peak mine.

Then I told them what the report had been about the discovery of gold at Cherry creek and Russel's gulch.

One man asked if I could tell them where Denver was, and that was a question I could not answer, for I had never heard of a place called Denver before.

I asked him what Denver was. A new mining camp that had just been named, or what.

"Why" he said, "Denver is a city close to Pike's Peak."

I answered, "Strange, you must have made a mistake in the locality of the city you are seeking. I have traveled all over this country for years, and I never saw or heard of a place called Denver in my life."

Then they told me that Dr. Russel, one of the discoverers of the gold mine, had staid all night at the town where they came from in Missouri.

When he, the Dr., was on his way home to Georgia, last fall he had told them what wonderful gold mines had been discovered up in the mountains, and there was a large city building in the valley that was going to be the queen city of the west, and they had named the city "Denver."

I was young then, and of course my experience was limited, so I believed the story that the man told, not stopping to think that it might be exaggerated, as an older person might have done.

I was going down the Arkansas river on my last trading trip with the Indians for that season, and the story of the wonderful gold mines made me anxious to get back to Bent's Fort. I had very good success in this trade, and in two weeks I was back to the fort with my pack horses loaded down with Buffalo robes.

After I had settled with the Col., I said, "I reckon you would have won the wager if we had made the bet last fall, Col., for I am afraid I have a touch of the gold fever."

Col. Bent laughed and said, "I thought you would not escape, Will, but you are not the only one affected. I have news for you. Kit Carson and Jim Bridger will be here in a few days from Taos, on their way to the gold mines, and so you are just in time to go with them."

I then told Col. Bent the story the gold seekers had told me when I was on my way to trade with the Indians this last time.

He said, "You must not believe all the stories that are floating about, Will. If you do, you will only be disappointed, for in a time when people are excited, as they are now over the finding of gold, there will be all kinds of exaggerated stories told. Some of them will be told in good faith, and some will be to merely mislead too credulous people. So take my advice, Will, and keep cool and don't get rattled."

The next day, after I had the talk with Col. Bent, Uncle Kit and Jim Bridger stopped at the Fort on their way to the new gold field. Of course, Uncle Kit was as glad to see me as I was to see him, and was rather surprised when I told him that I was all ready to go with him to the mines.

Jim Bridger said, "What are you going there for, Will?"

I said, "I am going to help you pick up gold. I haven't any use for it myself, but I just want to help you, Jim."

Uncle Kit said, "I guess, what gold we pick up won't hurt any of us."

The morning after this we three pulled out, and on the fourth day out we landed on the ground where the city of Denver now stands.

It was the first of June in the year of fifty-nine, and as near as I can remember, there were six little log shacks scattered around the west side of Cherry creek, which at that time was called "Arora," and the east side of the creek was called "Denver," and this was the Queen city of the west that I had been told about and had come to see, and it was amazing to see the number of people that were coming in there every day. They came in all shapes. They came in wagons, in hand carts and on horse back.

The hand carts had from four to six men to pull them, and I saw a few that had eight men pulling one cart.

Uncle Kit, Bridger and I remained there four days, just to see the crowds that were coming in. We found out the way to Russel's gulch, and we decided to go up there.

We went by the way that is called "Golden" now, but of course there was no such place then, that being the general camping place before going up into the mountains.

When we made our camp on the bank of Clear creek, where the city of Golden now stands, I think we could have counted two hundred wagons in sight of our camp. Close to us there were four men in camp, and they had one wagon and two yoke of cattle between them.

The next morning they were up earlier than we were and were eating their breakfast when we crawled out of our blankets.

As soon as they finished eating, they hooked up their ox teams and drove down to the creek and stopped at the bank and commenced to throw their provisions into the water. As soon as Uncle Kit saw the men doing this, he said, "What do they mean? Are they crazy? I will go and see what is the matter."

As soon as he got in speaking distance, he asked them what they were throwing their provisions to the creek for.

One of the men stopped and answered, "We are going back to Missouri, and our oxen's feet are so tender that they can hardly walk, let alone pull this load."

Uncle Kit said, "Why don't you throw the stuff on the ground? If you don't want it yourselves, do not waste it by throwing it in the creek. Someone else may want it."

One of them said, "I had not thought of that," and they threw the flour and bacon and coffee and other small packages of food on the ground.

There must have been as much as twelve hundred pounds of provisions laying on the ground when they got through, and I saw the contents of two other wagons share the same fate that same day. How long that stuff lay there I do not know. We left there the next morning, and I noticed that it had not been touched.

I never saw so many discouraged-looking people at one time as I saw in those wagons that were camped around Clear creek. I visited a number of camps where six or eight men would be sitting around a little fire talking about their disappointment in not finding gold to take home to their families, and some of them were crying like children as they said the expense of fitting out their teams and themselves had ruined them financially.

This spot on Clear creek seemed to be the turntable for the gold-seekers. They either went up the mountain to the mines or became discouraged and turned around and went home, and I do not believe that one out of ten ever left the creek to go up the mountain.

The way from Clear creek to the mines at Russel's gulch was through the mountains, with nothing but a trail to travel on and the roughest country to try to take wagons over I ever saw.

I do not know how many miles it was, but I do remember that we had a hard day's ride from Clear creek to Russel's gulch, and we did not ride a half a mile without seeing more or less wagons that had been left beside the trail, and in many of the broken wagons the outfit that the owner had started with was in the wagon.

[Illustration: I bent over him and spoke to him, but he did not answer.]

CHAPTER XII.

The night we struck the mines, we camped near the head of Russel's gulch. The next morning, after we had eaten our breakfast, we started out to take a look around, and Bridger said, "Where in the name of common sense do these people come from?" For look in any direction we would, there was a bunch of men with pick and shovel slung over their backs, and every little while we came on a bunch of men digging a hold in the ground.

Later in the forenoon we went to Green Russel's cabin, he being the man who had discovered the gold in that country. He had never met Uncle Kit before but had heard a great deal about him. When Carson told him his name, he invited us into his cabin. After we had talked with him awhile, he said, "I suppose you all think that I am to blame for all of this excitement, but if you think so, you are mistaken, so I will clear your mind and vindicate myself. A year ago last spring my brother, myself, and five other men came out here to prospect for gold. After we had prospected all over the country, we discovered this gulch, and we struck good pay dirt in the first hole we sank. We fixed up a couple of rockers and went to work, and the first week we took out a hundred dollars to a rocker. I told the boys that this was good enough for me, so each one of us staked off a claim, and to prove that each of us had a good claim, we sank a prospect hole on every claim, and we found that one claim was as good as another. There was only one of the party who had a family, that was my brother, the doctor, and as we all thought that we had a good thing, my brother concluded that he would go home and fix up his affairs this winter and bring his family out here in the spring, and he agreed to keep our finding a secret from everyone but his own family, but it seems that he did not keep his word but spread the news of our luck broadcast as soon as he struck the first white settlement, and the waste and destruction which you saw all along the trail from Clear creek to the gulch are the effects of his folly, although I believe that there are other mines as good as this in other parts of this country, but mining for gold is like other kinds of business. Only one man out of a hundred makes a success out of it."

The next day we were looking around, and we came upon two young men who said they were brothers, and they were so excited when we came near them that they could scarcely talk. They had been sinking a prospect hole and had just struck pay dirt.

We watched them pan out a couple of pans, and they certainly had struck it rich. After they had staked off their claims, Bridger asked them what name they would give their new discovery. They said, "There is a spring at the head of this ravine where we have often drunk and cooled ourselves, so we shall call our mine 'Spring gulch,'" and I was told by miners afterwards that these brothers had surely found a rich mine, for it extended the whole length of the ravine.

I met one of the brothers a number of years after the time I saw them panning out the gold, and he told me that he and his brother took twenty thousand dollars apiece out of that mine.

The next day we were knocking around the mining camp, and we ran across a man whose name was Gregory. He was from Georgia, and he had just discovered a quartz lead which proved to be very rich in gold.

He showed us some of the quartz that he had taken from it, and we could see the gold all through the rock. He said that when he sank down a hundred feet, it would be twice as rich in gold as it was at the top.

There was a town built at this place, and it was called Gregory, and in two years there were a half a dozen quartz mills built in that vicinity and quite a number more quartz ledges had been discovered, and they all paid well.

We had been in this region about two weeks, when I met one of the men that came with Capt. McKee. We were both surprised to see each other. I asked him what he was doing, and he said he was mining. He said the whole company was mining together on a claim they had taken up on south Clear creek about twelve miles from Russel's gulch, and they had fifty feet of sluice boxes and were taking out from five to seven dollars a day to a man, and had ground enough to last them two years.

He insisted on my going back with him to see the mine and said that I could have an equal interest with the others of the company if I would join them, and I have always regretted that I did not go and make them a visit at least for I never saw Capt. McKee again.

I was told afterwards that he made quite a good stake, and then went back to Texas and married and bought a home and lived and died on it about seven miles northeast of where Mineral wells is now, and I will say here that Capt. McKee was like many of his noble statesmen. He was brave, kindly, honest and true. One of nature's noblemen. He did not interfere with any man's business and allowed no one to meddle with his business, and if he professed to be a friend, he was a friend indeed, one that could be trusted in foul weather as well as fair.

Carson, Bridger, and I remained at Russel's gulch about three weeks, and we visited many claims and heard the shouts of the successful and the groans of those who failed, and we all three decided that we had got enough of mining by looking on without trying our hand at it, so we left the mining camp and pulled out for Denver, and from Russel's gulch to the foot of the mountain.

We were never out of sight of teams of every description, and nearly every person we met asked us how far it was to Russel's gulch.

We were about ten miles on the trail towards Denver when a man asked us this question, and Jim Bridger answered that if we were anywhere else in the United States it would be ten miles to Russel's gulch, but by that trail he reckoned it was about fifty.

The man said, "Doesn't the road get any better?"

Jim said, "I don't call this path a road, but if you do I will tell you that it gets worse all the way up."

When we reached the foot of the mountains at the crossing at Clear creek, we found more campers there than when we had left three weeks before. As we were riding along, Bridger said, "Where, do you suppose all these people came from?" Kit Carson answered, "Oh, they have come from all over the east. This excitement has spread like wild fire all over the country."

Up to this time we had seen but very few families in the crowds of gold seekers, but when we got to Denver on our return from the mines, we saw that a great many of the emigrants had their whole families with them, and it was surprising to see the number of cabins that had been built in so short a time, and we saw a number of teams hauling logs from the foot of the mountains to build more cabins, and there had been several little buildings built and furnished with groceries and dry goods since we had left there.

The evening we got to Denver we went a little ways up the Platte river to find a place to camp, and whom should we meet but our old friend Jim Beckwith. As Carson shook his hand, he said, "Why, Beckwith, I thought you had more sense than to be caught in a scrape like this."

Beckwith laughed and answered, "Well, Kit, I see I am not the only durned fool in the country. You seem to be caught in the same scrape with me," and for the next half hour it was amusing to hear the jokes these three old friends tossed at each other, for, of course, Bridger joined in.

After they had their fun with each other, Carson asked Beckwith what he was doing there. Beckwith answered, "I have staked off a claim here, Kit. It is not a claim either. It is a farm," and he pointed to a little bunch of timber a short distance from our camp. "I intended to build a cabin in that grove of timber," which he afterwards did, and he lived there about thirty years and died there about fourteen years ago as I was informed a year ago, when I was in Denver for the first time since Carson, Bridger and I camped on his claim.

When Jim Beckwith told us that he had taken up land and was going to build on it and make himself a home there, I wondered what he would do to make a living. The land seemed to be fertile enough, but I did not see any chance to sell what he might raise if he tried farming, but I was told that he cultivated the land for awhile and then it was too valuable. So he cut it up into lots and sold it, and now it is covered with business houses and residences, and all this change has taken place in forty-nine years.

As I stood and looked at the streets and blocks of houses, I found myself almost doubting that that was the spot where we had camped forty-nine years ago. When memory called back to my mind what a barren, desolate country it was at that time, it almost seemed incredible that such a large city could be built and such a vast change be made in less than fifty years, and not only in this particular spot but for miles and miles all through the surrounding country.

While we were in camp, I was down on the banks of Cherry Creek one day, and there were fifteen or twenty Indians sitting on the bank, and among them was a squaw who had a pistol in her hand. She seemed to be playing with it when several white men came along, and one of them was intoxicated. This one went up to the squaw and, taking hold of the pistol, tried to wrench it from her hand, and in the struggle the pistol was discharged and the man dropped dead. Some of his companions threatened to take vengeance on the Indians, but there were so many other white men standing around that had witnessed the whole affair and knew the Indians had done nothing to be molested for, they would not allow the Indians to be troubled. So the men took the body away, and that was the end of the affair.

That evening a band of Kiawah Indians came into the town and camped where the statehouse now stands. I happened to meet some of them, and being acquainted with them I stopped and talked with them, and they told me that they were going to have a peace smoke and a dance next day, and they wanted me to join them, which, knowing it would not be wise to decline, I promised to do.

When I went back to camp, I told Uncle Kit and the others of the invitation I had received and accepted. Uncle Kit said, "I guess we are too old to take a part in the dance, but we can go and look on and watch the fun." We did not go to the Indian camp until near noon the next day; and I think there were two or three hundred white men, women and children standing around the camp when we got there, and the majority of them had never seen an Indian before.

As Uncle Kit and Bridger and Beckwith did not wish to take a part in the performance, they kept out of sight of the Indians, and I went into the camp, and as soon as I arrived the Indians commenced to form the circle for the peace smoke.

We had all just taken our seats, and the head chief was in the act of lighting the pipe when he sang out, "O Wah," at the top of his voice, and in an instant every Indian sprang to his feet and started to run. I could not think what was the matter until I looked around and saw a man a short distance from us with a camera in the act of taking a photo of us, but he never got the picture, for not an Indian stopped running until his wigwam hid him from view.

The man with the camera looked the disappointment he felt as he came to me and asked if I were acquainted with those Indians.

He said, "What in creation was the matter with them? What made them get up and run? I would rather have given fifty dollars than miss taking that picture."

I could scarcely answer him I was so choked with laughter. But I managed to tell him that I reckoned the Indians thought that he had some infernal machine pointed at them that would blow them all to the happy hunting grounds.

He asked me if I would go and tell the chief that the camera would not hurt them and try to make them understand what he was doing with it. He said, "If you can persuade them to let me take a photo of them, I will pay you well for your trouble."

I told him I would try, but I was doubtful of his getting the picture.

So I went to the chief's wigwam and tried to explain to him and to persuade him to have him and all the band sit for their pictures to be taken.

The chief shook his head and said, "Hae-Lo-Hae-Lo white man heap devil," which meant "I will not that the white man would do them some evil," and then he said he was afraid that the white man with the big gun wanted to kill all his warriors, and all that I could say would not change his mind.

Carson, Bridger and I staid at Denver three weeks, and then we went back to Bent's Fort, and when we left Denver, the town and the country in every direction was covered with wagons belonging to emigrants that the excitement about gold having been discovered in the mountains had brought to Denver and the surrounding country.

We reached Bent's Fort late in the afternoon and had not been there over an hour when three men and a boy came in on foot and brought the news that the Indians had attacked a train of emigrants and killed them all. The emigrants were on their way back east, from Cherry Creek, where they had been led to believe that gold had been discovered.

The men that brought the news of the massacre were so excited that they could not tell how many people had been killed or how many wagons were in the train. They said that the train had just broke camp and started on their way when they heard the report of guns at the head of the train, and in a moment more the Indians came pouring down upon them, shooting everyone they met with their bows and arrows. "And," continued they, "when we saw them shooting and yelling, we broke and run before they got to us, and we did not stop until we got here." They said all this in a frightened, breathless way, that showed how excited they were.

Col. Bent sent the men and boy into the dining room to get something to eat, and Uncle Kit followed them, to try to get some more definite information regarding the massacre. After awhile Uncle Kit came back, and Col. Bent asked him what he thought of the news the men had brought. Carson answered that the men in the dining room did not know anything, and that he thought they were a party of emigrants who were disappointed and angry at their luck, and they had tried to vent their spite on some Indians they had met by firing on them, and had got the worst of the fight.

"You know, Colonel, that the Comanches have not troubled any white people in a number of years without they were aggravated to do so."

Col. Bent said, "Well, Kit, are you going down there to investigate the matter?"

Carson answered, "Yes, and won't you send three men along to bury the dead?"

Col. Bent said, "Certainly, Kit, and anything else you want. When do you want to start?"

Carson said, "We will start now."

Carson, Bridger, myself and three other men left the fort for the scene of the massacre, which we reached at the break of day the next morning, and the sight that met our eyes was a horrible one. We found twenty-three dead bodies close together, apparently where the attack had commenced, and down near the river, in the brush, we found five more, and also four living men who were not hurt, but frightened nearly to death.

After Carson had talked with these men a while and they had recovered a little sense, they told how the dreadful thing occurred.

They had just pulled out from camp that morning when they met the Indians. There were several men on horseback riding on ahead of the wagons. When they met the Indians, they commenced to shout "How-How," and the horsemen began to fire on the Indians without the Indians doing a thing to provoke them, and then the Indians had turned on them and killed every white person they could find, but that they had not been seen by the Indians, as they ran down the river and hid in the brush.

We searched thoroughly the brush all around for quite a distance, but we could find no more living or dead.

We could not find out by these men how many there were in the train any more than we could of the men that came with the news to the fort.

We began to bury the dead, and the four men commenced to look after the teams and wagons.

In a little while they came back driving three teams, and said they had found them hooked together, feeding along quietly, and they found that nothing had been touched or carried away from the wagons.

After Uncle Kit had learned the cause of the massacre, I think he was the most out of humor that I ever saw him. He said, "Such men as the ones who fired on those Indians deserve to be shot, for they are not fit to live in any country," and turning to Bridger he said, "Jim, it has always been such men as they that has made bad Indians and caused most all the trouble the whites have had with them, and still the Indians are blamed for it all, and have to suffer for it all. I hope I shall live to see the day when these things will be changed in this respect, and the Indians will have more justice shown them."

But I am very sorry to say that Uncle Kit did not live to see this accomplished. It was fifty years ago that Kit Carson expressed that wish in regard to the Indians, but it has never been gratified, for in all that time the Indians have been driven from one place to another and not allowed to rest anywhere long at a time, and in my opinion certainly have not had justice done them by the white race, and I will say this from my own experience, that when an Indian professes to be a friend he is a friend indeed, in storm as well as sunshine.

I will tell an instance that occurred four years ago when I was in Indian Territory. I was sitting on the street in one of the towns when an old Kiawah Indian came along, and looked at me quite sharply and walked on a few steps, then turned and looked at me again, and then he came back to me and slapped me on the shoulder and said, "A-Po-Lilly," which meant "Long time ago me know you." I looked at him and said, "No, you are mistaken, I do not know you," and then he told me where he had met me and what I had done for him, and as he recounted what had happened I remembered the incident.

The time I had first met him I was out hunting and met him in the forest. It was in the Territory of Wyoming, and he had had a fight with the Sioux, and they had shot his horse, and he was hungry and tired and footsore. I took him to my camp and fed him and kept him all night, and the next morning I gave him a horse so he could ride back to his tribe in more comfort, and I had not seen him since that morning, and this happened forty years before I saw him again, and he remembered me. He shook hands with me, which is a custom the Indians have not outgrown, and left me, but in a few minutes he returned with at least forty of his tribe with him, and I had to shake hands with every one of them. Some of them could speak good English, and they told me the story he had told them about my being kind to him, and they all called me their friend. This incident shows that the Indian appreciates kindness.

After we had buried the emigrants, which took nearly two days to do, Carson asked the men who had escaped being massacred where they were going and what they intended to do.

One of them answered, "If you men will stay with us all night, we will talk it over and decide what we had better do."

Carson said we had better stay with them that night, so we made a fire and prepared supper, and while we were eating we saw several more wagons coming down the trail near the river.

Uncle Kit said to the men that were with us, "Now is your chance, boys. You can join this train and go home with them."

When the teams drove up, the three men and the boy we had left at the fort were with them.

They all camped there with us, and after talking with the men, we found out that none of them claimed the teams and wagons that had been found. The owners of them had all been killed. The survivors did not know what to do with the wagons and their contents, and they appealed to Uncle Kit for advice in the matter.

Carson said, "I do not see that you can do better than take them along with you. If you leave them here, somebody will come along and take them, and they belong as much to you as to anyone."

So the next morning they rigged up five wagons with three yoke of cattle to a wagon, leaving eight wagons with their contents standing where their owners had left them when the Indians had killed them.

As they were ready to pull out, Uncle Kit went to them and asked them to give him their names and where they lived, "for," he said, "if I ever hear where any of the people lived who owned the property you have taken with you, I want to write to you so you can give them to their families."

We then bid them all good bye, and they started on their journey home, Carson having advised them not to molest the Indians no matter how many or how few they might meet on their way, and then the Indians would not molest them, as they were a friendly tribe, and that was the last we ever saw or heard of that party.

We now turned back to Bent's Fort and reached there just before night. Col. Bent's herder took care of our horses.

That night Carson, Bridger and I consulted together, and Bridger and I decided to go with Uncle Kit to his home at Taos, Mexico, and stay a month with him, but fate seemed to step in and change my plans.

The next morning when the herder went out to get our horses he found a man crawling along, trying to get to the Fort, who was nearly starved and so weak that he could hardly speak.

The herder put him on his horse and brought him to the Fort, and we gave him some food. He said this was the first time he had broken his fast in four days, and then he went on to tell that he and his comrades, which were four altogether, had been among the first to come out to Cherry Creek in search of gold the spring before, and after they got there, they were so disappointed to find that there was not enough gold there to pay them to stay that they concluded to go and prospect on their own hooks. Each of them had taken as much provisions as he could carry, with his gun and blanket, pick and shovel, and they had struck out into the mountains. They had kept on at the foot of the mountain until they passed the Arkansaw river, and here they went up into the mountains and soon lost their way.

"How long we were traveling or where we went, I do not know," continued the unfortunate man, "and finally we forgot the day of the week. As long as our ammunition lasted, we did not lack for something to eat, and foolishly we sometimes shot game we did not need, and after a while our ammunition gave out, and when that happened it was not long until all the other stuff was gone, and we could not tell where we were until we got out of the mountains and saw Pike's Peak, as we knew what direction Pike's Peak was from Cherry Creek.

"We knew then what direction to take to get back. The second night after we left the mountains, one of the boys was taken very sick, and as we could not think of leaving him to die alone, and we had nothing to eat for him or for ourselves, and I being the strongest, they picked me to go and try to get relief. It has been four days and nights since I left them, and I do not believe I have slept over two hours at a time since I started, I was so anxious to find help to go to them. And besides, I was so hungry I could not rest. Many a time I have walked as long as I could keep my eyes open, and I would drop down beside a log and fall asleep before I struck the ground and slept an hour or two, and then awoke with that dreadful gnawing in my stomach. Then I got up again and struggled on, but I could not have gone much farther when the herder got up to me, for my strength was nearly gone, and I should have given up and died very soon. Nobody knows what I have suffered on this trip, except they that have gone through the same ordeal. We have about one hundred dollars between us, and we are willing to give it to anyone who will go and carry something to eat and help my comrades to come here."

The looks of the man and the pleading way he talked and the faithfulness to his friends in trying to get help to them was more pathetic than any romance could describe it, and could not help but appeal to the heart of any man.

With the light of deep sympathy in his eyes, Uncle Kit stepped forward and, stretching out his hand toward the unfortunate, exclaimed, "Do not worry another moment; your comrades shall have assistance at once, or as soon as I can reach them," and turning to me, Uncle Kit said, "Willie, come outside with me a moment," and when I looked at him after I had followed him, I saw the tears on his cheeks. I had known Kit Carson several years, but this was the first time I had seen him moved to tears. He said, "Willie, my boy, can't you find these men as well as anyone?"

I answered, "Yes, sir; if this man can give me any clue to follow, I will find them in short order, for I have been all over those mountains and through the valley several times, and know the country well."

He said, "Well, I thought you could fill the bill if any one could, Willie; and now go and have three horses saddled, and I will have some grub fixed up, and by that time the man will have finished eating and will be more fit to talk to you."

My horses were soon ready, and I went in to see the man. When I went into the room where he was, I found him lying on a cot, and after I had talked with him a few moments, I decided in my mind he had left his comrades not far from where the city of Trinidad now stands. He gave me the description of nearly all the mountains and streams he had crossed on his way to the Fort after he had left his friends, and I thought if he had been correct in his description of his route I could find the suffering men without much difficulty. When I went out to where the horses were waiting for me, I found Uncle Kit had packed about forty pounds of grub on one of the horses. Col. Bent handed me a pint flask of whiskey, saying, "Now, if these men are alive when you find them, give them a small quantity of this, but be very careful not to give them too much at a time, and the same care must be taken in giving them food."

As I was starting, Uncle Kit said, "Now, Willie, if you are successful in finding the men, I hope to hear from you in two or three weeks. Jim and I will leave here today for Taos, and you will find us there when you come home," and he gave me his hand, and with a lingering pressure said, "Goodbye, and God speed you on your errand of mercy, my boy."

And I mounted my horse and left the Fort, and was off on my long, lonely journey over trackless prairies and through mountain passes that had perhaps never been trodden by a white man beforehand. No one can realize how lonely this journey was. I did not think much about it myself until I made my camp the first night. After I had staked out my horses and built a fire, I began to realize what a dreadful state the lost men must be in, for if I was so hungry, who had eaten a good meal at noon, what must they be suffering who had had nothing to eat in five days? The thoughts of the suffering men whom I hoped to rescue from death kept me awake most of the night, and I fully decided that this was the last time I would try to sleep until I knew whether they were living or dead. I was up with the dawn the next morning, and on the way, and I thought if I did not meet with any bad luck to detain me I would be in the vicinity of the men I sought by night.

From this time out I knew I must be very careful to look for signs of the lost men, as hunger might drive them to leave the place where their comrade had directed me to look for them. When I was a little west of where the city of Waltzingburge now stands, and the darkness was beginning to close down, I saw the glimmer of a little fire off to the right, at what looked about a half mile from me. I thought it might be an Indian camp and directed my course that way, but when I was within sight of it and was within a hundred yards or so of the fire, I could not see a soul stirring around it, but I kept on up to the fire, and suddenly my horse came near stepping on a man who lay on the ground with bare feet and nothing under or over him. I sprang from my horse and bent over him and spoke to him, but he did not answer or move. I then took hold of his shoulder and shook him gently, and he seemed to rouse up a little. I said, "What are you laying here for?" and he murmured in a voice so weak I had to bend my ear close to him to hear, "I have laid down to die."

I pulled the flask of whiskey from my pocket and raised him on my arm and wet his lips with a few drops of the whiskey. I repeated this several times, as he seemed to have relapsed into unconsciousness, and I was afraid I was too late to save him or bring him back to consciousness.

I laid him down and built the fire anew and unpacked my horse and got my blankets and made a pallet and lifted him on it. Lifting him seemed to revive him, and the firelight showed me that he had opened his eyes, and he put his hand on his stomach and whispered, "Oh, how hungry I am."

I gave him a small sup of whiskey, and, taking a piece of buffalo meat from my pack, I soon had it broiled, and with some bread I began to feed him in small morsels. I continued to do this for perhaps half an hour, as he was too weak to swallow much at a time, and I had to wait some moments before giving him another morsel, and between times I gave him a taste of the whiskey. Up to now I had no idea he was one of the men I was hunting for.

It was perhaps an hour from the time that I commenced to feed him when he seemed to come to himself, and I thought that he was strong enough to answer me, so I asked him how he came to be here in the weak, almost dying condition that I had found him in, and then he told me who he was and how he came to be there, and I knew he was the only survivor left alive of the three whom I had started out to find.

He said that he had not had a bite to eat in seven days, only what nourishment he could get by chewing his moccasins.

He had soaked them in water until they were soft and then broiled them on the coals and eaten them.

I told him how his comrade had been picked up near Bent's Fort in an exhausted condition, and how he had begged someone to go to the relief of those he had left starving, and that I had started out to find them if I could.

He said the one who first fell sick died the same night their comrade left them to get help, and that the other one and himself were not strong enough to dig a grave to bury him in, so they left him just as he had died and crawled away, and they kept on together until near the next night, when the one that was with him took sick and could go no further.

"And," said he, "I built a fire and we lay down, and I was so weak that I fell asleep and slept until morning, and when I awoke my companion was dead and cold. So I was all alone. I could do nothing for him any more than he and I could for the other one. I left him also and started on alone, but I could not go far, for I grew so weak. Then the thought came to me that I could eat my moccasins if I soaked them soft and broiled them over the coals. After I had eaten them, I was a little stronger and kept on until I reached this place, when my strength gave out again, and I built a fire, as I thought for the last time, for I did not expect to ever leave here. When you came, I heard your voice, but I thought I was dreaming."

After I had listened to his sad story, I gave him some more to eat and more whiskey, which seemed to revive him, and he gained strength very fast, and when the morning came he could sit up and seemed quite composed, although he was no more than the shadow of a man. But by noon he could walk around and seemed very anxious to be moving. Late that afternoon I saddled the horses and assisted him to mount one of them, and we left the place. He said he had thought that place would be his last resting place.

We had ridden slowly for about five miles when we came to a stream of cool water, and where we could have a shady place to lie down and rest, and I made a camp there and spread a blanket for my sick man and prepared some supper for us both. I had to remind him many times to be careful and not eat too much in his weak state, for he was so hungry and the food tasted so good that he found it difficult to restrain himself from eating more than was good for him.

For two days it seemed almost impossible for him to get enough to eat, and although I pitied him, I knew I must not give him all he would have eaten.

The morning of the third day after I found him, he seemed more rational than he had since I had been with him. That morning he asked where we were going, and when I told him we were going to Bent's Fort, where his comrade was waiting for us, he seemed surprised. He did not remember that I had told him how the herder at the Fort had found him, and that it was through his faithful struggle to get help for his starving friends that I had started out to find them. When I told it all to him again, he sat and cried like a child.

He said: "How can I ever pay this friend for suffering so much for me, and you, a stranger, for seeking to find me in the trackless wilderness?"

And then he told me what each of his comrades said before they died.

He said they were all raised together in one town in Missouri and were as dear to each other as though they had been brothers, and all their parents were in Denver, Colorado, where the four sons had left them when they started out prospecting for gold, and he said with tears in his eyes, "How can I ever tell their mothers what we all suffered, and how the two died and their bodies left laying unburied?"

After we had talked as long as I thought was best for him to dwell on the sad events, I cheered him up as well as I could. I assisted him to mount the horse I had selected for him to ride, and we pulled out on the trail for the Fort.

He was so weak that we could not ride over ten miles a day, and we were seven days going back the same distance that I had traveled in two when I struck out to find them.

The day before we reached Bent's Fort, I shot a young deer just as we were going into camp, and as he was eating some of it, he said it was the sweetest meat he'd ever eaten.

We landed at Bent's Fort on the evening of the seventh day after I started back with him. His comrade was sitting outside of the Fort when we came in sight, and when he saw us he hurried to meet us, and when we were in speaking distance of each other he said:

"Bill, I had given up all hope of ever seeing you again," and he did not wait for his friend to dismount, but reached up and took him off in his arms, and men who were used to all kinds of sights turned away with tears in their eyes at the sight of that meeting.

After they were seated together in the Fort and were more composed, they began talking about how they should tell the parents of the comrades who had died in the mountains.

One said, "I can never tell them," and the other said, "We must, for they will have to be told, and who else will do it?"

They now turned to me and asked if I would take them to Denver, and what I would charge them for doing it. I said, "Boys, I will take you to Denver, and when we get there you can pay me whatever you can afford to pay, be it much or little."

So it was decided that we should leave the Fort in the morning, and, as we were nearly ready to start, the man who had brought the news and had remained at the Fort while I went to find his comrades asked Col. Bent how much his bill would be for the time he had staid there. Col. Bent said, "You do not owe me a cent," and taking a twenty-dollar gold piece from his pocket, the Colonel handed it to one of the men, saying as he did so, "But you can give this to Mr. Drannan, for he is the one that deserves this and more for what he has done." We mounted our horses and left the Fort and struck the trail for Denver.

Nothing occurred to impede our journey, and we arrived at Denver on the third day after we left Fort Bent.

We camped on Cherry Creek on the edge of town.

I said: "Now, boys, I will take care of the horses and cook supper, and you two can strike out and see if you can find your folks, and if you have not found them by dark, come back here and get your supper and stay with me tonight."

They had not been gone more than half an hour when I saw them coming back, and an elderly man and woman and a young lady were with them.

When they came to me, the man whom I had found unconscious in the mountains said:

"Father and mother, this is the man who sought and found me and saved my life."

The father took my hand, and, in a voice that trembled with emotion, said, "I can never thank you enough for what you have done for my boy and his mother and me, for he is our only son, and I think our hearts would have broken if he had shared the sad fate of his two comrades."

The mother gave me her hand without speaking, but her tear-stained face and smiling lips thanked me more than words could have done. The young girl, whom the elder man presented as his daughter, thanked me in a sweet voice for bringing her brother back to them, and when all got through, I felt almost overpowered with their gratitude.

They insisted on my going home with them to stay all night, which I did, and the next morning I had the pleasure of meeting the father and mother and two brothers of the other man.

After I had talked with them all a while, one of the young men asked me what they should pay me for all the trouble I had taken upon myself in their cause.

I told them that I would take the twenty dollars that Col. Bent had given him for me, and as the morning was wearing away, I bid them good bye and left them and started on my journey to Taos, New Mexico, and my much-looked-forward-to visit to Uncle Kit, and that was the last time I ever saw any of these people. But a year ago I was at Denver and had occasion to call at the office of *The Rocky Mountain News*, which, by the way, is the oldest newspaper published in the state of Colorado, and while I was talking with the editor, he alluded to the incident I have just spoken about and said that the man whom I had found unconscious at the camp fire in the mountains lived and died at Denver, and that he was always called "Moccasin Bill," from the fact that he ate his moccasins while trying to find his way out of the mountains, and that for several months before he died he seemed to dwell upon that event and always mentioned how I'd rescued him from certain death on that to him never-to-be-forgotten occasion.

When I arrived at Taos, I found Uncle Kit and his family all in good health, and I found Jim Bridger there having what he called a grand good rest.

As soon as I had been greeted by Uncle Kit and the others of the family, he asked me how I had succeeded in my quest of the lost, and when I told him all the particulars, he said:

"Willie, my boy, that was one of the best things you have ever done, and it is something for you to be proud of doing, and I am proud of having a share in directing you what to do, and I am very proud of my boy."

I answered, "Uncle Kit, you have always taught me to do my duty on every occasion, as I have noticed you always do yourself, and it has been the example you have set before me as well as the instruction you have given me from my boyhood until now that has made me what I am, and I should be very sorry to do anything to make you ashamed of or cause you to regret that you took the little homeless, wandering orphan and gave him a father's care and protection, and I shall always try to make you love me whether I can do what will make you proud of me or not."

THE END.

www.ingramcontent.com/pod-product-compliance
Ingram Content Group UK Ltd.
Pitfield, Milton Keynes, MK11 3LW, UK
UKHW040752060225
454761UK00004B/293